RESTORING ISRAEL'S
KINGDOM

by

Angus Wootten

Restoring Israel's Kingdom

by Angus Wootten

Published by:
Key of David Publishing, Saint Cloud, FL
Distributed by:
House of David, PO Box 700217, Saint Cloud, Florida 34770
http://www.mim.net

Printed in the United States of America.
All quotations used by permission.

Unless otherwise noted, Scripture quotations are from the *New American Standard Bible* (NASB), © 1960, 1995, The Lockman Foundation, published by Holman Bible Publishers, Nashville; and the *New New American Standard Bible*, Quick Verse for Windows, © 1992-1999, Craig Rairdon and Parsons Technology.

Verses marked KJV are from the *King James Version* Bible.

Verses marked *Lamsa* are from *The Holy Bible From Ancient Eastern Manuscripts*, © 1968 by A. J. Holman, Nashville.

Verses marked NIV are from the *New International Version*, © 1995 by The International Bible Society, published by Zondervan Publishing House, Grand Rapids.

Verses marked TAB are from *The Amplified Bible*, © 1964 by the Zondervan Publishing House, Grand Rapids.

Verses marked TNKH are from the *Tanakh, A New Translation of The Holy Scriptures*, © 1985 by The Jewish Publication Society. New York.

Verses from *26 Translations of the Holy Bible*, © 1985 by the Zondervan Corporation, Mathis Publishers, Atlanta, are marked according to the particular translation.

Note:

To emphasize some Scriptures, italics or an alternate word choice has been used, especially for the names of the Father and Son. Also, with all verses, except the Amplified Bible (TAB), brackets [] indicate text added by the author.

ISBN 1-886987-04-1

ONE STICK IN HIS HAND
EZEKIEL 37:15-28

**Limited Edition Full Color One Stick Print
In Exciting Flaming Colors—**
by Crystal Lenhart

The Cover

"One Stick" painting contributed by
Crystal Lenhart, Sheridan, WY.
One Stick prints available (see previous page).

The following is from a letter that accompanied Crystal's generous contribution:

Dear Angus and Batya,

I hope you're pleased with the picture. As I said, I'm honored to be a part of this project....

I went through the book of Ezra a while back as a study on the restoration process. The first two points the Father showed me were that the people need to support the restoration process with their physical means according to their ability (Ezra 1:4, 2:68-69), and that He will stir the hearts of those who are to be part of the process (Ezra 1:5). I know my heart has been stirred and I must do what I can to contribute. So, it's with joy that I bring this freewill offering. Be blessed.

On a side note, here's the "little loaf of bread" the Father gave me this morning:

If Genesis 1:11 and Galatians 6:7 are true; if Yahweh planted/sowed Israelites in every nation, would He not reap Israelites rather than Gentiles? The fields are white unto harvest and we're part of a threshing team to reap what Yahweh has sown: Israelites!

In Yeshua,
Crystal
Sheridan, Wyoming

Dedication

To our Father in heaven who has given me the unmerited opportunity to serve His purposes, as He begins to gather the remnant of His people and thus restore His Kingdom here on Earth.

To my wife Batya who has truly been a faithful *helpmeet* in my efforts to accomplish that which our Father has given me to do. Her support and her help, which includes extensive editing to all my writings, have made this book possible. In addition, her obedience to the leadings of the *Ruach ha Kodesh* (Holy Spirit) have been an example and an inspiration to me.

To all who have helped along the way, especially those who have been supportive of the House of David over the years—and have so given me the encouragement and opportunity to work toward restoring the Kingdom to Israel.

" And so when they had come together,
they were asking Him, saying,
"Lord, is it at this time You are
restoring the kingdom to Israel?"
(Acts 1:6)

Contents

Forward

We all spend our lives "preparing." Our first five or six years of life are spent preparing for twelve years of schooling. We then spend twelve years preparing for four years of college. These four years often are spent preparing for two to four years of post graduate work. In all, we spend from twelve to eighteen years preparing for our careers, which normally will span some fifty years.

Then, we spend those fifty-some years preparing for our retirement years—which will hopefully span some twenty years. Most will spend these "golden," (or rusty years), fighting life's final battle, old age, and, also, by refraining from contemplating their next phase of existence.

We have all seen the need to prepare for the various phases of our life. But our most important phase is yet to come: eternity! So, how much time should we spend preparing for our eternity?

How *much* time? We have no choice. Whether realized or not, we will spend our lifetime "preparing" for eternity. Whether aware of our final outcome or not, our eternal fate will be determined according to our "deeds" (Greek: *ergon*)—by our work, toil, labor, done here on earth (Revelation 20:11-15).

But if so, then *how* we will spend our lifetime?

It is my prayer that the time you spend reading this book will not only help change your life, but will change your eternity.

Plan of the Book

Part One
In The Beginning God Created The World...Why?,

This section lays a foundation by defining our purpose and mission. It also provides an understanding of the problems and challenges we face in fulfilling our Father's desire to have a people for His own possession (Deuteronomy 4:20; 7:6, 14:2; Ezekiel 46:18; Titus 2:14; 1 Peter 2:9).

Part Two
Building on a Sure Foundation

This section focuses on our problems and challenges, and offers the necessary understanding that will help us accomplish our mission. This segment includes a selection of articles previously published in the *House of David Herald*—albeit with a some editing and revision.

These *Herald* articles deal with various aspects of the end-time gathering of the Father's remnant. Each examines key topics from different standpoints.

While there is some repetition of certain subject matters, the hope is that it will enhance the understanding as well as help us to see the importance of these vital subjects.

Part Three
The Gathering of the Remnant

This section outlines how we can accomplish our mission. It helps to set in motion the process of gathering the remnant of Israel into her restored Kingdom. Again, articles previously published in the *House of David Herald* will serve as the foundation to present this vital information.

Introduction

There are few truer or sadder words written than those long ago spoken by our Heavenly Father:

"My people are destroyed for lack of knowledge."

Sadder still are the words that follow those woeful words:

"Because you have rejected knowledge, I also will reject you from being My priests. Since you have forgotten the law of your God, I also will forget your children" (Hosea 4:6).

Looking back on over seventy years of sojourning, and on my own personal battle to recover from being one of those "forgotten children," I can only wish that I had known at the beginning what I know today. Fortunately, our Heavenly Father has been merciful to me. He has even caused many things in my life to work together for my good. In showing me His mercy, He has increased my love for Him, and He has helped me to truly understand that I have been "called according to His purpose" (Romans 8:28).

Looking back, I can see the influence of a childhood spent between two monasteries. Also, I see the impact of a twenty-two year service career—one that gave me a variety of opportunities to grow in the knowledge of my Heavenly Father. My formative years spent in the service included three and a half years service (during the Forties) at the United States Army Chaplain School. There, one of my jobs was to help publish and distribute a monthly publication called *The Chaplain's Hour.*

Now, half a half century later I am still publishing a monthly publication: For years now, my wife Batya and I have published a cutting-edge Newsletter called *The House of David Herald*— which is now in the process of becoming *The Messianic Israel Herald*—an informative, challenging *Magazine*.

I consider this part of my life my more important assignment —my more important "service."

I say this because, participation in six wars gave me the full opportunity to see not only the futility of man's ways, but also his deplorable condition: What can favorably be said of any society that can sacrifice its youth on the field of battle while the home fires burn merrily, and most of the "old folks at home" are concerned only with their own personal desires, ambitions and goals?

While I believe that as far the nations on this Earth go, America is still the best,[a] still, who wants to give their life for anything less than a people who are totally devoted to the Holy One of Israel, to His Son, and to His Holy Nation?

Nonetheless, I do not feel my Army career was a "total loss." In fact, I had some very positive service related experiences. Looking back, I now realize that one of the most important of those experiences was one that I did not truly appreciate at the time.

Back in 1962, while stationed in Ethiopia—one of my duties was serving as a Military Attache to the now deceased Emperor, Hailey Selassie [b] —I met two Israelis. This "chance" meeting later helped me to better understand the "how" of the task the Father (Yahveh) was giving, not only to me, but to all whom He has foreordained to help "gather the remnant of Israel and to restore its Kingdom." It also helped explain why my wife Batya and I wound up in Orlando.

Orlando, Florida is said to be the world's number one destination. Due to its influx of millions of visitors each year, it has

---

a Understandably so, the modern State of Israel gives something less than a "warm welcome" to those who believe in Yeshua, the Messiah of Israel. And, at least America still offers "religious freedom."
b Selassie claimed to be a descendant Menelik I, son of a union between the Queen of Sheba and King Solomon of ancient Israel. "According to Ethiopian tradition, Sheba (called Makeda) married Solomon, and their son, Menelik I, founded the royal dynasty of Ethiopia." *The New Encyclopaedia Britannica*, 29 Vol., 1985, Vol. 10, *Sheba*, p 714.

an extraordinary number of fine lodging and meeting facilities. Supposedly, this vast complex, which is growing daily, was put together for the "mouse" (Mickey). But, perhaps the future will show that many of these facilities will be used for another, greater purpose: that of providing the logistical support required to fulfill many of the Biblical prophecies concerning teaching, training, and ultimately, the final gathering of the scattered tribes of Israel (Jeremiah 31:18-19). In Orlando, many may well be trained before their final return to the Land long ago promised to their forefathers.

I dare say this because, I once saw that just as the Addis Ababa Airport was built to serve the capital city of Ethiopia, it was one day used for another, far greater purpose: It served as the host site for "Operation Solomon." There, in a thirty hour period in 1991, 14,400 Ethiopian Jews were airlifted to Israel, as a rebel army was descending on the city.

After some twenty-nine hundred years of exile, Yahveh chose to return a remnant of King Solomon (through the Queen of Sheba) to the Promised Land. What is most interesting is that: this return was triggered in 1962 by two Israelis. Two Israelis came to Ethiopia carrying a message to the exiled Jews living there. These men told the Ethiopian Jews that they needed to "recognize their heritage," and that they needed to begin to "prepare to return to the land of Israel."

Their actual exodus commenced sixteen years later, with the inauguration of "Operation Moses"—which exodus was culminated in the above mentioned "Operation Solomon."

In a twenty year period, some seventy thousand Ethiopian Jews —twenty percent of them in a thirty hour period—were returned to their ancient homeland. Many of these returning Ethiopians, like their Russian counterparts, were not practicing Jews, some were even Believers c in the Messiah. Just as in the exodus from Egypt, Yahveh was delivering a mixed multitude.

---

c We use "Believer" to describe those purchased by the blood of the Messiah (Christ) of Israel rather than "Christian" because the latter title is so often misused (Mat 7:23; 1 Cor 6:20; 1 Pet 1:17-19).

It was far more than mere coincidence that I was in Ethiopia in 1962, and that I met with the two Israelis who were investigating the claims and origins of these Ethiopian Jews. I will never forget their answer to my question of "why" they were carrying out their investigation. They said, "If these people are in truth Jews then they need to recognize that they are part of the people of Israel. And, they need to return to the land."

Now, decades after that fateful meeting, I find myself carrying forth a similar message to other exiled Israelites.

I wish I had stayed in contact with these two messengers, and that I had followed exactly how Israel's plan for gathering the Ethiopian Jews developed. Exactly how did these two forerunners end up being responsible for the return of seventy thousand? What happened in the sixteen years leading up to Operation Moses —when Ethiopian Jews were returned to Israel through the Sudan? How, in a primitive country, stricken with poverty, drought and famine, did 14,400 Ethiopian Jews wind up at the airport for that miraculous thirty hour airlift?

A question that is now more important to me is: How will we, the forerunners of Messianic Israel who are charged with taking the message of heritage and return to the exiles, going to end up with the millions and millions of returnees required to fulfill the end-time prophecies concerning the gathering of the remnant of Israel?

How? How will it all come to pass?

In 1967, Jerusalem was delivered from Arab control, and, I retired from the Army. Even as Jerusalem was "delivered," so I had several life-changing experiences over the next few years. The one that was most beneficial and had the greatest impact was, marrying my Batya, and putting our two families together.

Two people meshing their lives together can be a traumatic experience. Add ten children to the mix and you will get some heavy-duty teaching about the necessary principles of, and preparation for, the reunion of the two houses of Israel.

Batya and I launched our lives together by immediately becoming involved in the Catholic Charismatic Movement, and at the same time, in the very foundation of the Messianic Jewish Movement. Our involvement with the move that became known as "Messianic Judaism" led to our founding the House of David in the Mid-Seventies. In its early years, House of David's mission was to publish a catalog that offered Messianic Materials to all who were being piqued with a budding interest in the Jewish people, the State of Israel, and in their own heritage.

Those of you who have read any of Batya's books: *In Search of Israel* (in 1988), *The Olive Tree of Israel* (in 1992), *Who Is Israel? And Why You Need To Know* (in 1998), and *Who Is Israel? (Enlarged Edition)* in 2000, know that it was putting books about Israel in the catalog that led her to a fuller understanding of the identity of Israel. (If you have not yet read these books, you should. You should at the very least, read her latest book, *Who Is Israel?* In fact, you really need to read that foundational book before you read this book.)

Batya's questioning of the various theories and teachings regarding "Israel" and the "church" led her to cry out to our Father for the truth about "Israel." In response to her cry for understanding and wisdom, the Father gave her Scriptural insight—which led to her writings about the two houses of Israel—which ultimately aided in the foundation of Messianic Israel.

It is my hope that, by sharing this latter-day understanding about "both the houses of Israel" we will help others in their battle against ignorance and rejection—and thus cause the whole house of Israel to cease "stumbling" and to truly become all that they have been divinely appointed to be: a Chosen Race, a royal priesthood, a holy nation, a people for our Father's possession (Genesis 48:19; Isaiah 8:14; Romans 11:25; Jeremiah 31:18,19).

May we come to a place wherein we truly begin to proclaim the excellencies of Him who has called us out of darkness into His marvelous light. (I Peter 2:9).

Restoring Israel's Kingdom

Part One

In The Beginning God Created The World...
Why?

1

Are You Prepared?

Long ago Messiah Yeshua's (Jesus') [1] disciples asked Him: *"Lord, is it at this time You are restoring the kingdom to Israel" (Acts 1:6)?*

Yeshua's answer to them was:

*"It is not for you to know times or epochs which the Father has fixed by His own authority; but you shall receive power when the **Ruach ha Kodesh** (Holy Spirit) has come upon you; and you shall be My witnesses both in Jerusalem, and in all Judea and Samaria, and even to the remotest part of the earth" (Acts 1:7-8).*

If we asked the same question of Yeshua today, what would His answer be? What if it were:

*"**Yours** is the generation the Father has fixed for the restoration of His eternal kingdom to Israel"?*

Are *you* prepared for that answer? Are *you* prepared to enter into His eternal kingdom?

Life is a preparation for eternity! This is not a question but a statement of fact. The only questions are: "Will you be prepared?"

---

1 *Yeshua* (ישוע) is Messiah's given Hebrew name meaning "He is salvation" (Mat 1:21). *Jesus* is derived from the Greek transliteration of *Yeshua*, *Iesous* (Ἰησοῦς).

And, "Exactly *what* eternity will you have prepared for?"

Someday, in the not too distant future, this question will be answered for you. In that day you will receive the eternal consequences of your preparations—good or bad.

How can you prepare for your future in a way that will be most beneficial to you? The first step in answering this question is to ask yourself, what future you are preparing for? How can you best do that? By starting at the beginning.

In the beginning, GOD (Yahveh) created the heavens and the earth (Genesis 1:1).

Why?

What was His purpose for His creation?

In particular, what was His purpose in creating *you*? Can you know when and how your Creator plans to fulfill His purposes? Why are the answers to these questions important to you?

Why? Because knowing the correct answers to these questions will assist you in accomplishing that which your Creator purposed for your sojourn in this world.

On the other hand, if you do not know your Creator's purposes, it is extremely unlikely that you will be used to fulfill them. Yet, your life will eventually run its course, and that fateful day will come when you find yourself at your "heavenly rewards celebration" (exit interview, final judgment, call it what you may).

It would certainly be a sad commentary on your life to find that you were not prepared, to the best of your ability, for the eventuality that becomes *your* eternal reality!

We need to examine, from the perspective of the Judeo/Christian experience, not only the why? and what? of our Creator's purposes for His creation, but the when and how of His plans to fulfill His purposes.

If you have any concern regarding your current answers to why, what, when, and how, then you need the satisfaction that comes from knowing who you are, and having a sense, and understanding of the purpose for which you were created. [2]

Our God, the Holy One of Israel, created each one of us for a purpose. That purpose was to satisfy His desire to have a people for His own possession. His ultimate goal is to place His sanctuary in the midst of a people who have determined of their own free will that He is their God, and then, He will acknowledge that they are His people (Ezekiel 37:25-26).

Fulfillment of our Father's creation objective requires a covenant people who exercise dominion over the earth as His representatives, and who follow His ways. These people will not only walk as Jesus (Yeshua) walked, but they will be unified even as Yeshua prayed: "That they may all be one; even as You, Father, are in Me and I in You, that they also may be in Us, so that the world may believe that You sent Me" (John 17:21).

Two thousand years have come and gone since the Apostle John wrote these words. And yet, Yeshua's prayer remains unfulfilled. So, today, you, like all who have gone before you, find yourselves still looking for the return of our Messiah and for the establishment of His kingdom on earth.

But take heart, for you are a member of the "Jubilee Generation" (1996 - 2036)—the fiftieth generation [3] from Yeshua. As a consequence of having been given this unmerited opportunity, you may very well be among those who see the kingdoms of this world become the Kingdom of our Messiah.

Yeshua came to this earth in the fiftieth generation from Noah, which also was the first Jubilee Generation after the flood. Yeshua described His mission, in the synagogue at Nazareth, when He read the following verses from the prophet Isaiah:

"The Spirit of the Lord is upon me, because He anointed me to preach the gospel to the poor. He has sent me to proclaim release to the captives, and recovery of sight to the blind, to set free those who are downtrodden, to proclaim the favorable year of the Lord"

---

2 To better understand who you are to the Holy One of Israel, see *Who Is Israel?*, by Batya Wootten, 2000, Key of David, St Cloud, FL. Hereafter, *Who Is Israel?*

3 For a more complete discussion See Chapter 14, *The Jubilee Generation*

When Yeshua finished this reading, He then announced, "Today this Scripture has been fulfilled in your hearing'" (Luke 4:18-21).

According to the rabbinical custom of His day, reference to these verses in Isaiah would have been understood as including the entire passage. Therefore, if we continue to read the chapter, we see that Yeshua was declaring that He had been sent "To proclaim the favorable year of the Lord, and the day of vengeance of our God; to comfort all who mourn...giving them a garland instead of ashes, the oil of gladness instead of mourning, the mantle of praise instead of a spirit of fainting. So they will be called oaks of righteousness, the planting of the Lord, that He may be glorified. Then they will rebuild the ancient ruins, they will raise up the former devastations, and they will repair the ruined cities, the desolations of many generations. And strangers will stand and pasture your flocks, and foreigners will be your farmers and your vinedressers. But you will be called the priests of the Lord; you will be spoken of as ministers of our God. You will eat the wealth of nations, and in their riches you will boast. Instead of your shame you will have a double portion, and instead of humiliation they will shout for joy over their portion. Therefore they will possess a double portion in their land, everlasting joy will be theirs" (Isaiah 61:2-9).

The favorable year of the Lord is the year of Jubilee.

The Concept of Jubilee

At the core of the idea of "jubilee" is the Mosaic doctrine that all things, all creatures in the world, do not belong to men at all, but to Yahveh alone.

The biblical law of redemption makes "jubilee" possible. This jubilee law deals with the fact that the land should not be sold in perpetuity, for it belonged to Yahveh, and those in bondage should, and could, be redeemed. The redemption of land and of those in bondage could be accomplished at any time by a "kinsman redeemer." Otherwise, in the year of Jubilee, the land would revert back to its owner, and those in bondage would be freed (Leviticus 25:23-55).

4

Biblically, the year of Jubilee is celebrated in the fiftieth year. In this "Jubilee year," agricultural lands sold during the past 49 years are returned to their original owners, and any Israelite that is in bondage is set free.

Seventeen Jubilees were celebrated from the time Joshua took the land until the destruction of the First Temple. Then upon Judah's return from Babylon, the count began again, and it stopped with the destruction of the Second Temple.

In 1998 the State of Israel celebrated the jubilee of its founding in 1948. However, it was not considered a Biblical jubilee. Perhaps the reason Jewish religious leaders have not yet called for a Biblical jubilee is because, according to the Talmud[4] (rabbinical Jewish tradition), the Jubilee Year laws are in force, *only when all the tribes are living in "Eretz Israel"* (land of Israel) (TB Ar. 32b).

Yeshua came in the first Jubilee generation (the fiftieth generation from Noah). Yet, His generation did not experience the ultimate jubilee. But He set the stage for that "favorable year" when, at His second coming, He would assert His ownership of all the earth, and its population. And, all creation would acknowledge His Lordship.

At that time, every knee will bow and every tongue will confess that He and He alone is Lord!

Yeshua came in the fiftieth generation, or first jubilee generation: 6 B.C. to 34 A.D.

The first generation after Yeshua began in 35 A.D., which year is also thought to be the year of Paul's conversion.

Paul's conversion is key to, and the spearhead of, the almost 2000 year effort to renew the world *spiritually*, and to regather Yahveh's people. This mission stands in contrast to the mission of Noah's sons, which was to repopulate the world *physically*.

If we count forward from this point, we see that the *fiftieth generation from Yeshua, meaning the second jubilee generation,*

---

4 The collection of ancient Rabbinic writings consisting of the Mishnah and the Gemara, constituting the basis of religious authority in Orthodox Judaism. [Mishnaic Hebrew *talmûd*, learning, instruction),

began in 1996 A.D.!

Today (2000), we live in the fourth year of the fiftieth generation from Yeshua, and in the one hundredth generation from the flood!

Are there other events that validate that this is the generation that will see the "favorable year of the Lord?"

In the past century, we have seen the tents of Judah come up first (Zechariah 12:7). We have seen Jerusalem be essentially freed from hundreds of years of Moslem domination. And we have seen the foundation of a Jewish state.

But note, this was not the establishment of the "State of Judea," but rather the establishment of the "State of Israel!" Surely, this was a foreshadowing of the gathering of the end-time remnant of Israel prophesied by the Prophet Jeremiah (Jeremiah 23:1-8).

This foreshadowing is becoming reality as we see the dry bones of Joseph, Judah's brother, emerging from some twenty-seven hundred years of obscurity. The stick of Joseph, and his companions of Israel, is now in the hands of Ephraim. And, the Holy One of Israel is in the process of making it one with the stick of Judah, and his companions of Israel (Ezekiel 37:15-22).

The first event of the "this" Jubilee generation was the end of Israel's (Ephraim's) punishment.[5] After twenty-seven-hundred and thirty years, Ephraim's blindness to his heritage was being removed. He was being freed from the sentence of being a people who were "not a people" (Hosea 1:9, Ezekiel 4:5). Messianic Believers,[6] from a non-Jewish ancestry, were coming to an understanding of their Israelite identity. They were being instructed in the truth of their heritage (Jeremiah 31:18-19). Truly, this was a favorable year for Ephraim!

This was also a favorable year for Judah. For it is only when the "whole house of Israel" is united that we will have a people who can fulfill our Father's desire of having a people for His own possession.

---

5 For a more complete discussion see Chapter 11, *Ephraim, Once Again A Mighty Man*.

6 We use "Believer" to describe those purchased by the blood of the Messiah (Christ) of Israel rather than "Christian" because the latter title is so often misused (Mat 7:23; 1 Cor 6:20; 1 Pet 1:17-19).

2

Can We Make A Difference?

How do you and those of your generation—how do we—make a difference?

We, like every generation before us, are commanded to do that which Adam in Eden, and Israel in Canaan, failed to do. We have been summoned to create the society required to meet our Father's creation goals.

What will history say about our generation? It is up to us.

If our generation is going to experience different results from those who went before us, we truly need to be different! We must change! And then, we must encourage others to change. For our spiritual culture to change, it must change one heart, one soul, one conscience at a time. While our secular culture can provide many material advantages, it cannot put a sense of eternal hope in our hearts, nor can it put a sense of our Father's purposes in our lives.

To accomplish these essential purposes, we must learn the lessons of history. We must insure that we do not repeat history's mistakes. This axiom is doubly important for Israelites. For, if you do not know your history, then you are a branch that doesn't know it's part of the tree whose root is Yeshua (Revelation 22:16).

We need to understand that the people of Israel[7] went into exile and were scattered among the nations—where they remain to this day. More importantly we need to see that they are there because of their lack of knowledge (Isaiah 5:13). We must acknowledge the indictment with which our Father charged His people Israel:

"There was no faithfulness or kindness or knowledge of Him in the land. Instead there was swearing, deception, murder, stealing, adultery, violence, and bloodshed. The worse part was that, none found fault with this deplorable situation, and none offered reproof.

"Because of this lack of knowledge His people are destroyed. And, because they had rejected knowledge of Him, He also would reject them from being His priest. Further, since they had forgotten His commandments and were not walking in His ways, He would not only forget them, but also their children" (Hosea 4:1-10).

The punishment of His people Israel, those whom He had chosen to be a people for His own possession out of all the peoples on earth, was a reduction in the fulness of their status as "Yahveh's most favored people" (Deuteronomy 7:6).

This reduction of most favored status happened in stages. For the Northern Kingdom of Israel (Ephraim),[8] their degradation was completed by 722 B.C.. And, their fall from grace was drastic.

Our Father declared that they would no longer be His people, and that He would no longer be their God (Hosea 1:9).

This happened because, they, like those at Babel, had been building for themselves and not for our Father. So their Father did with them as He did with the rabble at Babel, He would scatter them among every nation, tribe and kindred on the face of the earth (Genesis 11:8-9; Hosea 8:8; Amos 9:9).

---

7 Those of the former Northern Kingdom of Israel
8 See Chapter 11, *Ephraim Once Again A Mighty Man.*

For those of Jewish Israel (Judah),[8] their reduction in status was meted out in two stages. With the destruction of Solomon's temple, coupled with a seventy year exile in Babylon, the glory and presence of Yahveh lifted from all Israel. His glory and presence that had filled the Tabernacle in the Wilderness, and also Solomon's temple, was not evident in the Second temple (Exodus 40:34; 1 Kings 8:11; Ezra 6:15-18).

Why? Because the presence and unity of all twelve tribes is required for the corporate presence of the glory of the Holy One of Israel. This was the case in the wilderness and at the dedication of Solomon's temple. However, during the times of the Second temple Judah is the primary presence recorded.[9]

The second stage of Judah's reduction in favorable status occurred in the first century. In 70 A.D., with Rome's destruction of Herod's temple, coupled with Judah's (majority) rejection of Yeshua,[10] they were left without a temple, without a sacrifice and without a priesthood. While the people of Judah retained the benefits of knowing their national identity, those who refused to accept Yeshua as Israel's promised Messiah would not experience the God of Israel in His fulness as Father, Son, and Spirit.

The earthly manifestation of Yahveh as the "Son of Man" (Yeshua) began His "Joseph role." In this role He began the process of gathering the lost sheep of the house of Israel. For the past two thousand years, this process has maintained a "remnant." According to Yahveh's gracious choice, Yeshua has been gathering a remnant from among those of Ephraim, along with those of Judah (Romans 11:5). This remnant, though lost to the benefits that come from a knowledge of national identity, has had the Hope of Glory!

"The mystery which has been hidden from the past ages and generations; but has now been manifested to His saints, to whom

---

9 David Pavlik's talk at AMI 2000, MIA Conference, Orlando, FL.

10 This is not to deny that many of Judah did opt to follow the Messiah. For even though the religious leaders, and a majority of the seven million Jews scattered throughout the Roman world in the first century, chose not to follow the Messiah, a large number of them did elect to follow Yeshua.

God willed to make known what is the riches of the glory of this mystery among the Gentiles (nations), which is Christ (Yeshua) in you, the hope of glory" (Colossians 1:27).

The purposes of Yahveh's punishments were for the "instruction" of His people. However, the Father also promised that the day would come when He would have compassion on the house of Judah and deliver it (Hosea 1:7). It would be a day when the descendants of those who had rejected their Messiah would instead say of Him, "Blessed is He who comes in the name of the Lord" (Matthew 23:39).

After Ephraim, after he turns back, repents, and receives instruction, the Father declares of him, "Yet the number of the sons of Israel will be like the sand of the sea, which cannot be measured or numbered; and in the place where it is said to them, 'You are not My people,' It will be said to them, 'You are the sons of the living God'" (Jeremiah 31:19; Hosea 1:9-10).

Also, the Prophets foretell of a day when the sons of Judah and the sons of Israel will be gathered together. They will come up from all the lands where they were scattered and experience the fulness of Jezreel—the final harvest. They will be gathered back to their own soil in such numbers that there is no more room in the land promised to the Patriarchs. It promises to be a day when our ancestral exodus from Egypt pales in memory in the light of this final gathering. (Isaiah 11:12; Jeremiah 23:8; Hosea 1:11; Zechariah 10:6-10).

Since a lack of knowledge was the cause of Israel's being scattered, it follows that a primary prerequisite for gathering scattered Israel would be to regain wisdom and knowledge. And, where better to begin a search for wisdom and knowledge than from Yeshua's answer to His disciples question, "What will be the sign of Your coming, and of the end of the age?"

Yeshua's answer to all of His disciple down through the ages is recorded in Matthew, Chapters twenty-four and twenty-five. There, Yeshua offers not only a variety of signs that will herald His return, but He gives examples of the type of people we need to be, and the way in which we must walk, if we are to enter into His kingdom.

Unfortunately, those who claim to be His people seek after signs rather than to walk in His ways. This is understandable, for the requirements to prepare to get on a "rapture bus[11]" that will take them away from trouble, or to prepare for great tribulation and the seven year reign of an anti-Christ, are minimal.

On the other hand, preparing to be involved in the gathering of the end-time remnant back to its own soil, and participating in the defeat of Israel's enemies, will require maximum effort.

Basically, the decision that we each have to make is, are we going to be an "actor" or a "reactor"? Are we going to live our lives reacting to events, or are we going to act in such a way that we cause events?

If our decision is to be an actor, then we need to follow the advice that Yeshua is giving to those who will be on stage for the final act.

Yeshua entreats those who will experience His return to see to it that no one misleads them. Since we may very well be the "those" whom He is entreating, it is imperative that we have the spiritual discernment, and the common sense, to weed out the false brethren and the shepherds who would mislead us.

One good way for us to discern truth is to ask, "Where, and how, are we being led?"

Where? If the ultimate goal is not the return of our King and the establishment of His kingdom here on earth, then we are on the wrong road (Revelation 11:15).

How? If the "how" is not by the restoration of **all things** about which Yahveh spoke by the mouth of His holy prophets from ancient time, then even though we might essentially be on the right road we are not moving, or at least not moving in the right direction. (Acts 3:21).

---

11 See HDH's *Rapture or Transformation? Escape or Victory?* and *Should I Believe In A Pre-Tribulation Rapture?*

The "things" which have yet to be accomplished in our day is the gathering of the remnant (Jeremiah 23:1-8; 24:5-7; Ezekiel 37:15-28). How important is this ingathering?

It will result in the fulfillment of prophecy and, thus, the restoration of the kingdom to Israel.

Having insured that we are not being misled, we can now be on the alert for the next pitfall of which Yeshua warned us. That is, not being prepared for our King's return. For, we do not know when He will return!

Yeshua told five stories that give us the wisdom and understanding needed to help prepare us for His coming (Matthew 25-26).

The first story tells of the head of the house who, had he known at what time of the night the thief was coming, would have been on the alert and would not have allowed his house to be broken into. The second story describes the consequences of a servant not being prepared for his master's return.

The third story is about ten virgins, who took their lamps and went out to meet the bridegroom. Five of them were prudent and took extra oil with them, and five were foolish and took no oil with them, The bridegroom was delayed, and the lamps of the foolish were going out, and the supplies of the prudent were not sufficient for both them and the foolish. So the foolish were forced to go to the dealers for more oil. While they were gone the bridegroom came, and those who were ready went in with him to the wedding feast and the door was shut. Later, when the foolish virgins returned, they said, "Lord, lord, open up for us." But He answered, "Truly I say to you, I do not know you."

The lesson we should gain from this story is not only to be on the alert for our Master's return, but to realize that attendance at the wedding feast requires that our lamps have sufficient oil. In other words, we need to be sufficiently prepared, in advance, to meet the challenges we can expect to face.

The fourth story tells of a man about to go on a journey. He called in his servants and entrusted his possessions to them. To one, he gave five talents, to another two, and to another one, each according to his own ability; and he went on his journey. The one who received the five talents went and traded with them, and gained five more talents. In the same manner, the one who had received the two talents gained two more. But he who received the one talent went away, dug a hole in the ground, and hid his master's money.

After a long time, the master of those servants came and settled accounts with them. The one who had received the five talents reported that he had gained five more talents. His master responded with, "Well done, good and faithful servant. You were faithful with a few things, I will put you in charge of many things; enter into the joy of your master."

Also, the one who had received the two talents reported that he had gained two more talents. His master also said to him, "Well done, good and faithful servant. You were faithful with a few things, I will put you in charge of many things; enter into the joy of your master."

The one who had received the one talent came up and said, "Master, I knew you to be a hard man, reaping where you did not sow and gathering where you scattered no seed. I was afraid, and went away and hid your talent in the ground. See, you have what is yours." But his master answered and said to him, 'You wicked, lazy servant, you knew that I reap where I did not sow and gather where I scattered no seed. Then you ought to have put my money in the bank, and on my arrival I would have received my money back with interest. Therefore take away the talent from him, and give it to the one who has the ten talents. For to everyone who has, more shall be given, and he will have an abundance; but from the one who does not have, even what he does have shall be taken away. Throw out the worthless servant into the outer darkness; in that place there will be weeping and gnashing of teeth."

The wisdom to be gained from this parable: Do not bury your

talent! Our Master expects a return on the investment He has made in each one of us!

Surely, we can all agree that if we live our lives and make no use of the talent(s) given us, it would be ludicrous for us to expect a reward when our Master returns..

The fifth story recounts the day when the Son of Man comes in His glory, and all the angels with Him. In that day He will sit on His glorious throne, and all the nations will be gathered before Him. Then, He will separate them from one another, as the shepherd separates the sheep from the goats; and He will put the sheep on His right, and the goats on the left.

Then, the King will say to those on His right, "Come, you who are blessed of My Father, inherit the kingdom prepared for you from the foundation of the world. For I was hungry, and you gave Me something to eat; I was thirsty, and you gave Me something to drink; I was a stranger, and you invited Me in; naked, and you clothed Me; I was sick, and you visited Me; I was in prison, and you came to Me."

Then, the righteous will answer Him, "Lord, when did we see You hungry, and feed You, or thirsty, and give You something to drink? And when did we see You a stranger, and invite You in, or naked, and clothe You? When did we see You sick, or in prison, and come to You?"

The King will answer and say to them, "Truly I say to you, to the extent that you did it to one of these brothers of Mine, even the least of them, you did it to Me.

Then He will also say to those on His left, "Depart from Me, accursed ones, into the eternal fire which has been prepared for the devil and his angels; for I was hungry, and you gave Me nothing to eat; I was thirsty, and you gave Me nothing to drink; I was a stranger, and you did not invite Me in; naked, and you did not clothe Me; sick, and in prison, and you did not visit Me."

Then these rejected ones will respond, "Lord, when did we see You hungry, or thirsty, or a stranger, or naked, or sick, or in prison, and did not take care of You?"

Messiah will answer them, "'Truly I say to you, to the extent that you did not do it to one of the least of these, you did not do it to Me." These will go away into eternal punishment, but the righteous into eternal life.

The moral of these five stories is simple: be on the alert, and be prepared. Clearly, we have been forewarned that we must always be ready. For, the Son of Man is coming at an hour when we do not think He will. And, when He comes, He will expect us to be ready to enter into the wedding feast, having oil in our lamps and having made good use of our talents.

The wisdom of these five parables also is summed up by Yeshua, when He says to the church at Laodicea, "I know your deeds, that you are neither cold nor hot; I wish that you were cold or hot. So because you are lukewarm [indifferent], and neither hot nor cold, I will spit you out of My mouth (Revelation 3:14-15).

It is wisdom to be "hot." It is far better to be prepared, and not called upon, than to be called upon and found unprepared.

How then do we prepare?

Obviously it would be beneficial if we could have been with Yeshua's first group of chosen followers and personally received the orders and instructions He gave them. However, the **Ruach ha Kodesh** is now available to each of us. And, we have the Gospels and Luke's account in the first Chapter of Acts about all that Yeshua began to do and teach. We also know that Yeshua presented Himself alive to His disciples after His resurrection, by many convincing proofs, appearing to them eleven times over a period of forty days and speaking of the things concerning the kingdom of God.

During these teaching sessions, Yeshua's emphasis regarding the restoration of the Kingdom must have been significant. For, when they had come together for what turned out to be their last instruction class, they asked Him, "Lord, is it at this time You are restoring the kingdom to Israel?"

Yeshua's answer to them, and to the next forty-nine generations, was, "It is not for you to know times or epochs which the Father has fixed by His own authority. It is for you to be My witnesses both in Jerusalem, and in all Judea and Samaria, and even to the remotest part of the earth" (Acts 1:1-8).

Forty-nine generations have come and gone since then. Throughout these generations our forefathers have been a "witness" throughout the earth. Those of Ephraim have witnessed to our Father's way with the emphasis on grace and salvation, and to His provision for us to have an individual, or **personal**, relationship with Him, through Messiah Yeshua. Those of Judah have attested to the Father's high standards, and served as a visible proof of His covenant with Abraham, Isaac and Jacob and His desire to have a **people** for His own possession.

The torch that lights the way for us to understand the mystery of our "Hope of Glory," by actually realizing the fulfillment of our hope, has now been passed to us—to those of the fiftieth, or Jubilee generation (Colossians 1:27).

Could this be *the* generation of which Yeshua spoke—the generation which the Father has fixed by His own authority for the age-ending epoch of fulfilling our *Hope of Glory*—which comes to pass by fulfilling His *Hope for Messianic Israel?* [12]

The signs of the times, and prudence, both dictate that we answer, "Yes, it is the time. Yes, it is time for us to prepare for our King's return."

---

12 See *The Hope of Messianic Israel*, page 259

3

Learning The Lessons of History

It has been said that if we fail to learn the lessons of history we are doomed to repeat them.

It is wisdom for us to know both those lessons we want to repeat, and those that we do not want to repeat. In other words, to the extent that we desire the results obtained by our forefathers, we emulate them. To the extent that we desire results different from the results obtained by our forefathers, we do not emulate them.

Therefore, it is incumbent upon us to have a knowledge of history. The past is important because, people who lived before us discovered truths from which we can learn, and thus, we can avoid repeating their mistakes.

If we join with those who consider the past a relic unworthy of their attention, we, like they, will find our short-term memory growing shorter, and our ignorance growing larger.

Unfortunately, we are seeing our generation focus increasingly on the future, while forgetting the past. This will undoubtedly make our future more dangerous. This is a warning given by Professor Stephen Bertman in his book *Cultural Amnesia: America's Future and the Crisis of Memory* (Praeger 2000).

Bertman argues that there is a tremendous cost to be paid when we overlook our past:

"The life of an individual is measured in years and decades; the life of a culture, in centuries and even millennia. A culture maintains its identity by passing on the sum of its values and experiences from one generation to the next. Its memory must be organic and temporal, else the culture dies or survives only as a hollow shell."

Memory loss distorts how we view everything: our country, its culture, our faith, our relationships with others and with our God. If no stories from the past about overcoming are recalled, then where is the appeal to self-sacrifice, hard work and individual responsibility, marital faithfulness, and accountability?

Nobel laureate John Eccles reminds us, "Without (memory) we are hollow persons, not only empty of a past, but lacking a foundation upon which to build the future. We are what we remember."

Bertman puts it this way: "If the memories of the past are not passed on, for all intents and purposes, they cease to exist." He warns, "By creating the impression that the new is intrinsically superior to the old, science and technology have effectively dethroned tradition. Simultaneously, they also elevate the stature of the present and future in the human mind."

We are becoming a society that worships the computer. However, while the computer has memory, it has no remembrance. It allows us to mistake access to recent information for wisdom. Students are majoring in technology skills, because they feel it is the quickest way to make money. They are mostly forgetting the humanities that help create a well-rounded life. This has led, in Berman's words, to a "materialistic creed that celebrates transience, and an electronic faith that worships the present to the exclusion of all other dimensions of time. Indeed, it is these forces, more than any others, that will govern the course of American history in the 21st century."

Materialism does not produce a meaningful philosophy of life. Most modern teaching, even at the college level, is about isolated facts disconnected from a philosophy of the whole. For example, America was founded on a philosophy. And, for those of us living in America, our faith, liberty, sense of justice, and our economy flowed from that philosophy. If we forget it, we forget America.

And yet, more and more people, especially the young, no longer think our past is important. Give them money and a temple on Wall Street, that is inhabited by a healthy bull. That is what they want.

Bertman's diagnosis of our present condition is not only true of our secular society, but also of our spiritual community. Earlier we acknowledged Yahveh's indictment of that same condition: "My people are destroyed for lack of knowledge. Because you have rejected knowledge, I also will reject you from being My priest. Since you have forgotten the law of your God, I also will forget your children" (Hosea 4:6).

The increasing breakdown of law and order must first of all be attributed to the churches and their persistent anti-nomianism.[13] If the churches are anti-law, or even lax with respect to the law, will not the people follow suit? Moreover, we must realize that civil law cannot be separated from Biblical law. For, the Biblical doctrine of law includes all law, civil, ecclesiastical, societal, familial, and all other forms of it. The social order which despises God's law places itself on death row. It is marked for judgment.

Fortunately, we have a good starting point to begin our search for wisdom. It being the past.

---

13 The doctrine or belief that the Gospel frees Christians from required obedience to any law, whether scriptural, civil, or moral, and that salvation is attained solely through faith and the gift of divine grace.

Restoring Israel's Kingdom

4

A Brief History of Israel

In the beginning, the Eternal God, the "I AM WHO I AM" (Yahveh), through His Word (Yeshua), created the heavens and the earth (Genesis 1:1; Exodus 3:14; John 1:1-3).

Our God made the light, the waters, all vegetation, and all living creatures (Genesis 1:2-26). The culmination of His creation being man, male and female, whom He created in His own image (Genesis 1:27).

Yahveh blessed man, and He said to them, "Be fruitful and multiply, and fill the earth, and subdue it; and rule over the fish of the sea and over the birds of the sky and over every living thing that moves on the earth (Genesis 1:28).

Now it came about when men began to multiply, Yahveh saw that they had corrupted themselves (Genesis 6:11). Only one man, Noah, was found to be righteous (Genesis 6:9). So, Yahveh blotted out every living thing upon the earth. Only Noah was left, together with those who were with him in the ark (Genesis 7:23).

Then Yahveh instructed Noah to be fruitful and multiply and populate the earth abundantly and multiply in it (Genesis 9:7).

Later, some of the sons of men said, "Come, let us build for ourselves a city, and a tower whose top will reach into heaven, and let us make for ourselves a name, otherwise we will be scattered abroad over the face of the whole earth" (Genesis 9:4).

Yahveh, seeing the city and the tower which the sons of men had built for themselves, was not pleased. So He confused their language and scattered them abroad from there over the face of the whole earth; thus ending their building program (Genesis 11:5-9).

But one man, Abram, found favor with Yahveh. Of him Yahveh said, he obeyed Me and kept My charge, My commandments, My statutes and My laws (Genesis 14: 18-24; 26:5). Yahveh chose Abram, so that he could command his children and his household after him to keep the way of the Lord by doing righteousness and justice. And so the Lord could bring upon Abraham those things that He ultimately spoke over him (Genesis 18:19).

Yahveh considered Abram to be righteous because he "believed" God. Specifically Abraham believed that, from his own loins, would come offspring as numerous as the stars of heaven, the sand by the seashore, and the dust of the earth (Genesis 15:4; 17:2-6; 22:17; 25:60; 26:4, 24; 28:3,14; 35:11; 46:3; 48:19).

In addition, Yahveh covenanted with Abram to be "God" to him, and to his descendants after him, and to give to Abram and his descendants, all the land from the river of Egypt as far as the great river Euphrates, for an everlasting possession (Genesis 15:18; 17:7-8; 26:4; 28:13; 35:12).

Throughout Scripture we see Yahveh's affirmation of His promise to Abraham—that Abraham would be fruitful, and that from his own loins would come myriads. Yahveh would be a personal God to those who came forth from Abraham's loins, and He would give them a piece of real estate. Yahveh then established the linage through which He would fulfill these promises.

The promise went from Abraham, to Isaac, then to Jacob, and then to Joseph, and finally, to Ephraim (Genesis 12:3; 15:5; 17:4; 26:4; 24:24,60; 28:3,14; 32:12; 48:4,16,19.)

Ephraim was designated as Jacob's firstborn heir (Genesis 48:1-22; Deuteronomy 21:17; 1 Chronicles 5:1-2; Ezekiel 37:19.) And, Ephraim's seed was destined to become a company of nations, a *melo hagoyim*, a fullness of Gentiles (Genesis 48:19; Romans 11:25; Isaiah 8:14; for *melo*: see Psalm 24:1).

In Yahveh's divine plan, the next step in developing a people for His own possession was to send them down to Egypt for four hundred years. To accomplish this portion of His plan, Joseph was sent down to Egypt as a forerunner to prepare the way for the House of Jacob (Israel). And the house of Israel, arriving in Egypt some seventy strong, would grow into a numerous people over the next four centuries.

When Israel's time in Egypt was fulfilled Yahveh appointed Moses to deliver His people out of the iron furnace of Egypt, that they might be a people for His own possession.

So Moses led them out, performing wonders and signs in the land of Egypt and in the Red Sea and in the wilderness for forty years (Exodus 15).

Unfortunately, the people of Israel, whom Yahveh had chosen as His inheritance, were unwilling to be obedient to Him, but repudiated Him, and in their hearts turned back to Egypt. While Moses was on the mountain receiving the Covenants of Promise the people said to Aaron, 'Make for us gods who will go before us; for this Moses who led us out of the land of Egypt—we do not know what happened to him. So, at that time they made a calf and brought a sacrifice to their idol, and were rejoicing in the works of their hands (Exodus 32).

So, Yahveh turned away from His people, saying to them, "It was not to Me that you offered victims and sacrifices forty years in the wilderness, was it, O house of Israel? 'You also took along the tabernacle of Moloch and the star of the god Rompha, the images which you made to worship. Because of this I will remove you beyond Babylon'" (Acts 7:43).

Israel's disobedience in the wilderness was a harbinger of its future conduct, which conduct would eventually lead to their being exiled from the land that it was about to enter.

Israel, to its detriment, has continually attempted to mix the gods of this world with the God of Israel.

But Moses successfully handled this first act of disobedience when he came down from the mountain. He destroyed the golden calf and the people were punished. Then the people built the tabernacle of testimony of Israel in the wilderness to the glory of the Holy One of Israel, according to the pattern which Yahveh had given Moses (Exodus Chapters 36-40).

Then Israel, led by Joshua, an Ephraimite, crossed the Jordan and took possession of the Land from the nations whom Yahveh had driven out before His people (Book of Judges).

After the time of Joshua, Israel was ruled by a number of Judges. Like the Kings who would follow them, some were good and some were not. The problem which has plagued Israel to this day is that they could not do away with other gods (Books of Judges, Samuel, Kings and Chronicles).

Then David found favor in Yahveh's sight. And David asked that he might find a dwelling place for the God of Jacob. But it was Solomon, David's son, who built a house for the Holy One of Israel (1 Kings 8:18-20).

Unfortunately, it was not enough for Solomon to build a temple for the Holy One of Israel. In addition, to please his many wives, he build places to honor their "gods." As punishment, after Solomon's death, Yahveh divided Israel into two houses: Israel (Ephraim) and Judah (1 Kings 11:11-13,26,31-35; 12:15,24; 2 Chronicles 11:4; Isaiah 8:14). Then these two house were sent into exile. The last vestige of the Northern Kingdom (Ephraim) was sent to Assyria around 722 B.C. The Southern Kingdom (Judah) was sent to Babylon during the period of 585 to 575 B.C. (1 Kings 14:15; 2 Kings 17:6,24; 1 Chronicles 5:26; Ezekiel 1:1).

Those of Ephraim became *LoAmmi—Not A People.* And, they were swallowed up among all nations, thus losing touch with their Israelite identity (Hosea 1:10; 2:1,21-23; 8:8; Romans 9:23; Amos 9:9).

While Israel is forever chosen to choose, each Israelite, **of his own free will**, must choose to follow, or not to follow, the Holy One of Israel (Deuteronomy 28:1-68; 30:19; Joshua 24:15).

There is an eternal call on all descendants of Israel. Moreover, their biology does not change, regardless of faith or the lack thereof (Deuteronomy 4:37; 7:6-8; 10:15; Exodus 19:4-6; Jeremiah 31:37; 33:25-26; Romans 11:28-29). Ephraim, like Judah, was scattered. But, in addition Ephraim became lost to his Israelite heritage (Hosea 1-2; 4:1,6: Jer 31:18-19). Yet, the people of Ephraim continue to be physical Israelites (Jeremiah 31:20; 2 Kings 17:23; Zechariah 11:14; Daniel 9:7; 1 Chronicles 5:26; Ephesians 2:17.Hosea 5:3; 8:8; Amos 9:9; Deuteronomy 28:64).

Israel has not as yet been reunited. For, a reunited Israel will be sinless, will not be uprooted from the Land, and Yeshua will reign over them (Isaiah 11:11-14; Jeremiah 3:14-18; 16:11-16; 50:4-5,20; Zechariah 8:3,7,13; 9:13; 10:7,8,10; Hosea 11:10; Obadiah 1:18; 1 Samuel 17:45; Ezekiel 37:22-26; Isaiah 27:9).

After seventy years in Babylon, a remnant of Judah returned to the Land, and rebuilt the temple. For the next four centuries, Judah struggled, first under Greek oppression and then Roman, to maintain a presence in the Land.

Then, in the fullness of time Yeshua was born, fulfilling the words spoken by Moses to the sons of Israel: "Yahveh, the Lord your God, shall raise up for you a Prophet like me from your brethren; to him you shall give heed in everything he says to you. And it shall be that every soul that does not heed that Prophet shall be utterly destroyed from among the people."

It was this Prophet whose presence was manifested to the congregation in the wilderness. It was He who spoke to Moses on Mount Sinai and gave Moses the living oracles to pass on to the people of Israel (Deuteronomy 18:15; Acts 3:22-23).

The Angel Gabriel said of Yeshua:

"He will be great, and will be called the Son of the Most High; and the Lord God will give Him the throne of His father David and He will reign over the house of Jacob (Israel) forever; and His kingdom will have no end" (Luke 1:32-33).

Yeshua said of Himself, "I was sent only to the lost sheep of the house of Israel (Matthew 15-24). And, My sheep know My voice. I know them, and they follow Me" (John 10:27).

Yeshua conferred the kingdom of Israel on His disciples: "Your Father has been pleased to give you His kingdom. He did this by conferring on them the kingdom which His Father conferred on them (Luke 12:32; 22:29). Yeshua also told them that, in His kingdom they would eat and drink at His table and sit on thrones, judging the twelve tribes of Israel" (Luke 22:30).

Yeshua said to Pilate, "You say correctly that I am a king. For this I have been born, and for this I have come into the world, to bear witness to the truth. Everyone who is of the truth hears My voice" (John 18:37).

Caiaphas the high Priest, "not on his own initiative, but being high priest that year: prophesied that Yeshua, 'was going to die for the nation, and not for the nation only, but that He might also gather together into one the children of Yahveh who are scattered abroad'" (John 11:52-53).

Peter said of Yeshua, "Thou art the Anointed One, the Son of the living God" (Matthew 16:16).

The *ami* (people of Israel) said of Yeshua, "Blessed is the King who comes in the name of the Holy One of Israel" (Luke 19:38).

Yeshua summed up His ministry in His report to His Father in His (Highly Priestly prayer):

"Father, I glorified Thee on the earth, having accomplished the work which Thou hast given Me to do. And now, glorify Thou Me together with Thyself, Father, with the glory which I had with Thee before the world was.

26

"I manifested Thy name to the men whom Thou gavest Me out of the world; Thine they were, and Thou gavest them to Me, and they have kept Thy word...for the words which Thou gavest Me I have given to them; and they received them, and truly understood that I came forth from Thee, and they believed that Thou didst send Me.

"I ask on their behalf; I do not ask on behalf of the world, but of those whom Thou hast given Me....keep them in Thy name, the name which Thou hast given Me, that they may be one, even as We are.

"I do not ask Thee to take them out of the world, but to keep them from the evil one. They are not of the world, even as I am not of the world. Sanctify them in the truth of Thy word. I do not ask in behalf of these alone, but for those also who believe in Me through their word;

"That they may all be one; even as Thou, Father, art in Me, and I in Thee, that they also may be in Us; that the world may believe that Thou didst send Me....I in them, and Thou in Me, that they may be perfected in unity, that the world may know that Thou didst send Me, and didst love them, even as Thou didst love Me" (John 17:4-23).

Then Yeshua went to the cross, and His last words before giving up His Spirit were "It is finished" (John 19:30).

But, thanks be to our Father in Heaven these were not His last words, for the tomb was empty!

After His resurrection, Yeshua presented Himself alive to His disciples. After His suffering, by many convincing proofs, He appeared to them over a period of forty days, and taught of the things concerning the kingdom of God. In response to His teachings His disciples asked Him, "Lord, is it at this time You are restoring the kingdom to Israel" (Acts 1:6)?

Yeshua's answer was, "It is not for you to know times or epochs which the Father has fixed by His own authority; but you shall receive power when the Holy Spirit has come upon you; and you shall be My witnesses both in Jerusalem, and in all Judea and

Samaria, and even to the remotest part of the earth. And after He had said these things, He was lifted up while they were looking on, and a cloud received Him out of their sight" (Acts 1:7-9).

Thus, Yeshua, having finished His work, was seated in heaven at the right hand of the Father. There He will remain until the period of fulfillment of all things about which Yahveh spoke by the mouth of His holy prophets from ancient time (John 17:4, Acts 3:21; Ephesians 1:20).

With Yeshua's death and resurrection, and the destruction of the Second Temple in 70 A.D., another division occurred in Israel. The various elements of First Century Judaism, that had been held together by a temple, a priesthood, and sacrificial system, split into two major segments: Rabbinical Judaism and Christianity. And for the next two thousand years the people of Israel have continued to divide.

However, our Father's has declared a latter day plan to reunite the two houses of Israel (Zechariah 8:23; Isaiah 8:14; Jeremiah 3:17-18; Daniel 7:27; Hosea 11:8-10; Amos 9:11; Luke 12:32; Romans 11).

And, as we—His people—enter the seventh millennium, He is beginning to gather the remnant of Israel from the places where He scattered them (Jeremiah 23:1-8). From this remnant He is calling forth the two houses of Israel, His two congregations of peoples, or two chosen families—Ephraim and Judah, and their companions of Israel—and He is making these two sticks, or trees, one in His hand (Ezekiel 37:15-28).

In the day when we see Israel is truly "One Stick in His Hand," Judah will believe in Messiah. This will happen when he sees Ephraim properly representing both the Messiah and Yahveh's Torah. Even as Judah has been blind to the Messiah, and Ephraim has been blind to his heritage and the truths of Torah, so both must begin to see, and it is wild branch Ephraim who must help bring this to pass (Matthew 23:37-39; Romans 11; Isaiah 8:14).

When Ephraim and Judah are united in Yahveh Elohim, when

their reunion is fully manifested, they become an invincible army—one that is empowered to fight, and win the battles of the God of Israel (Isaiah 11:14; Zechariah 9:13-10:10; 13:2; Hosea 1:11; Amos 9:10; Zeph 3:11-13).

Also, a day will come when the seventh angel will sound his trumpet. On that day, the kingdoms of this world will become the kingdom of our **Adonai** (Lord). As the greater Son of David, Yeshua will reign forever and ever. At this time, the dead will be judged. It also will be the time for Yahveh to give the rewards due to His bond-servants the prophets, and to the saints who fear His name, the small and the great, and to destroy those who destroy the earth (Revelation 11:15-19).

"Then a loud voice will be heard from the (Yahveh's) throne, 'Behold, the tabernacle of Yahveh is among men, and He shall dwell among them, and they shall be His people, and Yahveh Himself shall be among them, and He shall wipe away every tear from their eyes; and there shall no longer be any death; there shall no longer be any mourning, or crying, or pain; the first things have passed away.'

"And He who sits on the throne will say, "Behold, I am making all things new....It is done. I am the Alpha and the Omega, the beginning and the end. I will give to the one who thirsts from the spring of the water of life without cost.

"He who overcomes shall inherit these things, and I will be his God and he will be My son" (Revelation 21:3-7)

Until all these things have come to pass, it remains for us to *Shema Yisrael...*

Hear and obey O Israel! (Genesis 49:2; Deuteronomy 6:4; Hosea 5:1; Ezekiel 36:1).

Restoring Israel's Kingdom

5

Lessons Learned

Our God, the Holy One of Israel, created each one of us for a purpose. That purpose was to satisfy His desire to have a people for His own possession. He wants a people who are unified even as Yeshua prayed: "That they may all be one; even as You, Father, are in Me and I in You, that they also may be in Us, so that the world may believe that You sent Me" (John 17:21).

Thousands of different denominations and cults (which are continually multiplying), do not answer this prayer. Neither do the thousands of "religious Robinson Crusoes," each of which have his own island, an individual relationship with Yeshua, and little or no relationship with the people on the other islands. Our problem is a dysfunctional "Robinson" family: the family of Israel is divided, and it must be put back together before we can hope to fulfill our Father's desires of having a people for His own possession.

Unfortunately, the Church—by placing its emphases primarily on individual salvation based on "belief," and by ignoring the importance of heritage and national identity—has helped perpetuate the problem. She has enabled, even fostered divisions among the people of faith—who are for the most part unaware of their Israelite heritage. Thereby, she has encouraged dysfunctionalism.

The **Ruach ha Kodesh**, speaking through Paul, in his letter to the Ephesians, emphasizes a requirement for both individual and national relationships. Paul said, "Remember that you were at that time separate from Yeshua, excluded from the commonwealth of Israel, and strangers to the covenants of promise, having no hope and without God in the world" (Ephesians 2:12).

Paul gives three reasons why the Ephesians previously had been without hope, and without God in the world:

The first reason is because they were **separated from Yeshua**: this means, they were not saved, or born again. However, while we all can agree that not having obtained individual salvation is any individual's greatest problem, it was, according to Paul, not their only problem.

And Paul also gives a second reason: they were **excluded, or alienated, from the commonwealth of Israel**. In other words, in addition to not having individual salvation, they did not have national salvation. They were not part of a people set apart for the Holy One of Israel.

The third reason given was that they were "**strangers to the covenants of promise**." Paul spoke of the covenants that will one day culminate in the fulfillment of the Messianic Promise—which is the hope of glory—which is that the fulness of our eternal inheritance will be consummated at Yeshua's promised coming.

To make the family of Israel a functional family, forerunners must arise who will stop being "enablers." And, if **we** are these forerunners, then we cannot continue the failed policies and theology of generations of Christian and Jewish forefathers who enabled the divisions among the people of Israel to flourish.

Replacing a divided house that cannot stand with a united house that cannot fail may seem like an impossible mission. Yet the present day Messianic Israel explosion is proof that, under the guidance of the Ruach ha Kodesh, we can together accomplish the task of gathering the end-time remnant of Israel back to the land promised to our forefather Abraham. We can gather them in such numbers that there will seem to be no more room. And, in the land and in light of the enormity of this final ingathering of all Israel, we will no longer remember our ancestral exodus from Egypt (Jeremiah 23:2-8).

Working togther we can make a dysfunctional family functional!

6

The Voice of The People

In Yahveh's continuing and cumulative revelation to His covenant people, He not only speaks through leadership to the people, but he speaks through the people, to the people. And, through the people to the leadership. In other words, change most often starts at the root and works its way up. Those who recognize change become part of that change, and in turn nurture the changing process in others. Thus, they become the leaders and forerunners of a new move. This is true in both the secular and non-secular arenas.

We saw an example of this process in Moscow, when on August 19, 1991, tens of thousands, in response to an attempted coup, gathered around the Russian parliament building. Boris Yeltsin, recognizing and manifesting the desires of the people, climbed on a tank and became the leader of the former Soviet Union.

We also see a somewhat similar situation in the Book of Acts, wherein Paul addressed the desires of the "God fearers," meaning those "Gentiles who were called by Yahveh's name," and so were appointed to eternal life.

In an unexplained phenomenon of the period, God fearing Gentiles were found in the synagogues and cities of the diaspora that Paul visited.[14] And they, along with Jewish followers of Messiah, became the core of the First Century Church.

We also can see an example in the opinion process in the public body in the United States today, where formerly stable beliefs are now being challenged by one or more contradictory views. Excellent examples are the controversy between the Choice vs. the Right to Life movements of Abortion, and the Gay rights movement. These movements are part of the outward manifestation of the reformation of public morals presently taking place. These controversies were not started by those in power. They were initiated by an errant grassroots desire for change. Initially, those in control, State and Church, did attempt to maintain the status quo. However, we are seeing social acceptance of practices that were once taboo in our society: abortion, divorce, sodomy, homosexuality, casual sex, drugs, pornography, having children out of wedlock, etc.. And, without a Moses to control the non-secular, or a George Washington to guide the public, we are seeing a struggle among the leaders of both State and Church for power, as well as for the approval of the people.

In their attempts to guide and mold public will, most contenders become manipulative practitioners through publicity, advertising and pro**pagan**da (note what is at the core of this word). The apparent winners are reformers who are most sensitive to public will and desire. But, who controls public will? Where do the public desires that fuel demands for change come from? For example, whose idea was it to build a golden calf? Whose idea was it to deliver Israel from Egypt? Based on the answers to these two

---

14 *See the map, Atlas of Jewish History, by Martin Gilbert, reproduced by permission in IWho Is Israel? Also see Acts 9:15; 10:22,45; 11:1,18; 13:16,26,42,46,47; 14:27; 15:3,7,12,14,17,19,23; 18:6; 21:19, 25; 22:21; 26:20,23; 28:28.*

questions we see that the real contenders who would guide and mold public will are Yahveh and Satan. These two are now in the midst of the struggle that will end this age-old controversy. (This is not to imply that Satan has a power that is capable of contending with Yahveh. It is to say that Yahveh has for His purposes allowed this controversy.)

The degeneration taking place in the world today is the handi-work of none other than the "father of Lies" (John 8:44). This ultimate "manipulator" is spewing out his pro**pagan**da—and in and through its dissemination, he is gathering those who ultimately will worship and accept the mark of the beast.

The secret power of lawlessness is presently at work. The one who has heretofore held it back is being taken out of the way. We are seeing the lawless one revealed. We are seeing the work of Satan displayed in all kinds of counterfeit miracles, signs and wonders, and in every sort of evil that deceives those who are perishing. They will perish because they refuse to love the truth and so to be saved. For this reason, Yahveh is sending them a powerful delusion, so that they will believe the lie (i.e. social acceptance of abortion, divorce, sodomy, homosexuality, casual sex, pornography having children out of wedlock, etc.). They will be condemned because they have not believed the truth, but instead have delighted in wickedness (2 Thessalonians 2:7-12).

Evidence of The Coming Kingdom of Yahveh Is Exploding In Our Midst

We also see a similar opinion process in the Church, as the body of Messiah grapples with the evidence of the coming kingdom of Yahveh. We see certain signs of the times, such as: the reestablishment of the State of Israel, earthquakes, wars, famines, plagues, lawlessness revealed, all of which are part of the prophesied birth-pangs. Unfortunately, there is no consensus in the Church on how to handle these severe birth-pangs, nor how to comprehend how the Father will gather His people, and so bring His government into this world.

Thus, we see relatively stable religious beliefs being challenged by literally thousands of contradictory views. How else could we have some five-thousand denominations and cults in the United States alone (that being only the tip of the iceberg)?

We can group these contradictory views into several major categories. The largest portion of the Church (exemplified by the Roman Catholic Church) is attempting to keep and gain followers by holding on to its doctrines with minimal changes. The next group (which is best represented by the mainline Protestant World Council of Churches) is being more accommodating to the public's desire in their battle for membership. But, without the intervention of the Holy Spirit, the manmade doctrines of both groups will not be an effective defense against the lawless one.[15] And so, the vast majority of the members of these two groups, in a grand ecumenical movement, will ultimately worship and accept the mark of the beast. They will become the apostate church that serves the anti-Christ. They will be "those who have a form of godliness but in truth deny the power thereof" (Revelation 3:16,13:16-17; 14:9,11; 15:2; 16:2; 19:20; 20:4).

The remnant left over from these two giants, exclusive of many various cults, is made up of a mixture of Pentecostals, Fundamentalists, and Charismatics, etc. etc. etc.. It is primarily from this latter group that will come a faithful remnant that senses that the end is near, and that Yahveh is going to establish His kingdom. The major differences separating this group (other then battles over membership requirements) is whether or not they will participate in the final act here on earth. Many believe that, at some point, they will be "raptured," and will thus be spared all or part of the tribulations outlined in the Book of Revelation.

Certainly it would be wonderful if the rapture believers were

---

15 Throughout the history of Israel Yahveh has from time to time tolerated sin among His people for a season. But, the time always comes when He requires that iniquity be purged, and the full price paid for the pardoning of sin (Isaiah 27:9).

proven correct. However, if they are wrong, the consequences will be disastrous. Disillusioned and unprepared former rapture believers will be easy prey for the lawless one. Therefore, the prudent course of action for them would be to hope for the best, but to prepare for the worst.

We know the Father's desire is to give us the knowledge and discernment we require to guide us through these perilous times. However, knowledge and discernment are of little value if they are not received with correct goals and motives. For unlike the world system, Yahveh will not cater to, or be guided by, a public opinion process. Our wants must coincide with what He wants for us. His revelations will mean little or nothing to us until our wants coincide with His goals. Fortunately we do have His written Script, from which we may read, and so prepare for this final act. We can rely on the Ruach ha Kodesh to direct and guide us into all truth—including the increase of knowledge promised by Daniel (12:4)—as well as the confirmation by the threefold witness of the Spirit, the water, and the blood (John 16:13, 1 John 5:8).

When The Dust Settles We Will Be Known For Where We Stood

Alexander Pope once said: "The peoples' voice is odd; it is, and it is not, the voice of God."

Even so, the people are speaking today. From most, it is the voice of lawlessness. But, from a faithful remnant, it truly is the voice of God.

Obviously, making the wrong choice in this controversy will have eternal consequences. Ours will not be an easy choice. Even the very elect will be subject to great deception (Matthew 24:24). So, as we flounder in the indecision of our own desires and ambitions that are to be found in this Valley of Decision—even as we try to decide what we can individually make of, or do about, this proliferation of contradictory views—we must realize one vital point: the day will come when the dust of this vast controversy will settle, and then, each will be known for where he stood (Matthew 16:27, Romans 2:6).

So, we must become like the chiefs of Issachar. We also must men who understand the times, with knowledge of what Israel should do" (1 Chronicles 12:32). We must read the signs of the times and make our decisions based on the Word. However, we who are part of the remnant must realize that we are not alone. We are part of a growing army, whose lives are being dramatically changed, so as to enable them to stand in these trying times. One great change this body of Believers is experiencing is: we have received a "knowing" deep within our being that we are Israelites. This "knowing" is like the "knowing" we have regarding our personal relationship with the God of Abraham, Isaac, and Jacob.

This is the hour in which blindness is being lifted from the eyes of those of Ephraim. Thus they are gaining greater insight into their role as the other house of Israel (Isaiah 8:14; Romans 11:25). Yet, as the previously unidentifiable remnant of the covenant people of the Holy One of Israel, they have preserved the testimony of Jesus (Yeshua, the Messiah of all Israel).

Change also is coming to those of Judah: we will see the Jewish people, as a company, accept the Messiahship of Yeshua. That this process has already begun is indicated through a heightened Jewish interest in both the Church's concept of Messiah, and in their concept of the Messiah, and in the Messianic Judaism movement, wherein Jews are accepting the Messiah. As the identifiable remnant of the covenant people of HaShem (YHVH), they have preserved His Holy Torah (Law), His Holy Feasts, and His Holy Shabbat (Sabbath Day).

Answering The Call Placed Upon Our Lives

We note that, for the most part, the Bible only records those who answered the call Yahveh placed on their lives. While we do not fully know the Scriptural criteria for being called and chosen, we do know that "*many* are called, but *few* are chosen" (Matthew 22:14). And, we realize that the ranks of the chosen do not include those who did *not* answer the call placed upon their lives. Therefore, it behooves each of us to take advantage of every opportunity given us to fulfill our part in the divine destiny for this hour.

While it is an hour of divine destiny, it will also be an hour of trial and testing, when a "Church" that is but a godless shell will be spewed out of the Father's mouth. It is the hour in which we will each be asked to "lose our head for our God" (Revelation 12:11). It also is the time for the anxious longing of the creation to be fulfilled, by the revelation of the sons of Yahveh (Romans 8:19). We have come to a time when Ephraim is beginning to know himself. A remnant is being raised up, the veil is being lifted, its heritage and purpose is being restored to it (Jeremiah 31:18-19). At the same time, Judah is recognizing Yeshua *Ha'Natseret* (Jesus of Nazareth) as the true Messiah, the Lion of Judah, the Branch of Israel; he is seeing that He died and rose from the dead, and now lives at the right hand of the Almighty Father; and according to the ancient Holy Scriptures, the Messiah is **Adonai** (the Lord) appearing in the flesh, which Yeshua demonstrated in Himself (Isaiah 53; Micah 5:2-4).

A Messianic Vision

It is this restoration of these two houses of Israel that Ezekiel sees in his vision of the dry bones:

"The hand of the LORD was upon me, and He brought me out by the Spirit of the LORD and set me down in the middle of the valley; and it was full of bones. And He caused me to pass among them round about, and behold, there were very many on the surface of the valley; and lo, they were very dry... He said to me, 'Prophesy over these bones, and say to them, "O dry bones, hear the word of the LORD."' Thus says the Lord GOD to these bones, 'Behold, I will cause breath to enter you that you may come to life... and you will know that I am the LORD...' and they came to life, and stood on their

41

feet, an exceedingly great army. Then He said to me, 'Son of man, these bones are the whole house of Israel' (Ezekiel 37:1-15).

Yahveh declares that these bones represent the *whole house of Israel*. And in the balance of this chapter of Ezekiel, the Father reveals how He is going to accomplish this resurrection. It is by reuniting the two houses of Israel. The plan for reunification is outlined in Ezekiel's prophecy about the two sticks:

"The word of the Lord came again to me saying, and you son of man take for yourself one stick and write on it, 'For Judah and for the sons of Israel, his companions, then take another stick and write on it, 'for Joseph, the stick of Ephraim and all the house of Israel his companions.' Then join them for yourself one to another into one stick, that they may become one in your hand. And when the sons of your people speak to you saying, 'Will you not declare to us what you mean by these? Say to them, 'Thus says the Lord God, Behold, I will take the stick of Joseph, which is in the hand of Ephraim, and the tribes of Israel, his companions; and I will put them with the stick of Judah, and make them one stick, and they will be one in my hand'" (Ezekiel 37:15-28.)

Fulfilling Ezekiel's Messianic Vision

Building upon the foundation of the apostles and prophets with Yeshua as our the corner stone, we can create the arena wherein Ezekiel's prophecy can be fulfilled (Ephesians 2:20). In this arena, the two sticks can be symbolically joined in front of the people, and they can be instructed and prepared for the work of Yahveh. There, both Ephraim and Judah can be included on an equal and comfortable basis—with a common agenda of restoring the kingdom, by building a reunited house, thus preparing the way for the return of the Greater Son of David, and so they will fulfill the messianic vision.

The *Hope of Messianic Israel*[16] will accomplish these purposes.

---

16 See *The Hope of Messianic Israel*, page 259

As a people, our common hope will serve as an adhesive that will bind us together, and also will act as a solvent to remove the "blindness in part" which has happened to all Israel (both houses). As this blindness is lifted, non-Jewish followers in Yeshua will gain further insight into their role as Ephraim. They will become defenders of Torah, and of Judah, and so the numbers of Jewish people accepting the Messiahship of Yeshua will continue to increase.

Most importantly, Yahveh is calling His people of Israel together. Once again, He is speaking to the people, through the people. Yahveh is giving His faithful remnant a *Messianic Vision.*

Restoring Israel's Kingdom

7

Who Told You?

Yahveh is the "God of Israel," and His people are "the people of Israel." Thus, the identity of the people of Israel is extremely important: how we define Israel determines how we interpret Scripture. It sets the course for the path we take as we walk through the Word. It governs our interpretation of Yahveh's end-time plan for His people: For, it rules who we believe those people to be. Therefore, it is crucial that we ask ourselves: who told us about "Israel"? Did they tell us the truth? Were they building on a Scriptural foundation of truth?

A recent edition of the Encyclopedia of American Religions listed 1,586 different faiths in the United States—which number only continues to increase. Each of these religions in some way differs from the others, yet each claims to have the truth!

Do one or more of these faiths have the truth, or at least sufficient truth so their members won't be misled by lies and the father of lies? If so, which one, or ones?

We must be concerned about the consequences of being deceived by errors and misconceptions, for lies bring captivity and death, while truth brings freedom and life (John 8:21,32,44; 2 Timothy

2:26). With such high stakes riding on what we believe, we must ask ourselves: is what we believe true? Is the foundation on which we are building our understanding of Israel one of truthfulness?

In his book, *Ten Philosophical Mistakes*,[17] Mortimer J. Adler, one of America's foremost philosopher, explores the ten major errors in the development of modern thought, and he examines the serious consequences these errors have had in our everyday lives. He explains how the errors came about, and what we can do to avoid their snare. Adler takes on Locke, Hume, Rousseau, Hobbs, Marx, and a host of other post-16th-century thinkers, pointing out that: their common and disastrous mistake was to invent new kinds of wisdom which was used to continue building on a faulty foundation. For, they all failed to go back to ground zero and to begin to build on ancient and original truths!

In other words, the philosophers did not tear down the faulty structure far enough, they did not get to a solid foundation of original truth.

Adler begins his book by quoting a 4th Century B.C. assertion made by Aristotle: "The least initial deviation from the truth is multiplied later a thousandfold." Adler also paraphrases the words of Thomas Aquinas: "Little errors in the beginning lead to serious consequences in the end." Adler himself says: "Instead of retracing the steps that lead back to their sources in little errors at the beginning, modern thinkers have tried in other ways to circumvent the result of the initial errors, often compounding the difficulties instead of overcoming them."[18]

Do Christian theologians suffer from the same disastrous mistake? Did they invent new kinds of wisdom not built on original truths? If so, do their errors compound our problems?

The answers call for a resounding, "Yes! Yes! Yes!" The Church has never recovered from its early doctrinal divisions and theological mistakes. Especially crippling are the mistakes made

---

17 *Ten Philosophical Mistakes*, MacMillian Publishing. NY, NY,

18 *Ten Philosophical Mistakes*, pages xiii,xv

over the identity of Israel, for they blind us to a full understanding of Yahveh's plan for the whole house of Israel.

The truth is, initially, that all of Messiah's followers were physical Israelites who belonged to a sect of Judaism (Acts 28:22). Further, these Israelites had children. But somehow, somewhere along the way, we ceased to consider their physical descendants as physical Israelites. Also, the Church broke away from Judah and became a "Gentile Church."

How did this happen? What caused these changes?

An oversimplified answer is: It began when Believers in Messiah Yeshua were put out of the synagogues (John 9:22; 12:42). This exclusion was escalated when Rome sought to subdue Judea in the first century. After the Roman destruction of the Temple, in 70 A.D., some of the people of Judah began to develop and follow what was later called "Rabbinic Judaism." Others followed "the Way" (Acts 24:14), which ultimately developed into the "Westernized Christianity" of today. Also, in the second century, those of "Rabbinic Judaism" declared a man named Bar Kochva to be Messiah, one who would bring deliverance from their oppressors. Those who followed Messiah Yeshua could not endorse this false Messiah, nor his battle. Therefore, their Jewish brothers labeled them as traitors, or *meshumed*, and again put them out of the synagogues. Earlier, because the Jewish people put up a tremendous fight against mighty Rome, "anti-Jewishness" became rampant among the Romans. Roman converts gave vent to their ugly anti-Jewish attitude in their theology, and began to separate themselves from things considered "Jewish." The more they separated themselves, the less they were persecuted by Rome, and the less they were known as a "Jewish sect." Ultimately, the Roman converts outnumbered the Jewish Believers, and the Church traded their Hebrew orientation for one rooted in paganism. Thus Rome became the seat of power for the Greco/Roman Westernized Christianity of today.

The result?

Judah cut the Church off, and so she cut herself off from Judah. And, the more she was cut off from her roots, the more rootless, Gentilized, and paganized she became. And, the more pagan she became, the more Judah continued to cut her off. On and on the story goes, like the proverbial dog chasing its tail.

Little Errors: Serious Consequences

Initial deviation from absolute truth by the Early Church has been multiplied a thousandfold. Even the slightest retaliatory anti-Jewish errors made in the beginning have lead to serious consequences in the end. Today, the Church produces rootless children—children bored beyond belief with her elementary teachings—children who see through the lies of her often grossly distorted theologies.[19]

Due to her separation from her Israelite roots, physically, the Church became rootless, which led to her excessive emphasis on the "Spiritual Israel" title, which aided in blinding her to the truth of her physical Israelite roots, and to more of the dog chasing its tail syndrome (Isaiah 8:14; John 2:22; Romans 11:25).[20]

The Unchangeableness of Genealogy And of The Grafting Process

To stop chasing one's tail, and to build a solid foundation in one's understanding of Israel, one must tear down the faulty structure to a point of absolute truth. And, the truth is: what an individual believes, or fails to believe, has absolutely no effect on the facts about his biological descent! Faith, or a lack thereof, does not, cannot, change the actual identity of your grandfathers. True, the punishment for certain sins was to be "cut off" from the people, yet, the sinner did not cease to be a biological Israelite. Yahveh's call on the people of Israel is a call to be His "witnesses," and, it is

---

19 See the HDH's *Muddled Doctrines, The Crossroads At Laodicea,* and *The City of Truth.*
20 This is not to deny her Spiritual roots in the Messiah through the all-important second birth.

a call that is "without repentance." Though an Israelite can be a "bad witness," he remains nonetheless, a "witness," meaning he continues to be a biological Israelite (Numbers 15:30; Deuteronomy 11:26; Zechariah 8:13; Romans 11:20-29). Further, unbelieving Israelites can be grafted back into the living Olive Tree of Israel (Romans 11:23).

This truth about the unchangeableness of ones genealogy and his ability to be grafted in again, applies to the people of Judah and to the scattered sheep of the Northern Kingdom—to those destined to become the lost sheep of the house of Israel (Hosea 1-2; 8:8; Amos 9:9). For, Yahveh said the Ephraimites would become a "*melo goyim*," or, a "fullness of Gentiles" (Genesis 48:19).[21] Also, as many ancient Rabbi's taught, Yahveh determined that these scattered Israelites would "one day experience a second birth that would once again make them the people of Israel."[22] These "lost" tribes of Israel were not lost in the sense that we will find them on some as yet unchartered island. Rather, they were lost as to their identity—which "lostness" was part of their punishment (Hosea 1:9-11; 8:8; Romans 9:26).[23]

Further, Messiah's first followers were physical Israelites, and they numbered in the tens of thousands. Surely this vast host of first century followers results in millions of physical descendants being in the Church today.

Also, to His original followers, Yahveh has added myriads of so-

---

21 Jacob prophesied that those of Ephraim would become a "*melo goyim*." See Strong's Hebrew Lexicon , word #'s 4393 and 1471.

22 Alfred Edersheim, in his study of Rabbinical thought regarding the lost tribes, concludes: "As regards the ten tribes there is this truth underlying...that, as their persistent apostasy from the God of Israel and His worship had cut them off from His people, so the fulfillment of the Divine promises to them in the latter days would imply, as it were a second birth to make them once more Israel." See his book, *Life and Times of Jesus the Messiah*, page 15. Also see, *The Olive Tree of Israel,, In Search of Israel*, and *Who Is Israel?*. Chapter 7..

23 Orthodox Rabbi Isidor Zwirn says that in gathering the so-called Gentiles, Yeshua was actually preserving the whole house of Israel. See his Booklet, *Was Jesus A False Messiah?: Or, Did He Preserve (Netzer) The Whole House Of Israel?* Rabbi Zwirn also says: "Separateness, hostility and warfare continued between the Ephraimites and Judahites until, the first Holocaust of Israel [occurred]. The government of Northern Israel was wiped off the face of the earth." See the HDH , *What Motivates George Bush And His New World Order?*

called "Gentiles." However, many, if not the majority, of these Gentiles are undoubtedly physical Israelites! They are the manifestation of God's promise in Amos and Hosea to gather the scattered descendants of Israel (see John 10:16; Ezekiel 34:11).

As to any actual foreigners who might join themselves to Messiah's original followers, and as to any wild olive branches that He might be grafting back into the cultivated tree,[24] the laws for joining the house of Israel applied to them: Yahveh decreed three things one must do to be recognized as a physical Israelite: 1) Be circumcised 2) Observe Passover 3) Sojourn with the Israelites. Once they fulfilled these requirements, they were called "natives of the land." He even warned converts not to see themselves as separate from His people Israel (Exodus 12:48,49; Leviticus 19:34; Numbers 9:14; 15:15,16; Isaiah 56:3-8).

When Yeshua instituted the New Covenant in Israel, He changed these Laws to that of circumcision of the heart, with Him serving as our Passover Lamb, and His requirement for sojourning is with New Covenant Israelites (Jeremiah 31:33; Hebrews 7:12; Romans 2:29; 1 Corinthians 5:7; Hebrews 10:25).

Since the first Believers were physical Israelites, any who joined them also became physical Israelites. They were and are today, New Covenant Israelites; they are physical Israelites being called to abide by a spiritual covenant (Ephesians 2:11-19).

Two Houses—Two Lies

After King Solomon's death, the house of Israel was divided into the two houses of Ephraim and Judah. Though Ezekiel speaks of the day when Yahveh will make the "two sticks" that represent them, "one stick in His hand" (Ezekiel 37:15-28), presently, the house of Israel remains divided: Ephraim, the fullness of Gentiles, the Congregation of the First-born, the Church; and Judah, those of the rabbinical Judaism of today.

---

24 See Jeremiah 11:10,16; 2:18,21; Revelation 11:3-4, Romans 11:17, and The Olive Tree of Israel.

This divided house of Israel believes two lies:

1) The lie believed by the Jewish people is: You cannot accept Jesus (Yeshua) as the Messiah and remain Jewish!

2) The lie believed by the Church is: We are spiritual, rather than physical, descendants of Abraham, Isaac, and Jacob! Further, the matter of physical descent is not important!

Believing these lies has resulted in Jewish people cutting off those whom she should rightfully be calling her own. Because, it causes terrible hardship for Jewish Believers who want to embrace their Jewishness, their people, and the Jewish Messiah.

Regarding the Church, she does not see that, to believe anything less than the full truth about the identity of the physical Israelites is to be blinded by a lie, and, that her "little error," has "led to serious consequences in the end."

It resulted in a Church that is sitting on the street corner, waiting for a Rapture Bus—a Bus that will come and take them away from it all. But, in reality, as part of the people of Israel, she is called to stay and to be part of the solution. Sadly, she has not rightly discerned the Bus Schedule. For, the Rapture Bus will not come until the "sound of the last trumpet," and that trumpet will not sound until the pouring out of the last bowl (1 Corinthians 15:52; Revelation 11:15).[25]

Both houses cheat themselves by believing the above two lies, for these lies hinder Yahveh's reunion plan, and, only a reunited Israel will be manifested as the sons of God. Only they will achieve the promised victory over evil (Ezekiel 37; John 17; 1 Samuel 17:45; Isaiah 11:13-14; Obadiah 1:18; Zechariah 9:13).

Today, six thousand years from Adam, four thousand years from Abraham, and two thousand years from Messiah, Yahveh's people have not yet experienced the full manifestation of their sonship (Romans 8:19).

Why not? And, when will that happen?

---

25 See 2 Thessalonians 2:3-4, and the HDH's *Rapture Or Transformation?*, *Victory In The Gulf!* and *Restoring The Fallen Booth of David: The Tabernacles Celebration.*

Their sonship will be manifested only after Ephraim "comes to know himself," and only after he shakes off "the sins of paganism of his youth" (Jeremiah 31:18-19). When Ephraim "comes to know himself," he will exchange the lie he believes for the truth. When he shakes off the lie, then his "jealousy will depart." Then, he will be redeemed from the mistake of building on a faulty foundation. When these changes come to pass, then, Judah will begin to recognize him as a true brother (Isaiah 11:13).

Israel has not experienced the fullness of its long promised victory because Yahveh promised that victory to a united people! These people will not experience this victory in fullness as long as they are divided! For, a "house divided against itself cannot stand." The invincible army of Isaiah 11 speaks of a reunited house. The King of Kings will reign over a reunited, sinless Israel (Mark 3:25; Isaiah 8:14; Jeremiah 33:24; Ezekiel 37:15-28).

In summation, our concept of Israel becomes the map we use to navigate our voyage to our eternal destiny. Our opinion about the identity of Israel becomes the rule book we use to discern both who the players are, and Yahveh's game plan for the players. It is therefore vital that we exchange the lies we believe about Israel for the truth. For, only then can we begin to understand His Divine Plan for the whole house of Israel. And, only when we understand that plan will we be building on a sure foundation.

Part Two

Building On A Sure Foundation

8

Who Is A Jew? A Look At Israel's Bloodline

Y eshua said, "Let not your heart be troubled: believe in My Father, believe also in Me. I go to prepare a place for you in My Father's house" (John 14:1-2).

Our Father's house is the house of Israel. Unfortunately, for the past twenty-seven hundred and thirty years that house remains divided into two houses: Judah and Ephraim.

Yahveh's people are still the people of Israel, and His land is the land of Israel (Genesis 1:1-Revelation 22:21). To determine the place of the Ephraimite, or non-Jewish Believers in Israel—let us look at the bloodline of Israel.

We will examine this topic from an aspect of the question: "Who is a Jew?" For, if Ephraimites understand Judah's present concept of, and relationship to, the bloodline of Israel, Ephraimites will be better equipped to understand their own relationship to Israel.

Jews and Messianic Jews, for the most part, do not have a problem with the question, "Who Is A Jew?" Also, they see the title "Jew" as being synonymous with "Israelite." However, this definition has given Ephraimite/Christians a number of problems.

The Church's perception of Jewish identity has resulted in confusion about Israelite heritage and inheritance; and about the part the Ephraimites play in Israel.

It wasn't always this way. The Church really didn't have a problem with the question of "Israel" for its first nineteen hundred years. It resolved the question by fashioning a theology that had the Church replacing the Jew, and to strengthen their claim they attempted to do away with the Jew—he being the only other contender for the title.

By the middle of the twentieth century, the Church numbered over a billion and a half members, making it by far the largest religion on the face of the earth. Compare this number to the Jews who, at the same time numbered some fourteen million (hardly more than their number in the first century).

Definitely, these figures confirm that by comparison, the Church was as the stars of heaven, the dust of the earth and the sands of the seashore. Undoubtedly, based on numbers the Church was the Israel of God!

Then in 1948, out of the ashes of Auschwitz, Buchenwald and Treblinka, and from oppressed Jewish ghettos around the world, a Jewish State resurrected. It was reborn in the land which Yahveh gave to the people of Israel as an eternal inheritance. The birth of this new state was a giant blow to the Church's claim that the Jews had lost it all, and that they alone were Israel!

To make matters worse, instead of naming this Jewish State "Judah," the name the Jews had always called their portion of land, they named it "Israel," the name that was commonly used throughout history to signify the ten tribes who formed the Northern Kingdom of Ephraim.

Truly, what goes around, comes around. The wheel had surely made a full revolution in this instance. The Church had made it clear for centuries that she they was "Israel." Now, in one fell swoop, the Jews grabbed the title back. And, their claim was confirmed by a multitude of God-inspired miracles in their behalf.

What did the Church do about this challenge? For the most part, she played down the importance of a physical relationship with Abraham, Isaac, and Jacob—or a physical fulfillment of the promises Holy One of Israel made to her. Together with this 'sour grapes' approach, she simply ignored the Jewish State—and went right on with her claims that she was "Israel." However, she did begin to emphasize the concept and title of "Spiritual" Israel.

(The Catholic Church, which numbers two thirds of main-line Christendom, has only recently officially recognized the fact that a Jewish State even exists. The World Council of Churches, which represents a large portion of the other third of Christendom, is also no friend of the Jewish State.)

The Leopard Has Not Changed Its Spots

It would appear that "Christendom" continues to attempt to solve an old problem with an old unworkable solution. The nations of Christendom, promoting a New World Order, have joined with Israel's enemies in refusing to recognize its right to Jerusalem —as well as other portions of the land of Israel. Once again, "Christianity" is attempting to resolve the question of who Israel is, by doing away with the Jew. It is setting the stage for the reduction, if not the elimination, of the problem of a Jewish State.

On the other hand, there are Charismatics, Evangelicals, Fundamentalists and Pentecostals who have seen in the formation of the new State, a fulfillment of end-time Bible prophecy. Unfortunately, in their minds, they have given the physical title, and the land of Israel, to the Jew. In turn, they have opted for a bailout from the end-time stage by way of a pre, or mid-tribulation "rapture."

However, over the last quarter century there has been a small and growing remnant of non-Jewish Believers, who, knowing the consequences, refuse to give up their birthright. They want no part of Esau's folly. (Hebrews 12:16,17,23; Exodus 4:22).

These people see themselves as "Messianic Israelites," and they know that, somehow, in some way, they are a part of the people of Israel—and that someday they will have a portion in the land of Israel.

This remnant is moving on a companion course with a small remnant of Jews who have realized that the Jesus of the Christians, is likewise their Messiah (albeit with certain changes in understanding). These Jewish Believers have a far better grasp on their place in God's end-time plans for Israel; because, they have not only claimed their Messiah, but also their birthright—and the heritage that goes with it.

Awareness of their identity and heritage is a must for all Ephraimites who would accomplish that which the God of Israel would have them achieve in this last hour. To fully understand that heritage, they need to understand the mystery of the "fullness of the Gentiles" (Genesis 48:19; Romans 11:25; Hosea 1:-2).[26]

A helpful way to gain this awareness is to understand how Jews perceive their own identity, because Ephraimite conception of how Jews determine their own identity as Jews has greatly affected the way Ephraimites perceive their own identity. Therefore, we must question whether the Ephraimite perceptions are correct.

Popular Perception Does Not Equal Truth!

The following view is an excellent example that proves that popular perception, by itself, does not make something true, but can equate it with reality:

"In western civilization a popular perception is: 'It is better to be a man rather than a woman, white rather than any other color, and a mainline Christian Protestant rather than any other religion.' From this popular perception, we gained the expression "WASP," meaning "White, Anglo Saxon Protestant."

---

26 See the *Who Is Israel?* and Chapter 9 *The Hope of Glory and the Fulness of the Gentiles.*

While these perceptions are not true, biologically or spiritually—popular acceptance over the centuries has made them real life facts. Acceptance has made them reality.

Fortunately, in our day, in the non-secular arena, we have seen many women and non-whites refuse to accept these perceptions as a guiding factor in their lives. As a result, they are leading richer and more rewarding lives.

Believers should likewise refuse to accept false perceptions. Especially, perceptions that have in the past, and will continue in the future, deny them the fullness and abundance of life that is their promised portion.

The popular perceptions of identity that have hampered non-Jewish Believers continue to exist because they believe the following:

1. They are Gentiles. (The name means heathen, foreign to the God of Israel.)
2. They are bloodline descendants of anybody other than Abraham, Isaac and Jacob.
3. Bloodline descent is immaterial since they see themselves as Abraham's "spiritual, adopted heirs." They believe that, generation after generation, even if descended from generations of born-again, spirit-filled followers of Messiah, they must individually be grafted into a Jewish Olive tree.[27]

On the other hand, Ephraimites have perceived just the opposite about the Jewish people. No matter what the apparent linage, Jews are the real thing: "Cokes." They are "God's chosen people." These people ignore the probability that, at some point in the past 4000 years, Jewish physical ancestral lines have also been affected by conversions, adoptions and extra-marital sex (fornication, adultery or rape). Yet, we see them as "true bloodline descendants of Abraham, Isaac and Jacob." And, in the case of the Jew, we

---

27 See *Who Is Israel?*

believe physical descent is very important!

However, the truth is the havoc that extra-marital sex has wrought in family genealogies is stressed by a study conducted some years ago of middle-class families in England. For accuracy in this study, it was essential that the children be the biological children of both parents. This project had to be abandoned because blood tests proved that forty percent of the children could not be the biological child of the man they claimed as their father! This does not mean the tests proved the other sixty percent were the biological children of the men they claimed as their fathers. That fact could not be conclusively proven. Imagine the possible results today with DNA testing!

Results like this only emphasize the potential inaccuracy of all genealogy. This inaccuracy was recognized as early as the third century by the Talmudic Sage, Ulla. He concluded that many Jews were not the biological children of Abraham, Isaac and Jacob. Therefore, he noted in Kiddushin 31a that "Jews could no longer be sure of their pedigrees."

Think about it: It only takes one birth resulting from an extra-marital impregnation to change one's entire genealogy. Or, another way to look at the magnitude of this problem is to realize that only Yahveh, and perhaps your mother, know who your father is.

Is The Label Gentile, Like Wasp, A Badge Of Ignorance?

Are the popular perceptions about genealogy, which have become foundational stones of the theology of most churches, true? Or, is the label Gentile, like WASP, a badge of ignorance?

Let us examine the basis on which the Church decides that Jews are natural children. In addition, let us question if her popular teaching that adoption into the family of Abraham, Isaac and Jacob is the only way non-Jewish Believers can obtain an inheritance in Israel.

First, would any mother or father, under normal circumstances, prefer to adopt a child rather than have one naturally? Is there anyone who would claim that it is more advantageous to be an adopted child, rather than a natural one?

Abraham gave his opinion about adoption. He made it clear to Yahveh that without a natural heir he felt he was not blessed. Yahveh put a seal of approval on Abraham's attitude. And, He assured him that his heir would **not** be an adopted Gentile. Instead, his heir would come forth from his "own body." Also, he would not have just one heir, but would have descendants as numerous as the stars of heaven, the dust of the of the earth, and the sands by the seashore (Genesis 15).

Should we assume the unchangeable God has changed (Hebrews 13:8)? Could it be that under the New Covenant, Yahveh is fulfilling His oath to Abraham—the one who was upset over having one adopted Gentile heir. Could it be that our God is giving Abraham millions of "adopted Gentiles" as his promised heirs?

It Is Physically Impossible For Anyone To Trace His Genealogy!

On the other hand, if Yahveh is fulfilling His promise to Abraham with myriads of natural heirs—We are faced with the fact that the identity of these heirs remains a "mystery." Because, today it is **physically impossible** for anyone to trace his genealogy back to Abraham, Isaac and Jacob.

Only Yahveh knows where the descendants of Abraham, Jew or non-Jew, are today. Over the past 4,000 years, in performing His oath to Abraham, God has orchestrated and tracked the dispersion of Abraham's seed: conquering armies, migrating peoples, nomadic traders, and the proverbial wandering Jew, have all been poured into Yahveh's giant seed scattering blender. For He is fulfilling His word, that He would scatter the seed of Israel through "all nations" (Hosea 8:8; Amos 9:9).

King Solomon, with 600 wives and 300 concubines, is certainly a good example of how effective one man can be in dispersing seed. Imagine the number of descendants that it is mathematically possible for him to have today! Through the Queen of Sheba alone, he might very well have turned not only Ethiopia, but a large portion of Africa, into Abraham's promised seed. In spite of the fact that today, man cannot physically trace his genealogy—genealogy remains important to our God. And He can, and does, trace it. The New Covenant begins by establishing the genealogy of the Messiah, and it ends with His affirmation, "I am the root and offspring of David,"(Revelation 22:16). In Ezra and Nehemiah, those who aspired to the priesthood were excluded and considered unclean if they could not prove their genealogy (Ezra 2:62; Nehemiah 7:64). Also, the Apostle Peter calls Believers, "A Chosen Race, A Royal Priesthood, A Holy Nation, A people for God's own possession" (1 Peter 1:1, 2:9).

This New Covenant Priesthood will one day enter into the New Jerusalem. However, the New Jerusalem only has twelve gates—named after the twelve tribes of Israel. Through which gate will these New Covenant people enter?

They will enter through their tribal gate (Revelation 21:12; Ezekiel 47:22, 48:31).

Again, are we to assume that Yahveh, the God who is the same yesterday, today, and forever, has changed? Has He changed His requirements for the priesthood, or changed the definition of His nation, or changed the people He has chosen for His own possession, or changed how they will enter into the New Jerusalem?

The Leaders of World Jewry Answer The Question "Who Is A Jew?"

It is a fact that today we cannot use genealogy to determine Israelite bloodlines. To further confirm this, lets us review the answers David Ben-Gurion, at the time Prime Minister of Israel, received in 1958, from the leaders of world Jewry, to his question "Who Is A Jew?"

The book, *Jewish Identity*, published in 1970 by Feldheim Publishers, Jerusalem, Israel, is a documentary compilation of the responses to David Ben-Gurion's query, "Who Is A Jew?" It includes Ben-Gurion's letter, responses from eight Israeli, six European, and five American Rabbis; ten Israeli, five European, and seven American Scholars; and two Israeli Jurists. It also concludes with a summation of the key points made in the forty-three responses, and forty four opinions (Ben-Gurion also had an opinion).

The Summation Is:

1. The answer to the question, "Who is a Jew?" is two-fold:
    a. Anyone who is born of a Jewish mother is a Jew.

    b. Anyone who has embraced Judaism, giving up other religions, regardless of whether he observes or does not observe the precepts of Judaism, is a Jew.
2. Judaism is a universal religion, and a Jew cannot exclude himself, nor can he be excluded by secular or religious authorities. Only Yahveh has the right of exclusion.
3. The term Jews, like Christians, is a religious connotation. Unlike Christianity, Judaism is the creation of one people.

The last half of this last point, is another popular misconception. Christianity is likewise the creation of one—and the same people. They are an extension of the Patriarchs—even as is Rabbinical Judaism.

Now let us ask: Do the above conclusions of the book support the Christian perception "that the Jewish people are bloodline descendants of Abraham, Isaac and Jacob?"

Absolutely not. The following examination of these conclusions clearly shows that the Jewish people themselves are not supportive of a claim of bloodline descent:

Two major points are made in the summation:

Anyone who is born of a Jewish mother is a Jew, and—anyone who has embraced Judaism, regardless of whether he observes or does not observe its precepts, is a Jew.

Thus, according to Jewish experts, Biblical genealogy, or the requirement to be a bloodline descendent of Abraham, Isaac or Jacob, is not a factor in determining if one is a Jew!

Only A Descendant of Abraham, Isaac and Jacob Would Choose To Embrace Judaism?

Many Jews take the position that "only a descendant of Abraham, Isaac and Jacob would choose to embrace Judaism."

Perhaps there is more than a grain of truth to be found in their position. For the New Covenant reveals that "many are called and few are chosen" (Matthew 22:14). It confirms that it is "in Isaac" that all of Abraham's heirs will be called (Hebrews 11:18).

However, if the above point that "only a descendant would choose to be a Jew" were true for the people of Judah, would it not also be true for the people of Ephraim, the other House of Israel?

Another question:

Is anyone who is born of a Jewish mother automatically of the bloodline seed of Abraham, Isaac and Jacob?

The Jewish Talmudic approach of tracing bloodline descent through the mother came about because, in the diaspora, they were forced to live in societies where the laws and commandments of the God of Israel were not observed. The Sages reasoned: A child's mother is always known; but, you can never be sure of the father. Therefore, descent will be established through the mother.

In societies where extra-marital sex is commonplace (willing and unwilling), fatherhood can only be claimed by faith. While there are DNA tests today that can prove that a man is or is not the father of a child, we presently have no way of testing our ancestors.

Ezra 9:1-10:44 is used as the Biblical basis for the above Talmudic decision. However, in Scripture, genealogies are counted through the father. This is true in the Book of Ezra and the books written at, and after, the time of Ezra. This is also true in the New Covenant, where ancestral and genealogical references are through the male. Even in the so-called "Miriam genealogy of Messiah," only males are listed.

The New Covenant position is clear: Bloodline descent is through the father.[28] In Hebrews, Yahveh says He saw the seed that would become Levi, Abraham's great grandson, in Abraham's loins (vs 7:9-10).

This seed, that contained the life-force that flowed in Abraham's blood, was passed by Abraham to Levi in the following manner:

A) Abraham passed his seed through his wife, Sarah, to his son, Isaac.

B) Isaac passed the seed through his wife, Rebekah, to his son, Jacob.

C) Jacob passed the seed through his wife, Leah, to his third born son, Levi.

If a "bloodline" is conveyed by the woman, then we would have a problem with the virgin birth of Messiah. If Mary conveyed the blood of Adam to Yeshua, then He was just another Adam, or man. His offering on the altar that is above would have consisted of the sin-tainted blood of Adam.

If Yeshua were only a man, like other men, then any man could have gone to the cross.

However, the sinful blood of Adam carries the curse of death, and it could not be offered on the altar above. For the Psalmist says, "No man can by any means redeem his brother, or give to God a ransom for him" (Psalm 49:7).

Yeshua did not offer Adam's blood on the altar. He offered "His Father's blood" (Acts 2:28; Hebrews 9:14). For, He was a new Adam. He was a God/man.

---

28 See *Who Is Israel?*, Chapter 10, *The Blood, The Redeemer, And Physical Israel,*

What Bloodline Did Messiah Receive?

Yeshua received the bloodline of His Heavenly Father, when the Holy Spirit came upon Mary (Luke 1:34-35). Therefore, it was this sinless blood, that carries the promise of eternal life, that He offered on the heavenly altar.

It is through the father's seed: a seed made of water and blood that the bloodline is passed. Yeshua came by just such a seed. John tells us there is "one who came by blood and water—Yeshua" (1 John 5:6).

Sarah, from just such a seed deposited in her by Abraham, formed and gave birth to Isaac. Rebekah, in the same way, received the seed from Isaac.

Question: If you remove Isaac, how can you get Abraham's seed to Jacob?

Isaac is the physical link between Abraham and Jacob, and he is the physical link between the two women. Remove Isaac from the above example and you remove the physical link that existed between them. Without a physical link, Abraham's seed could not be passed from Sarah's womb to Rebekah's womb.

Substituting another man, to serve as the physical link between Sarah and Rebekah, would only work if this man had Abraham's seed in him. For that is the seed that Yahveh saw in Abraham loins—the seed that Yahveh destined would become the person that was Levi.

However, changing the woman would not affect the bloodline. Change Rebekah to another woman, and she could have passed Abraham's bloodline from Isaac to Jacob.

So, what bloodline have Jewish mothers been passing along for centuries?

Only God in Heaven knows.

Only God in heaven knows one's genealogy. This is true for the Jew and non-Jewish Believer alike. Paul made this point in his first letter to Timothy. He instructed him to ignore endless genealogies, never-ending pedigrees, endless records of ancestors, and myths.

Rather, Timothy was to realize that Yahveh's administration and stewardship was to help people accept His plan of faith! (1 Timothy 1:4).

The only way we can determine today whether one is a bloodline descendant of Abraham, Isaac and Jacob is through faith in Yahveh and in His Word! So, let us not put our confidence in the misconceptions of man. Rather, let us trust in our God!

You Will Know By Faith, Not By Red Lights

As a Believer, you can trust that, if you were lost, and have been found, and now know the voice of Messiah, then, you must be one of the lost sheep of Israel. Yeshua made it clear that He came only to the lost sheep of Israel. And, only His sheep know His voice (Matthew 15:34; John 10:27). That is the truth. If not, then the God who declares that, "He is the same yesterday, today, and forever," changed His mind.

Paul confirms that if you belong to the Messiah then you are Abraham's seed ("sperma"), and like Isaac (who was a physical heir), you are children of the promise (Galatians 3:29 and 4:28).

Further, if you have received the "Spirit of adoption," then you are a son of Israel. For, "the adoption as sons, belongs to the sons of Israel" (Romans 9:4).

If you receive this as truth, a red light will not go on in the center of your forehead—one that will tell the world that you are an Israelite. Likewise, a red light did not go on when you were born again into God's family. Rather, by faith you knew that you knew that you were a new creation! And, a red light will not go on when you accept the reality of your physical heritage. Again, by faith you will know that you know that you are an Israelite!

The acceptance of the above in no way limits Yahveh. The fact that He is keeping the oath He swore to Abraham, does not restrict Yahveh, if He should so desire, from adding Gentiles as He wishes to His kingdom.

The Inclusion of Gentiles In The Kingdom of Israel Is Not Yahveh's Main Focus!

However, the possible inclusion of Gentiles in the Kingdom of Israel is surely not the main focus of the God of Israel.

Scripture verifies that His primary goal is the multiplication and salvation of the seed of Abraham, Isaac and Jacob.

And, that seed was scattered among the "Gentile Nations." Thus, the need for the "Great Commission" to send forth His call among the Nations.

Yahveh's Requirements For Israel:

Both Jews and Ephraimites must keep His requirements to be an Israelite in good standing, lest they be broken off of the tree for unbelief (Romans 11).

For those with personal doubts about their heritage, they may take advantage of Yahveh's circumcision/ passover/sojourning safety net.

Yahveh decreed there were three requirements one must meet to be recognized as a physical Israelite: 1) Be circumcised, 2) Observe Passover, 3) Sojourn with Israelites. Once these requirements were fulfilled, they were called "natives of the land." He even warned the converts not to see themselves as separate from His people Israel! Scripture declares they were physical Israelites! (Exodus 12:48,49; Leviticus 19:34; Numbers 9:14; 15:15,16; Isaiah 56:3-8.)

The New Covenant further qualified these laws: From circumcision of the flesh to that of the heart. From a sacrificial lamb to Yeshua serving as our Passover. From sojourning with those who followed the Old Covenant to sojourning with those who follow the New Covenant. (Jeremiah 31:33; Hebrews 7:12; Romans 2:29; I Corinthians 5:7; Hebrews 10:12.)

Yahveh has kept, is keeping, and will keep His Word. It is impossible for Him to lie (Hebrews 6:18). Therefore, He will accomplish all that He has spoken by the mouth of all His holy prophets since the world began (Acts 3:21). He is raising up from the seed of Abraham, Isaac, Jacob, Joseph and Ephraim, a *melo ha goyim*, a fullness of Gentiles, a company of nations (Genesis 48:19). Yahveh is keeping His word to Rachel. Her (grand) children, Ephraim and Manasseh, shall return to their own land. And, Ephraim (the firstborn) is once again becoming a mighty man (Jeremiah 31:9; 15-20; Zechariah 10:70).

The Jews, who primarily descend from Jacob's son Judah, do not fulfill these Scriptures. While they absolutely are an integral part of Israel, and they were part of a congregation of nations prior to the division of Israel, after the division, they were not, and are not now, either a fullness of Gentiles or a company of nations.

Judah And Ephraim Are Equal Heirs!

Judah is one of the houses of Israel. The other house is that of Ephraim. And, we are living in the day when the Father is in the process of uniting the two houses. However, true unity calls for a common denominator. In this case, the denominator is the fact that both houses are joint **equal** Heirs. It is only when Ephraim realizes the truth of who he is as an Israelite that his brotherhood with Judah will be manifested. The Holy One of Israel has called many Israelites to accept His New Covenant (Jeremiah 31:31, 32:40-44). Those who answer this call will, like the first century Israelites, such as Peter and Paul, not be rewarded by being cut off from physical Israel. Rather, they are members of the general assembly of the Israel of God—the Church of the firstborn (Ephraim), and their names are enrolled in a heavenly list (Hebrews 12:23). In the Kingdom to come, the Heavenly gates are named after the twelve tribes of Israel. And the twelve apostles of the Lamb sit on twelve thrones judging the twelve tribes of Israel. They are recorded in the Book of Life—not as Gentiles—but as Israelites!

We pray that if you have not already done so, that you will shake off the shackles of adoption and its sister, the bonds and chains of the title of Gentile, and the subsequent fetters of second class citizenship.

We also pray you walk in the fullness of all the God of Israel has planned for you, guided not by popular misconceptions, but rather the Word of God and the witness of the Spirit!

9

Our Hope of Glory and The Mystery of The Gentiles

The Declaration of Independence of the United States, made in 1776, gives the hope of life, liberty, and the pursuit of happiness. All of which we receive by being citizens of the United States.

Comparatively, our God gives us the Hope of Glory: the hope of eternal life, liberty, and happiness. His is a promise made before the foundation of the world. And we receive these hopes by being citizens of His Commonwealth of Israel.

What is "hope?"

It is a feeling, a desire that what is wanted or expected, will happen. And we all want life, liberty and happiness. So, for an answer to life's most important question: "How do we realize these hopes, both in this world and in the world to come?" Let us look to the writings of the Apostle Paul:

"Brethren, it is by understanding the mystery of the Gentiles, which has been hidden from the past ages and generations, and which has now being manifested to His saints, that you will understand that it is Yeshua in you, that is your hope of glory.... However, to realize the hope that Yeshua has given you, you must be a citizen of the commonwealth of Israel and a partaker of the covenants of promise" (Colossians 1:25-28; Ephesians 2:12; Author's Personal Paraphrase).

Salvation: Being born again, accepting Messiah, being saved, call it what you may. It is this crucial message of personal salvation that the Church has heralded to the remotest corners of the earth for two millennia. Undeniably, it is the greatest, and most important message anyone could ever hear, because it gives one the hope of glory!

The Church started with the right message: personal salvation. However, because of her "blindness"she did not go far enough (Genesis 48:19; Isaiah 8:14; Romans 11:25). Thus, she lost sight of the "full" solution to the "mystery of the Gentiles," and consequently she also lost sight of her own ultimate mission, which is, the restoration of the Kingdom to Israel.

Make no mistake, it is the resolution of this mystery that will equip the elect to understand, and thus to complete the mission that will ultimately turn our hope into glory!

As we mentioned earlier, the *Ruach haKodesh*, speaking through Paul, in his letter to the Ephesians, emphasizes a requirement for both individual and national relationships. Paul says, "Remember that you were at that time separate from Yeshua, excluded from the commonwealth of Israel, and strangers to the covenants of promise, having no hope and without God in the world" (Ephesians 2:12).

Paul gives three reasons why the Ephesians previously had been without hope, and without God in the world:

1) They were separated from Yeshua. They were not saved. However, while we all can agree that not having obtained individual salvation is any individual's greatest problem, it was, according to Paul, not their only problem.

2) They were excluded, or alienated, from the commonwealth of Israel. In other words, in addition to not having individual salvation, they also did not have national salvation. They were not part of a people, set apart for the Holy One of Israel.

3) They were strangers to the covenants of promise. Paul speaks of the covenants that will one day culminate in the fulfillment of the Messianic Promise (Jeremiah 31:31-32; Hebrews 8:8-12). This is the hope of glory. It is this fulness of our eternal inheritance that will be consummated at Yeshua's promised coming.

Before we make a more detailed examination of Paul's three points, we first need to go back in history to determine why the Ephesians had been without hope and without God is this world. For we need to know the root cause of a problem if we are to solve it. Further, as stated earlier, if we will not learn from the mistakes of the past, we are doomed to repeat them.

Sadly, history reveals that we have not learned. For, generation after generation, and even in our generation, the majority of the people in the world have continued to be without hope and without God.

Why do the problems of hopelessness and Godlessness continue to plague the world?

Prior generations of Believers have run their lap of the race with limited success, while in effect passing on this problem to the next set of runners. And now, our generation has been given the baton. Now it is our turn to run. The question is, will we pass the baton in the same way as did our forefathers? Or, do we have a unique opportunity to actually finish the race?

Could we be the forerunners that cross the finish line? The signs of the times say yes. The signs being fulfilled Biblical prophecy in the past century indicate that such is the case (Matthew 16:3).

Yes, we are being given the extraordinary opportunity to serve as vessels of mercy—vessels the Holy Spirit can use to help gather the lost sheep of Israel to the Shepherd of Israel—thus giving them the hope of glory (Romans 9:23). And in this way, these found sheep will no longer be excluded, or alienated, from the commonwealth of Israel. Rather than being strangers to the covenants of promises, they will partake of the eternal pledges of assurance, which will give them the everlasting glory—which is the realization of their hope.

How Can We Meet This Challenge?

If ours is the last leg of the race, what are we to do?

To best answer this question, we first need to answer two basic questions: *Who are we? And why are we here?*

Who Are We?

Hopefully our answer to this question will not be like that of the pessimistic philosopher Schopenhauer, who, sitting all disheveled on a park bench, when asked who he was, said to the attendant, "I wish to God I knew."

This answer, along with one that is an even more pitiful cry, haunts all humanity. The other is a cry that is uttered by all who have lost their way, and it is, "I wish I knew God."

Why would any man question who he is? And why would any man question who is God?

Why? Because the modern world with all its advancements in science, technology, and philosophy, seems in many ways to have done away with a need for both God and man. Newton dismissed God by his theory of a mechanical universe. Darwin, by his view of evolution, dismissed man. Freud dismissed a reasoning mind by his insistence that man was but an animal, motivated not by reason but by hidden unconscious animal drives and instincts.

In the past century, we have quarreled, not over whether man is an animal, but as to what *type* of animal. Is he motivated by his collective ancestral impulses and manners (Darwin), by economic necessity and his stomach (Marx), or by his libido (Freud)?

Modern man, being told on one hand that he is but an animal, and on the other hand that he is a god, does not have a satisfying answer to the questions of why, what, when, and how. By his own confession, he is lost in a meaningless and hopeless moment between two eternities. He is lost and hopeless because the enlightenment from these great advancements in science, technology, and philosophy has led him to see his origins as being the chance multiplication of amoebas. His destiny is but to return to cosmic dust.

Those who reject the modern meaninglessness of a life without hope have turned, as man has done throughout history, to an ideology: a system of beliefs that provide the social needs and aspirations for an individual, a group, a culture, a people. And, the key to every ideology depends upon its genesis (beginning or origin).

In other words, every system of thought that attempts to explain the origins and destiny of man is dependent upon an original conviction regarding the nature of man. And, whether or not the system has any hope of being correct, first and foremost, depends on whether the original assumption is correct. Therefore, the continued failure of modern ideologies, and of many ideologies of the past, can undoubtedly be attributed to wrong assumptions as to man's genesis.

The Judeo-Christian ideology of man's genesis has him being created in the image of the One God of Israel, and, he is created with the hope of eternal life.

Yet, the proliferation of theologies, doctrines, denominations, and cults, to which these ideologies have given birth, all serve to bear witness to the confusion that still exists regarding who we are and where we are going!

The Truth Is...

We have all questioned the theologies and doctrines with which we were nurtured. Further, on a daily basis, we make decisions based on our current ideology. And these decisions have eternal consequences. So, we need to cut through the mass of divergent denominational and cultic theology and doctrines that represent "Christian" thought today, and we need to get to the **truth**. Especially, we need to get to the **truth** of **who we are!**

What is Truth?

Truth is the Father's reality behind our perception.

Further, the truth may frequently seem unreasonable; it may at times be depressing; sometimes it may appear to be wrong; but it has an eternal advantage: it is Yahveh's reality. And, what is built on His truth neither brings, nor yields confusion.

We must be concerned about the consequences of being deceived by errors and misconceptions, for lies bring captivity and death, while truth brings freedom and life (John 8:21,32,44; 2 Timothy 2:26).

With such high stakes riding on what we believe, we must ask ourselves: Is what we believe true? Is the foundation on which we are building our understanding of who we are, why we are here, and where we are going, one of truthfulness?[29]

In Chapter Seven, *Who Told You*, we pointed out that the post-16th-century philosophers who were responsible for the development of modern secular thought, devised new kinds of wisdom. Then, with their innovations, they began to build on faulty structures. Thus, they made a disastrous mistake, because they did not tear down their faulty structures to the point of a solid foundation; they did not go all the way down to ancient and original truths!

Even so, Christian theologians of the reformation, in their attempts to correct errors made by the early Roman Church, suffered from the same disastrous mistake: Instead of retracing the

---

29 See Chapter 7, *Who Told You?*

faulty steps all the way back to a solid foundation of original truth, modern theologians have tried in other ways to circumvent the result of the initial errors. Thus, they often compound their difficulties rather than overcome them.

It is because they have not dug down far enough that the church[30] has yet to recover from many of her early doctrinal divisions and theological mistakes. Especially crippling are the mistakes made over the identity of Israel. For they blind us to a full understanding of Yahveh's plan for the *whole* house of Israel, of which "whole" we are a part.

The truth is, initially, all of Messiah's followers were *physical* Israelites who belonged to a *sect* of Judaism (Acts 28:32). Undoubtedly, these Israelites had children.

But, as stated earlier, somehow, somewhere along the way, the church ceased to consider their physical descendants as physical Israelites. She further distanced herself from unbelieving Judah when she began to admit "Gentiles," who in turn **were not** seen as being physical Israelites (Acts 21:28-30).

Ultimately, the ties between the two were completely broken, and the followers of Yeshua became a "Gentile Church."

Today, we forerunners, those who have been commissioned to pick up the pieces and to put Israel back together again, are faced with an age-old question:

"Who is Israel?"[31]

---

30 "Church," like "Israel," is a multi-faceted name/title, and often one has to know what the author means with their use; and so we state that we realize there is an organized ecclesiastical "Church System" that ultimately will "persecute" true Believers (Rev 3:16; 2 Tim 3:1-12); and that there is a true *church*, an eternal *ekklesia*, a body of Believers who seek to follow the God of Israel (Acts 7:38; 2 Thes 1:1; 2:13).

Also, there is a "Synagogue of Satan" that opposes Messiah's claims (John 8:44; 10:33; Rev 2:9; 3:9). In this document, the term "Church" is used loosely, sometimes including those who "claim" to be part of "the church" (the true Body). This same loose standard is applied in references to "Jews/Judaism." We trust that in the end, the Holy One Himself will decide who among both peoples is acceptable to Himself (Mat 7:23).

Nonetheless, because the word "Church" is derived from the Germanic word, *kirke*, and was first used to speak of a ritualistic circle (see *Church*, Smith's Bible Dictionary, Fleming Revell), we prefer the Greek, *ekklesia* when referring to the true *called out ones* (Strong's word # G 1577).

31 See the books: *In Search of Israel*, *The Olive Tree of Israel*, and *Who Is Israel?*.

Am I An Israelite?

An even more pressing question that each of us should answer is: **"Am I an Israelite?"**

These questions, Who is Israel?, Who is an Israelite?, have been asked for thousands of years without a definitive answer. Since the exodus of a mixed multitude from Egypt, Israel has harbored the simultaneous convictions that: first, Israel was an entirely unique and separate community—a peculiar people—being descendants of Abraham, Isaac and Jacob; and secondly, Israel is a people, linked by faith in a common ideology. Both of these convictions have one commonality, they both require that Israel had to be set apart from the world. And yet, they were to remain in the world, both at one and the same time.

Like our forefathers, we continue to be faced with the apparent hopeless dilemma of two contradictory opposites. The solution, which the Church, Judaism, and Messianic Judaism, have bought, and which they in turn attempt to sell,—is to see these two convictions as the coexistence of two complementary, incompatible viewpoints—which can be successfully harmonized and united.

Now if this solution does not leave you confused, then you do not understand the situation.

Admittedly, we do not have all the answers today. "However, there is a God in heaven who reveals mysteries," and He promised to reveal them in the latter days (Daniel 2:28). Even so, the Father has begun to remove the blindness to the mystery concerning the identity of Israel—as well as the mystery surrounding the Gentiles.

So it is that, on a one by one basis He is revealing to many non-Jews that they are Israelites. Great numbers are now beginning to realize —based on the leading of the Holy Spirit—that they most likely are descendants of Abraham, Isaac and Jacob.

Those who believe this have a "conviction," a knowing that we know. It is not unlike the conviction and knowing we each have concerning our personal salvation.

What About The Others?

What about those who have not been convicted of the truth regarding their salvation? Most will answer: "I *know* I am saved, and I pray that my witness will lead others to salvation."

What about those who have yet to see the truth about our heritage?

Our answer should be:"I *know who* I am, and I pray that my witness will bring others to a knowledge of their heritage.

What about those who do not see us as we see ourselves?

We need to *know* in our hearts that the Holy One of Israel sees us as a full-fledged member of His people Israel, even though the Church at large, and many of our brothers and sisters in Messianic Judaism, do not recognize us as such. Instead, in their eyes we are "adopted Gentiles" who in some mysterious way have become "Spiritual Israelites."

However, their misunderstanding should not dictate our image of ourselves, nor should it shake our faith in the fact that we are who Yahveh says we are! Remember, "If you belong to Yeshua, then you **are** Abraham's offspring (sperm), heirs according to promise" (Galatians 3:29).

Just as Yahveh saw Levi in the loins of his father Abraham, He also saw us in our father Abraham's loins! For when the God who foreknew us before the foundation of the world said to Abraham that his seed would be as the stars of heaven, the sand by the seashore, and the dust of the earth, He was not speaking of a future event, but rather of an event that had taken place before the foundation of the world! (Ephesians 1:4, Hebrews 4:3, Genesis !5:5, 22:17, 26:4, 28:14, 32:12).

A People For His Own Possession

This world is not the result of chance, rather it was deliberately created by Yahveh for His good pleasure, which was, and is, to have a people for His own possession (Isaiah 46:10; Deuteronomy

4:20, 7:6, 14:2; Titus 2:14;1 Peter 2:9). His desire was, and is, that these people, whom He would call, would of their own free will, choose Him to be their God, and they would choose to be His people!

But, there is a difference between choosing Yahveh to be our God, and choosing to be His people.

The Church has placed emphasis on her choosing of God, meaning on individual salvation, but she has put little or no emphasis on choosing to be His people, or on national salvation. For the most part, the Church has taken the attitude that all, even if they might be descendants of generations of Believer's, start at ground zero in their relationship with Yahveh. It does not even occur to them that they may be descended from those who have been in the Olive Tree of Israel for generation upon generation.[32]

On the other hand, the Jewish people have placed their emphasis on national salvation—on being God's chosen people. And, it is this attitude that flames the fires of jealousy in the non-Jew—Ephraim. However, rather than be jealous, Ephraim needs to get with the program. He needs to realize that he will only attain the fulness of his hope when he recognizes that he too is an integral "part of" the Kingdom of Israel. (To be "part of" does not mean to be "all," nor does it mean to "replace" those of Judah.)

We need to understand that our names are not added to the *Book of Life*, rather, names are *erased* from the *Book of Life* (Psalm 69:28; Revelation 13:8, 17:8).

Moreover, branches are *broken off* the Olive Tree of Israel for unbelief. And, those who are "(re)grafted" into the root that is Messiah, are "olive" branches that became "wild." However, they are nonetheless "olive" branches, and, "Israel" is the "olive tree" (Jeremiah 11:10,16; 2:18,21; Romans 11:17-24).

---

32 In saying this, we do not mean to deny the need for each individual to be born from above, and thus to enter into a personal relationship with Messiah Yeshua. Instead, we speak for the need to begin to see ourselves as a "corporate," even national, people; that people being the chosen people of Israel (1 Pet 1:1; 2:9).

No Hope And Without God In The World

Again we emphasize the requirement for both individual and national relationships:

"Remember that you were at that time separate from Yeshua, excluded from the commonwealth of Israel, and strangers to the covenants of promise, having no hope and without God in the world (Ephesians 2:12).

As stated earlier, they were separated from Yeshua, and thus they were **excluded from the commonwealth of Israel**. The King James Version translates this as, **being aliens**, rather than **excluded from**. However, *Vincent's Word Studies of the New Testament* says, ***apallotriow*** (ap-al-lot-ree-o'-o), rather than being translated **alien**, would be better translated if given the force of the verb **alienated**; as if they had once been otherwise. They were once in a condition other than that of being alienated or being aliens.

Using **alienated,** rather than **excluded,** the verse reads: "Remember that you were at that time (prior to having hoped in Yeshua[33]) separate from Yeshua, alienated (with-drawn or detached[34]) from the commonwealth of Israel, and strangers to the covenants of promise, having no hope and without God in the world."

Truly, the translation of one word can make a profound difference in our belief structure.

The Mystery Is Solved!
We Are A "Returning" People!

Another example of how mistranslation of one word can make a profound difference in what we believe is found in the Greek word *epistrepho*. James uses this word when delivering the conclusions of the only recorded meeting of the Jerusalem council:

---

33 See Ephesians 1:12-15
34 Alienated: To cause to be withdrawn or detached, as from one's society, *Webster's New World Dictionary*.

"Therefore it is my judgment that we do not trouble those who are *epistrepho* to Yahveh from among the Gentiles" (Acts 15:15-19).

Most translate this word as **"turning,"** which translation indicates a process, rather than an accomplished fact.

James is referring to **Gentiles** who are in the process of *epistrepho* to the Father. The King James translate this as, **are turned**, which indicates an accomplished fact rather than a process. However, *epistrepho*, could just as well be translated *returning*, or *returned!* Strong defines "*epistrepho (ep-ee-stref'-o)* as, "to revert—come (go) again, convert, (re-) turn (about, again)."

What a difference between **turning, turned,** and **returning!** Surely it would rock the doctrines of Christianity if they accepted the translation, "Therefore it is my judgment that we do not trouble those who are **returning to Yahveh from among the Gentiles.**" Then they would see that through James, the Holy Spirit is solving the "mystery of the Gentiles!"

Another Scriptural nail that can be used to hammer home this truth (in love of course) that these so-called Gentiles were descendants of former members of the commonwealth of Israel, and were thus **returning**, is found in Romans Chapter Eleven. This Chapter deals with the retrieval of branches from the Olive Tree of Israel that had become wild, but were being grafted back into the cultivated tree.

Paul, speaking to these formerly wild branches, recalls Isaiah's prophecy, foretelling the day when Yahveh would deliver Israel and forgive Jacob's iniquity (Isaiah 27:1-9; Romans 11:27). Paul also says the gifts and the calling of God are irrevocable, and that, even though you wild branches were **once disobedient to God**, you are now being shown mercy (Romans 11:29-30).[35]

If Paul lumps the wild, or formerly **disobedient** branches, and the cultivated branches together, as being those on whom the Father is having mercy, then he is in fact saying they all are part of Israel. After all, to be **disobedient** to Yahveh one had to have known, at

---

35 See *The Olive Tree of Israel.*

some time in the past, His standards—which standards they were expected to obey.

Who better fits this bill than the lost, dispersed sheep of Ephraim—those once **alienated from the commonwealth** by being swallowed up among the nations, and yet in Paul's day, were being be regathered—**returning to Yahveh from among the Gentiles** (Hosea 8:8; Amos 9:9; Acts 15:15-19; Ephesians 2:12)? Who better fits this description than Ephraim, the "fulness of Gentiles" (Genesis 48:19)?

So why has the church missed the truth of the mystery of the Gentiles and the importance of being part of the Commonwealth of Israel?

Ephraim's LoAmmi Punishment

These returning so-called Gentiles were being punished! Their punishment was: "You are not My people and I am not your God"(Hosea 1:9).[36] Yet, the day would come when the Father would end their punishment and would once again consider them as His people and He would be their God (Hosea 1:10).

To understand the importance and difference between a corporate relationship and an individual relationship with Yahveh, we briefly recount His relationship with Abraham's descendants. From Abraham's descendants He choose Isaac, and from Isaac's descendants Jacob was chosen, then Jacob had twelve sons whom Yahveh called Israel (2 Kings 17:34). These twelve tribes served as the physically identifiable presence of Yahveh's corporate people on earth until the seventh century B.C. In that fateful century, Israel's first holocaust occurred: ten of the tribes were slowly absorbed into the nations and were no longer physically identifiable as part of the corporate people of the God of Israel. Then, the fifth century B.C. drew to a close, and the second holocaust took place, the Southern Kingdom, or Judah, was scattered among the nations;

---

36 See Chapter 11, *Ephraim, Once Again A Mighty Man.*

but, a remnant of Judah maintained its identity during its seventy year exile in Babylon, and this remnant has been known as Jews to this day.

However, these few Jews are not all Israel! Even today, with the establishment of a secular Jewish state, we do not have the promised restoration of the Davidic Kingdom. Having the tents of Judah go up first is the beginning, but not the end of the restoration process (Zechariah 12:7)! The fulness of the restoration will only be experienced when all Israel is once again physically identifiable, and physically occupying the land promised to the Patriarchs. It will be fulfilled only when all Israel is ruled by the King of Kings.

When did Ephraim's punishment start? No later then 722 B.C., which year marked the final fall of the last physical vestige of the Northern Kingdom. When will it end? When the descendants of those lost ten tribes are no longer lost, but are once again recognizable as the people of Israel!

Understand that this punishment meted out to the Northern Kingdom was a corporate punishment. Scripture records that Yahveh came to a point that His corporate relationship with the Northern Kingdom of Israel was such that, for a period of time, He would not recognize them as His people, and He would not be their God. They would be **alienated from the commonwealth of Israel** for a season. And, until our generation this punishment has remained in effect. However, we are now experiencing signs which indicate that we are in the day when Yahveh is ending His corporate punishment of Ephraim.

Fortunately, we have the unmerited opportunity to be living in the day when Messianic Israel—the restored Davidic Kingdom—is being formed. Daily, the numbers of Believer's, many of whom themselves or their forefathers, returned to Yahveh from among the Gentiles and are now understanding their heritage in ever growing numbers. And they are seeing themselves as "A chosen race, a royal priesthood, a holy nation, a people for Yahveh's own possession, that will proclaim the excellencies of Him who has called them out of darkness into His marvelous light" (1 Peter 2:9).

Strangers To The Covenants of Promise

Again, Paul said the "Gentiles" who are being gathered" were **strangers to the covenants of promise**. Fortunately, there seems to be universal agreement that the *Covenants of Promise* are the several renewals of Yahveh's covenant with the Patriarchs—which covenant will culminate in the fulfillment of the *Messianic Promise* —which is the basis of all the covenants.

However, receiving the manifestation of Yeshua in our lives is not the fulness of our hope of Glory! Rather, His presence gives us the hope that one day we will realize the fulness of our inheritance, which will be consummated at His promised coming.

It is to this divine Messianic perfection of all things that we look for fulfillment of our hope. For, at Yeshua's return, the prophecy He gave Ezekiel so long ago will no longer look to a future event. Rather, it will be a record of *an accomplished fact:*

*'Behold, **I have taken** the sons of Israel from among the nations where they had gone, and I have gathered them from every side and brought them into their own land; and they are now one nation in the land, on the mountains of Israel; and one king is king for all of them; and they are **no longer two nations**, and they are no longer **divided into two kingdoms**. And they no longer defile themselves with their idols, or with their detestable things, or with any of their transgressions; but I have delivered them from all their dwelling places in which they have sinned, and I have cleansed them. And they are My people, and I Am their God. And My servant David is King over them, and they have One Shepherd; and they walk in My ordinances and keep My statutes and observe them. And they live on the land that I gave to Jacob My servant, in which their fathers lived; and they will continue to live on it, they, and their sons, and their sons' sons, forever; and David My servant is their prince forever. And I have made a covenant of peace with them; it is an everlasting covenant with them. And I have placed them and*

85

multiplied them and have set My sanctuary in their midst forever'"
(fulfilled rendering of Ezekiel 37 21-27 according to the Author).[37]

Obtaining Our Messianic Hope

At this juncture in history, what can we forerunners reasonably
expect that the Church and the Jewish people will do to hasten
Yeshua's return and the restoration of the Kingdom to Israel?[38]

Not much, because the Church at large doesn't see the
restoration of a Davidic Kingdom as her goal. She is headed for a
Kingdom in heaven, not to one that will be established on this
earth.[39] On the other hand, the over-whelming majority of the
Jewish people do not envision a Messiah who is the Son of God.
So, an intelligent answer to the question of what we can reasonably
expect the parties to do to advance the cause of restoring the
Kingdom to Israel, is: Without the injection of dramatic change—
very little.

Yet, it is the Church and the Jewish people whose ranks contain
the remnant of Israel, the remnant Yahveh is gathering back to their
own soil (Jeremiah 23:8).

As Forerunners We Face...

By default, the ball is in our court. But what are we to do with
it? What are we who have been given the Hope of Messianic Israel
—the challenge of accomplishing the reunion of Ephraim and
Judah, and thus preparing the way for the restoration of the
Kingdom to Israel—to do? What can we realistically accomplish
towards these age ending goals? After all, we are pitifully few in
number, financially challenged [poor], already overworked and
over-committed, and, our vision is rejected by "the Church,"
Judaism, and by most Messianic Jews—who should be our co-

---

37 See Chapter 13, *Roman Roads And The World Wide Web.*
38 See Chapter 17, *The Messianic Vision.*
39 See HDH's *Rapture or Transformation? Escape or Victory?*; and, *Should I Believe In The Pre-Tribulation Rapture?*

workers in this restoration process.

Let's face it, there are giants in the land, and we are but grasshoppers in their sight. Worse than that, we are grasshoppers in our own sight.

Maybe we should go back to Egypt?

Does this account sound familiar? Is not our problem the same one our fathers faced in the desert when Yahveh placed before them the promised land?[40]

Giants In The Land!!!

You remember the story. "Yahveh said to Moses, 'Send out for yourself men so that they may spy out the land of Canaan, **which I am going to give to the sons of Israel**; you shall send a man from each of their fathers' tribes...'

"So, Moses sent a representative from each tribe to spy out their destination, the promised land of Canaan. Unfortunately, ten spies came back with a bad report:

"We went in to the land where you sent us; and it certainly does flow with milk and honey...Nevertheless, the people who live in the land are strong, and the cities are fortified and very large; and moreover, we saw the descendants of Anak there."

"Then Caleb quieted the people before Moses, and said, 'We should by all means go up and take possession of it, for we shall surely overcome it.' But the men who had gone up with him said, 'We are not able to go up against the people, for they are too strong for us.'

"So they gave out to the sons of Israel a bad report of the land which they had spied out, saying, 'The land through which we have gone, in spying it out, is a land that devours its inhabitants; and all the people whom we saw in it are men of great size...and we became like grasshoppers in our own sight, and so we were in their sight.'

"Then all the congregation lifted up their voices and cried, and the people wept that night. And all the sons of Israel grumbled

---

40 See HDH *Overcoming Religion—Possessing The Land.*

against Moses and Aaron; and the whole congregation said to them, 'Would that we had died in the land of Egypt! Or, would that we had died in this wilderness! And why is Yahveh bringing us into this land, to fall by the sword? Our wives and our little ones will become plunder; would it not be better for us to return to Egypt?' So they said to one another, 'Let us appoint a leader and return to Egypt.'

"Then Moses and Aaron fell on their faces in the presence of all the assembly of the congregation of the sons of Israel. And Joshua the son of Nun and Caleb the son of Jephunneh, of those who had spied out the land, tore their clothes; and they spoke to all the congregation of the sons of Israel, saying, 'The land which we passed through to spy out is an exceedingly good land. "If Yahveh is pleased with us, then He will bring us into this land, and give it to us—a land which flows with milk and honey. Only do not rebel against Yahveh; and do not fear the people of the land, for they shall be our prey. Their protection has been removed from them, and Yahveh is with us; do not fear them.'

"But all the congregation said to stone them with stones. Then the glory of Yahveh appeared in the tent of meeting to all the sons of Israel. And Yahveh said to Moses, 'How long will this people spurn Me? And how long will they not believe in Me, despite all the signs which I have performed in their midst? I will smite them with pestilence and dispossess them, and I will make you into a nation greater and mightier than they.'"

Fortunately, Yahveh honored Moses' intercession for the people and did not destroy them. However, He would punish them. He said to Moses, "I have pardoned them according to your word... Surely all the men who have seen My glory and My signs, which I performed in Egypt and in the wilderness, yet have put Me to the test these ten times and have not listened to My voice, shall by no means see the land which I swore to their fathers, nor shall any of those who spurned Me see it. But My servant Caleb, because he has had a different spirit and has followed Me fully, I will bring into the land which he entered, and his descendants shall take possession of it.'"

So Yahveh meted out two fates to Israel. For those who had grumbled against Him: "...your corpses shall fall in this wilderness, even all your numbered men, according to your complete number from twenty years old and upward, who have grumbled against Me. Surely you shall not come into the land in which I swore to settle you....

"Your children, however, whom you said would become a prey—I will bring them in, and they shall know the land which you have rejected. But as for you, your corpses shall fall in this wilderness. And your sons shall be shepherds for forty years in the wilderness, and they shall suffer for your unfaithfulness, until your corpses lie in the wilderness. According to the number of days which you spied out the land, forty days, for every day you shall bear your guilt a year, even forty years...I, Yahveh, have spoken, surely this I will do to all this evil congregation who are gathered together against Me. In this wilderness they shall be destroyed, and there they shall die" (Numbers 13:1-14-35).

Yahveh told our forefathers that He would give them the land of Canaan. The problem was that the people accepted the bad report of ten men, rather than the good report of two men. Once again the majority was wrong. Accepting the bad report caused **599,988 men of Israel to lose faith and not believe in His promises!** The solution to the problem was—**two men of Israel did believe Him!** The ten, plus the 599,988, or 599,998 unbelievers, died in the wilderness. The **two believers entered the promised land!**

Grasshoppers Or Good Witnesses?

Yahveh has promised that He will restore the Kingdom to Israel. "They were asking Him, saying, 'Lord, is it at this time You are restoring the kingdom to Israel?' He said to them, 'It is not for you to know times or epochs which the Father **has fixed** by His own authority'" (Acts 1:6-7).

It has been almost two thousand years since Yeshua spoke these words of promise, and millions of Israelites have walked this earth and have died in the wilderness. Now it is our turn to walk this earth. The question is, will we too die in the wilderness?

Our only hope to avoid this fate is the hope that we are the generation that has been foreordained to receive the restored Kingdom. Admittedly, we do not know for a fact whether or not we are that generation. However we have, as did our forefathers in the wilderness, a freewill choice to make.

We can believe or not believe our Father's promises! We can be grasshoppers or good witnesses!

Yes. We can elect to live our lives as if we are that chosen generation that will see the return of the Greater Son of David and the restoration of the Kingdom to Israel. And, if our lamps are filled with oil, and it turns out that we have labored to accomplish the right tasks in the wrong generation, we are far better off than having labored to accomplish the wrong tasks in the right generation.

By laboring to accomplish those tasks, which Scripture requires be completed prior to the Messiah's return and establishment of His kingdom, we will, at the very least, have been an example. We will have been an example that will help prepare the next generation to be on the alert and ready for the return of the Bridegroom. But, if our lamps are not filled, and the Bridegroom returns, we will, like our forefathers who did not believe, die in the wilderness.

We've Circled The Mountain Long Enough

After forty years in the wilderness, a time came when Yahveh said to Moses, "You have circled this mountain long enough. Now turn north" (Deuteronomy 2:2-3).

We too have circled our mountain long enough. It is time to turn east, time to answer the Father's whistle as He calls for Ephraim to come trembling from the west. It is time to return to the land promised to our forefathers Abraham, Isaac and Jacob (Isaiah 11:11; Hosea 11:11; Zechariah 10:7-10).

How do we answer the whistle? Obviously, at this time we cannot climb on a plane and in a mass move to Israel. For the most part, we cannot afford such a move, and we would not be welcomed in Israel anyway. But, these obstacles are the giants that Yahveh will overcome at the appointed time.

Our job is to prepare for our appointed time. But how?

Many will undoubtedly remember Operation Solomon from a few years ago. In it, the Israelis, ahead of a rebel horde marching on Addis Abba (the capital of Ethiopia), airlifted out some 14,400 Falashas (Black Jews) in thirty-six hours. Quite a feat. But an even greater feat was having 14,400 Falashas at the airport. Where did they come from? Why were they there? How did they get there?

In the early sixties, **two Israelis** (shades of Joshua and Caleb—two witnesses) were sent on a mission to Ethiopia to investigate the Falashas who claimed to be descendants of King Solomon. Why? Because if they were Jews, then they should have the opportunity to return to the land of Israel. These two witnesses were the initial link in a chain that, some thirty years later, would have 14,400 Falashas at the Addis Abba airport, who would in turn be airlifted out in an astounding thirty-six hours.

What did these two witnesses do? They instructed the Falashas as to their true identity, and they informed them about their inheritance: they planted a seed.[41]

The Forerunner's Mission

As forerunners, we too are links in the chain the Father is forging that He might deliver Ephraim from the nations and reunite him with Judah. So, let each of us be a strong link in that chain, and let us link-up with others. Let us begin to instruct other Ephraimites as to their true identity, and to inform them of their inheritance. For, in this manner, we will help fulfill Jeremiah's prophecy concerning

---

41 The author, having served in Ethiopia in the early sixties as a US Army staff officer, and as an advisor to the Ethiopian Army, can attest to these facts—having met and talked with the two Israeli witnesses.

the instruction of Ephraim (Jeremiah 31:19). Or at least, we will plant a seed.

Admittedly the task of instructing Ephraim holds the hope of advancing the **future** goal of Kingdom restoration. And, many have a problem of relating a **future** goal to everyday life and with the **ever-present** goal to love one another as Yeshua has loved us (1 John 4:10-19). So they concentrate their efforts and resources on the **present**, often at the expense of the **future**. Yet the day will come when the **future** becomes our **present**.

Can we at the same time pursue our **present** and **future** goals? Are these two goals compatible?

Yes we can. Yes they are. Indisputably, the solution to **all** this world's ills is for the kingdoms of this world to become the Kingdom of Our Messiah! Therefore, any and all efforts to further the cause of Kingdom restoration can surely be counted as acts of loving one another.

For example, in France it is a crime not to help someone you see in distress. Without a doubt Yahveh's compassion exceeds that of the French. And surely He expects us to help those we see in need and distress. For this is the theme of the parable of the judgement of the sheep and goats, and it is the very heart of love (Matthew 25:31-46; 1 Corinthians 13).

There is no shortage of those in need and distress. Daily we see a lost and hopeless world, suffering from the ravages of depraved men, groaning in futility under the sting of death (Romans 2, 8; I Corinthians 15:55-56). What can we do to help? What does Our Father expect from us forerunners?

A lot! Why? Because we have been given the key: that key being the key of David. For it is the return of the Greater Son of David—of Him who holds that key who will, at His return to a *united* people of Israel—reveal His sons, and thereby deliver creation from its futility, and destroy our final enemy—which is death—and thus, restore the Kingdom to Israel (Romans 8:18-20; I Corinthians 15:26; Revelation 3:7-8; Ezekiel 37:22-28).

Admittedly, the task of uniting Israel is by our standards an impossible task. Which, according to author Watchman Nee, assures us that it is a task from Yahveh based on the fact that we cannot accomplish it without Him. What is our part? What is Yahveh's part? How do we tell the difference?

One well known evangelist gave a good answer to these questions when he said, "The more I show my faith by my works the more I see the works of God accomplished." This should not surprise us, because Yahveh has a track record of working through men.

Passive or Involved?

Again the question: What can **we do** to help? We can be passive, and limit our involvement to prayer, and let the Holy Spirit accomplish the actual instruction of those Ephraimites that He wants returned to an understanding of their heritage and purpose. Or, we can pray *and* get involved. If we do get involved, we will find that the more we witness, the more people will be led by the Holy Spirit into an understanding of their heritage and purpose.

We can try. Therefore, let us take full advantage of every opportunity to help restore the Kingdom. At the very least, let us put as much of our energies and resources in attempting to attain our goals as did those who had a part in the building of great cathedrals and halls of learning, placing a church on every corner, and carrying the Gospel of personal salvation throughout the earth. After all, can we be critical of them and accomplish less?

If You Had A Million Dollars

One last thought. If you had a million dollars, and a whole year completely free to devote to Yahveh's purposes, what would you do with your time and money?

OK, you do not have a million dollars and a year. But you do have an hour, perhaps a day, or even a week. And, you always have sufficient resources to accomplish each and every job our Father will give you to do. Further, remember that Yahveh's rewards are not based on **what we have**, but rather on **what we do with what we have** (Matthew 25:14-30).

10

The Way of The Gentiles

Yeshua sent His disciples out and commanded them, "Do not go in the way of the Gentiles, do not enter *any* city of the Samaritans; but rather go to the lost sheep of the house of Israel."

What did Yeshua mean by this command? Why did He give it? What implications, if any, does this command have for us today?

These questions were raised during a question and answer session at a recent conference. The concern of the questioner was that these instructions appeared to confirm a belief widely held in the Church—that the Jewish people, and the Jewish people alone being the lost sheep of the house of Israel, are the physical Israel of whom this Scripture speaks. Naturally, this interpretation of the verse rules out the possibility that true non-Jewish Believers likewise are possibly physical heirs in Israel. Also, this concept leads to the non-Jewish Believers being forced to either accept the position of an adopted child, or, to create a "spiritual genealogy," and so to settle for being "spiritual Israel." Another alternative is to take the position, as some do, that the Church[42] is a completely different entity, having few ties with the physical nation of Israel and its covenant relationship with the God of Abraham, Isaac and Jacob.

Another concern of the conferees was the apparent differences between various versions of the Bible regarding the phraseology used in the above command. They wanted to know which of the diverse translations had the greatest validity in this case.

To answer these questions, we compare Matthew 10:5-7, as rendered in various versions of the Bible:

New American Standard Bible:

"These twelve Jesus sent out after instructing them, saying, **'Do not go in the way of the Gentiles,** and do not enter any city of the Samaritans; but **rather go to the lost sheep** of the house of Israel. And as you go, preach, saying, "The kingdom of heaven is at hand."

Bible of the Church of the East, or *Lamsa:*[43]

"These twelve Jesus sent out, and charged them and said, **keep away from pagan practices**, and do not enter a Samaritan city; but **above all, go to the sheep which are lost** from the house of Israel. And as you go, preach and say that the kingdom of heaven is near."

New International Version:

"These Jesus sent out with the following instructions: **'Do not go among the Gentiles** or enter any town of the Samaritans. **Go rather to the lost sheep** of Israel. As you go, preach this message: "The kingdom of heaven is near."

There seems to be as many versions of these verses as there are translations. For example:

King James Version: **"Go not into the way of the Gentiles."**

The New Testament, A New Translation (James Moffatt):

"Do not go among the Gentiles."

---

42 There is a true church to be found within the organized Church.

43 The Holy Bible From Ancient Eastern Manuscripts. Containing the Old and New Testaments translated from the Peshitta, The Authorized Bible of the Church of the East. Translated by George M. Lamsa. Published by Holman Company.

The New Testament in Modern English (J.B. Phillips):
"Do not turn off into any of the heathen roads.
The Four Gospels (E.V. Rieu):
"Do not stray into the pagan lands."
The Living Bible (Kenneth Taylor):
"Do not go to the Gentiles."
The Amplified Bible:
"Go nowhere among the Gentiles."

At this point, if you're not confused over what Yeshua commanded His disciples to do, then you don not understand the situation.

Why So Much Confusion Regarding These Verses?

Why and how did we arrive at such a confused state?

According to a recent edition of the Encyclopedia of American Religions, the Church in the United States is divided into some 1,586 recognized faiths (which does not include cults and thousands of unrecognized groups). Together, they represent a potpourri of sects offering an assortment of doctrines, laws, and traditions, which are selected from a smorgasbord of Scriptural translations —at the same time ignoring Yeshua's repeated calls for unity (John 17:11,21,23).

This maze of beliefs and understandings, which has been developed by the shepherds who control these sects, determines what their sheep believe. For, the beliefs of most Christians are unfortunately based on what they are told. Therefore, it is crucial that we ask ourselves: Who told us? Did they tell us the truth? Were they building on a Scriptural foundation?[44]

To ensure that our answers regarding Yeshua's command are built on a solid Scriptural foundation, let us lay aside our biases, prejudices and preconceptions, and let us take a more detailed look at these verses.

---

44 See Chaper 7, *Who Told You?*

The general sense to be gained from the above translations (excepting *Lamsa*) is that the disciples were to stay away from Gentiles (non-Jews). They were to go *only* to the lost sheep of the house of Israel, which title, so they imply, means the Jews. And, to these Jews, they should preach that the kingdom of heaven is near.

However, if preaching that the kingdom is near is in truth a mandate Yeshua was leaving to His Church, at best the Church has ignored it. Further, the Church has gone to the Gentile, not the Jew, and she has not preached to anyone that the kingdom of heaven is near—at least she has not preached it in the sense that the fulfillment of the Lord's prayer is "thy kingdom come **on earth.**" The mission of bringing His kingdom to earth should be a prime objective for every generation. However, the majority of the Church focuses on "going to heaven."

Come Let Us Reason Together

We can find the truth regarding these verses by being a diligent workman "who accurately handles the Word of truth" (2 Timothy 2:15). And, by following the prescription God gave Isaiah: "Come now, let us reason together" (Isaiah 1:18).

To find the truth, it would be good to go back to the original manuscript of the Gospel of Matthew. But, an original does not exist. Further, there is debate over just which language it was first written in: Greek, Hebrew or Aramaic. While we will not make an attempt to settle this controversy, we do want to put forth the understanding that there are potential pitfalls that can result when Scripture is translated from one language into another language.

For example, the American Constitution, which is written in English, will remain the same when new copies are made. However, even with an original in hand, today's English Constitutional commentaries dispute the exact meanings of the original words. Some six hundred members of Congress make this evident, by constant debate over the meaning of the constitution, under the watchful eyes of nine supreme court justices.

Translations into other languages only magnifies this problem. For, one language is not easily translated into another without loss or confusion of meaning. Further, translations are always subject to revision and dispute over exact meanings because words and terms of speech change over the years. This is why we have so many translations and revisions of early English translations, such as the 1611 King James version.

This dilemma grows when we add the fact that the translators of our English Bibles were not working with a single document. They worked with hundreds of documents in several different languages. These facts make our job of being a workman accurately handling the Word of truth even more difficult. In fact the miracle, and the evidence of the Hand of God at work, is seen in that general agreement does exist among the various translations.

What Is The Difference?

As to Matthew 10:5, let use examine the difference between the translations based on their translation of the Greek word *hodos*,.[45] We will again except the *Lamsa Bible*, which is the only translation of those being reviewed that is translated from Aramaic sources.

Strong's Concordance defines *hodos* as a "primary word; a road; by implication a progress (the route, act or distance); figuratively, it designates a mode or means, journey, (high-) way." Other reference works, i.e., Abbingdon's *Interpreter's Dictionary of the Bible*, *The Zondervan* Pictorial *Encyclopedia of the Bible*, Eerdmans' *International Standard Bible Encyclopedia*, and the *Theological Dictionary of the New Testament*[46] go into greater detail in defining the various ways in which *hodos* is translated into English. However, the ten volume *Theological Dictionary* goes into the greatest depth, over sixty pages, in its discussion of the various ways *hodos* is used in Scripture.

---

45 Strong's number 3598G.
46 *Theological Dictionary of The New Testament*, Kittel/ Friedrich, Eerdmans, Grand Rapids.

The *Theological Dictionary* gives the following definition of *hodos*: "The 'way' or 'street' in its many possible forms, e.g., the narrow path trodden by those who have gone before, or the broad roads made for the traffic, on which chariots can travel, troops can march, pilgrims can travel, and processions can be held. The word can also be used for the route taken by ships, the course of a river, the course of a journey, and the flight of birds.

"Metaphorical or figurative use generally has the sense of 'way and means' to achieve or do something. For example, Plato used the word to mean 'the characteristic manner of life which a leader exemplifies for his followers.' The word is used some 880 times in the Septuagint (Greek Old Testament), and some 104 times in the Greek New testament. It is often used to serve the proclamation of God's will. Many verses speak of the *way* or *ways* of God, and even the *ways* which God Himself takes, i.e., His dealings, purposes and acts. The context always makes it clear whether this is the sense or whether one is to think of human conduct. The *ways* which men walk can be called the *ways* of the Lord because they are *ways* which He has commanded."

Following are some metaphorical and figurative New Testament uses of the word *hodos*:

Matthew 3:3 For it was he of whom it was said by the prophet Isaiah, The voice which cries in the wilderness, prepare the *way* of the Lord, and straighten his highways (Lamsa).

Luke 1:79: "To give light to them that sit in darkness and in the shadow of death, to guide our feet into the *way* of peace" (NIV).

Luke 20:21: "So the spies questioned him: 'Teacher, we know that you speak and teach what is right, and that you do not show partiality but teach the *way* of God in accordance with the truth'" (NIV).

John 14:6: "Jesus saith unto him, 'I am the *way*, the truth, and the life: no man cometh unto the Father, but by me'" (KJV).

1 Corinthians 12:31: "But eagerly desire the greater gifts. And now I will show you the most excellent *way*" (NIV).

From the above, we see that *way* is used in the New Testament to speak of the *way*, or *ways*, of God and man, meaning in the sense of *mode* or *conduct*. Further, the context of the sentence always makes it clear whether it speaks of conduct, or whether one is to understand a physical road, path or distance.

For example:

Matthew 8:30: "And there was a good *way* off from them an herd of many swine feeding" (KJV).

Matthew 13:4: "And when he sowed, some seeds fell by the *way* side, and the fowls came and devoured them up" (KJV).

Mark 10:17: "As Jesus started on his *way,* a man ran up to him and fell on his knees before him..." (NIV)?

Mark 11:8: "And many spread their garments in the *way*: and others cut down branches off the trees, and strewed them in the *way"* (KJV).

Now, we are ready to take another look at "the *way* of the Gentiles" as used in Matthew 10:5.

After the above review, ask yourself, can we use the *literal* meaning of *hodos* and say it speaks of a physical road belonging to the Gentiles? Would it make sense for Yeshua to instruct His disciples: "Do not use the roads that belong to the Gentiles when you take out the message of the Kingdom"? Hardly. The Roman roads are often given as one reason Yeshua came when He did. And, the early Church made great use of this excellent transportation system in proclaiming the "Good News."

The Church Could Be In Big Trouble

Obviously, the context does not allow using *way* in its literal sense. So, let us look at it in its metaphorical or figurative sense as way, means, or mode: "Do not go in the *manner* or *mode* of the Gentiles."

In other words, Yeshua said, "Go out and preach the Kingdom the *way* I taught you, and do not use *pagan methods* and *practices* in attempting to achieve your goals."

If not using "pagan practices" is in truth what Yeshua meant, then the Church is in big trouble; because, that is just what it has done! Greek/Romanized Christianity is built on an extensive foundation of pagan methods and practices!

In saying, "Do not go *among* or *to* the Gentiles," The NIV, Living Bible, and Amplified translations, are using *hodos* in a physical sense—not as a title. However, Scripture uses *hodos* as a title for the early followers of Yeshua. And, this God-given title is based on "The *Way*, or belief system they were following:

Acts 9:2: [Paul] "asked for letters to the synagogues in Damascus, so that if he found any there who belonged to the *Way*, whether men or women, he might take them as prisoners to Jerusalem" (NIV).

Acts 19:23: "And at that time there was a great uprising against those who followed in the *Way* of God" (Lamsa).

Acts 22:4: "I persecuted the followers of this *Way* to their death..." (NIV).

The very essence of the New Testament is that the "Good News" is to be preached to all creation. Therefore, it does not make sense to have Yeshua say in the preamble to His longest and most comprehensive instructions to His disciples: "Do not go among, or to, the Nations."

Also, their translation of this passage is not consistent with the major emphasis they put on everything else in their translations. It being that the Church *has* been called to go to the Gentiles (rather than to the Jews). Yet, in their translations, in this instance, we find the reverse: Do *not* go to the Gentiles, but go to the Jews.

Using *hodos* strictly as a physical title or designation, as these translations have done, is not warranted.

The interpretation of the NASB and KJV, "Do not go in *the way* of *the* Gentiles," rests with how one defines or understands the word *way*. However, the fact that these versions join NIV, Living Bible, and Amplified Bible in the manner in which they translate Matthew 10:6, "but rather go to the lost sheep of the house of

Israel," puts them in the same camp. They all translate the Greek word *mallon,*[47] as *rather,* instead of using a word or phrase that indicates *more of the same,* or *in a greater degree.* And, this is the way Lamsa correctly translates this verse: "But *above all*, go to the sheep which are lost from the house of Israel."

While NASB and KJV are vague about the meaning of *way*, they mistakenly make it clear that they think the disciples should go only to Jews.

Translating this passage this way well illustrates the fact that they are adhering to preconceived prejudices and positions. Their primary error being that they think only the Jewish people are physical Israel, and that the Church is "Spiritual Israel." The Church, so they think, is made up of people descended from anybody *but* Abraham, Isaac and Jacob.[48] They erronously see the Church as being comprised of people who have been grafted into a Jewish olive tree, and adopted into the family of Abraham, Isaac and Jacob. Had they understood the following three points they would have translated this passage as did Lamsa:

1) In Scripture there were, and there still are, two houses of Israel (Isaiah 8:14).

2) The olive tree of Israel has two branches (Jeremiah 11:10,16; 2:18,21; Romans 11:17).

3) The "spirit of adopion belongs to the sons of Israel" (Romans 9:4). Truly, it is as House of David has long proclaimed: "How one defines Israel determines how one interprets Scripture."

This critical analysis of some passages in a particular translation is not meant to condemn the entire translation. There are many different English translations of the Bible, and none are 100% correct, so the reader, with the help of the Holy Spirit, must carefully choose that which they do accept. Like eating chicken, you eat the meat and spit out the bones.

---

47 Strong's 3123. mallon, mal'-lon; neut. of the compar. of the same as G3122; (adv.) more (in a greater degree) or rather:--+ better, X far, (the) more (and more), (so) much (the more), rather.
48 See H DH, *Apprehending Abraham's Blessing.*

Do Not Enter Any City Of The Samaritans

When giving His instruction about their method of proclaiming the Good News of the kingdom, Yeshua also said: "Do not enter any city of the Samaritans."

What did He mean by this statement?

Zondervan's Encyclopedia tells us that at that time, Samaritans, Jews and Gentiles lived in the city of Samaria, and in the northern half of the province of Samaria. However, the southern half of the province was populated primarily by Samaritans. Josephus describes the city of Samaria in Herod's day as a cosmopolitan city of Jews, Samaritans, Greeks, Macedonians, and Romans. This mixture of Jew and Gentile was also true of the major population centers of Judea and Galilee.

Therefore, it is reasonable to conclude that Yeshua was referring to the cities that were populated essentially with Samaritans. Thus, He said, "any city of the Samaritans," rather than "any city of Samaria." So, the logical understanding of this phrase, taken in the context of the passage we are examining, would be that Yeshua was saying do not go to the Samaritans.

But, why did He include this statement in His instruction to the Apostles?

Samaritans: Lost Sheep Or Gentiles?

To answer this question, we first need to understand how Yeshua and the Twelve viewed the Samaritans: Were they lost sheep of the house of Israel, or were they Gentiles? If they were considered to be Gentiles, it would have been superfluous for Yeshua to say, "Do not enter any city of the Samaritans." Simply instructing the Twelve to, "Go *only* to the sheep which are lost from the house of Israel," would have sufficed. Based on this sentence alone, the Twelve, believing the Samaritans were *not* lost sheep would *not* have gone to them. However, if the Apostles considered the Samaritans to be lost sheep, and, if Yeshua did not want the

Apostles going to them—*at that time*—then it would have been necessary to include the statement: "Do not enter any city of the Samaritans." For, without these instructions the Twelve *would* have included the cities of the Samaritans in their itinerary.

Common sense, devoid of prejudice and preconceptions, clearly encourages the view that Yeshua and the Twelve considered the Samaritans to be lost sheep of the house of Israel. Further, history and Scripture both confirm this perspective.

History Of The Samaritans

In general, the secular history of this period records the inhabitants of Samaria as being the descendants of the polyglot of peoples who had inhabited the land in the preceding centuries. This would include, descendants of the Israelites (those left in the land after the Assyrian conquest of the northern kingdom of Israel), and descendants of the colonists imported by the Assyrians.

Abingdon's *Interpreter's Dictionary* says the historic Jewish view is that the Samaritans were only descendants of the colonists whom the Assyrians imported. *Zondervan's Encyclopedia* expounds on this Jewish view, saying they believed the Samaritans were the result of intermarriage between the colonist, whom the Assyrians planted in the northern kingdom, and the Israelite population that remained in the land. Either view makes it clear that the Jewish Religious Hierarchy of the day did not consider the Samaritans to be a legitimate part of the Religious Jewish community or the covenant people of Israel.

Their attitude would be similar to that presently held by the majority of the ultra Orthodox Jewish community regarding the Conservative and Reform Jews. They are not accepted as equal by the Orthodox. Further, these three branches of Rabbinical Judaism join together in refusing to accept the Messianic Jews. Opinions aside, in all these groups legitimate Israelites are found.

Regarding the Samaritan view of themselves as being part of the people of Israel, *Abbingdon's Interpreter's Dictionary* says the

Samaritans, for their part, dismissed this Jewish view as being malicious and fabricated. They claimed the deportation in 722 B.C., was neither total nor final. While they admit that pagan colonists were introduced by the Assyrians, they say they must not be confused with the true, native Israelites. *Abingdon Interpreter's Dictionary* makes the critical appraisal that there is much to support this Samaritan claim. It points out that the attitude of Samaritans and Jews toward each other is wholly and most naturally explained as a continuance of the ancient hostility that existed between Israel and Judah. Further, there is abundant Scriptural proof that the two houses of Israel were not joined at this time.

The most plausible conclusion regarding this population question is that, after the fall of Samaria in 722 B.C., the local population consisted of two distinct elements that were living side by side. They were a remnant of the native Israelites and the descendants of the foreign colonists. This is similar to the situation in Samaria today, with Jews and Arabs living side by side—albeit not peaceably. *Zondervan's* Encyclopedia suggests that, more than likely, the Samaritans were the pure descendants of the Israelites that were left in the land. For, it concludes, the theology of the Samaritans shows little sign of the influence of the paganism of the Assyrians, nor of the colonists imported by the Assyrians. Further, if there was any intermarriage, then the foreigners converted and the children were regarded as Israelites.

Old Covenant Scripture addressing this situation is sparse, but there is evidence that there was a remnant of the northern kingdom in the land after 722 B.C.. King Hezekiah, whose reign (715-687 B.C.) began seven years after the final Assyrian conquest of Samaria, held a great Passover in Jerusalem, which feast men from Manasseh, Zebulun, and Asher attended (2 Chronicles 30:10,11). As late as the time of King Josiah (640-609 B.C.), at least 82 years after the fall of the northern kingdom, Ephraim and Manasseh contributed to the repairs on the Jerusalem Temple (2 Chronicles 34:9). Jeremiah records that about 587 B.C. (135 years after the northern kingdom was no more), eighty men came from Shechem, from Shiloh, and from Samaria with their beards shaved off and their clothes torn and their bodies gashed, having grain offerings and incense in their hands to bring to the house of the Lord (41:5).

Furthermore, the post exilic prophets, in particular Jeremiah, Ezekiel, Daniel, and Zechariah, treated the tribes of the vanquished northern kingdom—those in the land, and those scattered abroad—as integral parts of the covenant people of Israel.

Our final point in this regard is two-fold. Point one is the fact that the bloodline comes from the father. The second point is that ones biology does not change, regardless of where the people were, or presently are, located—what one believes or does not believe cannot change ones genealogy. An Israelite forever remains an Israelite. Further, because bloodlines are passed from father to son, they remain direct descendants of their father.

Samaria And Samaritans: An Integral Part Of The Early Church

New Covenant Scriptures prove the inhabitants of Samaria were an integral part of the initial makeup of the church:

Acts 1:8: ".....and you will be my witnesses in Jerusalem, and in all Judea and *Samaria*, and to the ends of the earth."

Acts 8:1: "....at that time there was a great persecution against the church which was at Jerusalem; and they were all scattered abroad throughout the regions of Judea and *Samaria*."

Acts 8:5: "Philip went down to a city in *Samaria* and proclaimed the Christ there."

Acts 8:14: "When the apostles in Jerusalem heard that *Samaria* had accepted the word of God, they sent Peter and John to them."

Acts 9:31: "Then the church throughout Judea, Galilee and *Samaria* enjoyed a time of peace. It was strengthened; and encouraged by the Holy Spirit, it grew in numbers, living in the fear of the Lord."

It is important for us to note that in Acts 8:14, Peter and John, who were the recipients of the command, "do not enter any city of the Samaritans," are found doing just that—they are entering a Samaritan city. Obviously something had changed. Apparently, Yeshua's command was *temporary* in nature. Why was this *temporary* command given? And further, when was it changed?

Yeshua And The Woman At The Well

The Third Chapter of John describes Yeshua's visit to the Samaritan City of Sychar (verses 4-42). There, He is talking with a Samaritan woman at the city well who says to Him: "Our father Jacob gave us this well." And, "our fathers worshiped in this mountain" (Of necessity we must conclude that her "fathers" would have been Israelites of the northern kingdom, for it is they who "worshiped at that mountain"). Yeshua, by posing no objections to either of her observations, appears to be confirming their accuracy. Further, His two day visit ends with many Samaritans in Sychar confessing that He was the Messiah. Thus, He ended any ban at this time. Also, it is significant that this is the only record in the four Gospels of a group of people, other than His immediate disciples, accepting Him as the Messiah before His crucifixion.

In light of Yeshua's visit to Sychar, we can only assume the reason He initially instructed the Twelve not to go the Samaritans was because He was reserving that task for Himself. However, after His visit to Sychar, the door to the Samaritans was opened wide. And, it was opened by the same One who had earlier forbade its entry. To further confirm this point, note the time when the Jews said to Yeshua, "Aren't we right in saying that you are a Samaritan and demon-possessed?" (John 8:48-49). Yeshua answered, "I am not possessed by a demon." He did not add, "I am not a Samaritan." Perhaps He did not deny the accusation that He was a Samaritan because He knew the Samaritans were fellow Israelites.

Keep Away From Pagan Practices

It is always difficult to give greater weight or importance to a portion or passage of Scripture, because all Scripture is important. However, if one were going to pick out key portions of Scripture, the Tenth Chapter of Matthew, Yeshua's instructions to His disciples, would surely be included.

In this chapter He is equipping them, telling them where and how to go, and what to do. Also, these instructions are in complete harmony with Yeshua's instructions, or great commission, as recorded in Mark and Acts (Mark 16:15; Acts 1:8).

Clearly Lamsa's translation: "Keep away from pagan practices" is far more consistent with the whole of Yeshua's instructions to His disciples. Having arrived at this conclusion, let us now look at exactly what Yeshua meant when He charged His disciples to keep away from pagan practices.

Yeshua's first step in Matthew 10 is to empower the twelve by giving them authority over unclean spirits, and power to heal every kind of disease and sickness. His next step is to charge them to keep away from pagan practices, as they go to the lost sheep of the house of Israel proclaiming the "Good News" that the kingdom of heaven is near.

Why did Yeshua feel it necessary to include this charge to His disciples? Because His ministry was mostly conducted in Galilee of the *Gentiles*, and those of the former northern kingdom were regarded as Gentiles, and His disciples were men of Galilee of the *Gentiles* (Acts 1:11).

The title of 'Jew,' at the time of Yeshua, had a wider application than signifying one was a physical descendent of Judah. Also, there are instances of peoples joining themselves to Judah after the fall of the Northern kingdom of Israel. The book of Esther records that many of the people of the land became Jews (Esther 8:17, 9:27). Paul was of Benjamin, and Anna was of Asher yet they were considered Jews (Philippines 3:5, Luke 2:32). This broad definition of "Jewishness" also applied to those in Galilee.

Galilee Of The Gentiles

After the separation of Solomon's kingdom (936 B.C.), the region later known as Galilee, was the most northerly part of the northern kingdom of Israel. In 734 B.C. this area was absorbed into the Assyrian Empire by Tiglath-Pileser. Under Assyrian rule, Galilee, along with the other areas of the former northern kingdom, underwent a series of importations and deportations. Through the next six centuries the region passed in turn to Babylonia, Persia, Macedonia, Egypt, and Syria—all the while constantly experiencing infiltration and migration. This was happening because, as Yahveh had prophesied, He was sifting the house of Israel among all nations (Amos 9:9, Hosea 8:8).

Then in 80 B.C., Alexander Janneus, of Judah, subdued this region, and Judaized the mixed population. And, so many of these Galileans—farmers, herders and fisherman, became known as "Jews."

However, even though they were considered loyal to the Jewish state, they were always considered to be inferior by the "Judean Jews." I.E., "Can any good thing come out of Nazareth/Galilee?" (John 1:46; 7:52). This condescending attitude was likewise held by the many Jews who migrated from the south, settling in the Galilee, and thus becoming known as Galileans.

It is apparent that the Galileans were easily distinguishable to their fellow Jews by their speech. The classic passage is, of course, the accusation by the bystanders against Simon Peter regarding his denial (Mark 14:70; Luke 22:59). For, they said of him: "Your *speech* gives you away." This accent calls to mind the incident recorded in Judges—when 42,000 people of Ephraim were killed—because their speech gave them away (12:6).

It was from this mixed group of Galileans that the first disciples of Yeshua were drawn. From them the twelve were chosen. Yeshua was well aware that these Galileans, and the followers from Judea and Samaria would soon separate from those Jews who would reject Him. And when this happened, He did not want them following in the footsteps of their forefathers, and thus mixing pagan practices into the way He had instructed them to follow.

For, that is exactly what happened the last time there was a separation in Israel: Ephraim and Judah separated into two kingdoms—Judea and Israel. At the death of King Solomon, God fulfilled His Word to Solomon and tore ten parts of the kingdom from his son Rehoboam, and God gave those ten parts, or ten tribes, to Jeroboam (1 Kings 11:9-36).

God also promised Jeroboam,"If you do whatever I command you, and walk in my ways, and do what is right in my eyes, by keeping my statutes and commands, as David my servant did, I will be with you. I will build you a dynasty as enduring as the one I built for David and will give Israel to you (1 Kings 11:38).

But, Jeroboam did not keep the Lord's statutes and commands as David did. Fearing that his people would return to Jerusalem and thus follow after Rehoboam, he constructed two golden calves, which he set in Bethel and Dan. Jeroboam then presented them to the people as the gods who had brought them up out of the land of Egypt. He also established houses of worship on high places, and made priests of those who were not of the tribe of Levi, and he changed the feasts and feast days. Unfortunately, the Kings of Israel who followed after Jeroboam continued to lead Israel down this path of pagan practices—until the day came when the Lord said, "I will put an end to the kingdom of Israel" (Hosea 1:4).

It's Time To Bury Jeroboam

Bryan Hennessy, in his House of David Herald article, *It's Time To Bury Jeroboam*, says:

"The sin of Jeroboam is the fruit of the idolatrous religion which he craftily introduced into the Northern Kingdom of Israel. For, after the nation was split in two, the people of the Northern Kingdom, or those under Jeroboam's rule, were still traveling to the Temple in Jerusalem—to keep the Feasts, as required by the Lord. Jeroboam, fearing that he would lose his place if the people returned to Judah, devised a religious substitute—to keep his people at home. This substitute caused the people of Ephraim to worship and serve the Lord in the ways of the Gentile Nations, rather than *in the manner in which God had specifically instructed them* (1 Kings 12).

"Thus, did the people of Ephraim follow Jeroboam in apostasy—and sadly, they follow him to this day. And, we, those who in this Twentieth Century do follow the Messiah, we likewise are guilty of the same sin in that we continually put our religion, or the traditions and practices of Westernized Christianity, before His truth. This is idolatry by any definition.

"By choosing to be obedient to the dictates of the man-made traditions of Christianity, over the voice of Messiah—as expressed in the Bible and the spoken Word of His Holy Spirit —by this disloyalty, Yahveh does find us guilty of walking in the sins of Jeroboam."

Why Did The Lord Put An End To The Kingdom Of Israel?

The following are but a few of the reasons why the Lord put an end to the Kingdom of Israel according to Hosea:

- Harlotry, adultery, swearing, lies, deception, murder, stealing, bearing illegitimate children, mixing with the nations, being without sense, and acting like a silly dove.
- Establishing their own feasts, new moons, sabbaths, and festal assembles; making covenants with worthless oaths, making images and idols, and eating unclean foods.
- Rebelling against God, having a lack of faithfulness toward God, transgressing the covenant of God, regarding God's law as a strange thing, speaking lies about God, following man's commands, lack of, and rejection of, the knowledge of God in the land.

Hosea ends his charges against the Ephraimites saying, "Who is wise? He will realize these things. Who is discerning? He will understand them. The *ways* of the Lord are right; the righteous walk in them, but the rebellious stumble in them" (Hosea 14:9).

The verdict is clear! Yeshua wanted us to herald the kingdom of God in His *ways*, and not in the *ways* **of the heathen gentiles**.

The Deadly Mixture

What has the Church done with this verdict?

Calling a pig clean does not change the fact that the pig does not chew the cud. By Yahveh's definition, the pig is still an unclean animal (Leviticus 11.7). And, calling Sunday the Sabbath—or the Gentile festival of the sun god (winter festival) Christmas—or calling the festival of Ishtar (spring festival) Easter—does not make them feasts of Israel.[49] These changes of the ways of the God of Israel made by the Church, are no more pleasing to Him than were the changes Jeroboam made.

Westernized Christianity, as we know it today, is a product of a *mixture* of Christianity and paganism. This very mixture produced the Churches of the Dark Ages. Out of which came our modern Churches—changed, but not restored to the truth of their roots.

Church scholars recognize that the Church developed from this *mixture*, and from their point of view, Christianizing pagan practices was a *triumph* for Christianity! Adopted into the Church, along with the pagan feast days, were gentile ways of music, singing, lights, incense, ablutions, floral decorations, statues, water, oil, vestments, decoration of altars, crosses, order of service, repetitions, etc. In literally hundreds of ways, Gentile ways were merged into the Church and called "Christianity." Thus the Church paid the bill for her acceptance by the Roman Empire in the currency of compromise. This pagan currency continues in use to our day.

---

49 Yeshua's resurrection can and should be celebrated as the feast of the "First of the First Fruits" (Exodus 34:22).

The Old Covenant records that the apostasy into which our forefathers repeatedly fell was that of *mixture*. They did not totally reject the way of the God of Abraham, Isaac and Jacob. Rather, they *mixed Gentile **ways** with it*! Such was the case when they worshipped the golden calf: "These are your gods, O Israel, who brought you up out of Egypt" (Exodus 32:4). They mixed their commemoration of Yahveh's deliverance with paganism!

Such worship was—and still is—false, heathenistic, and an abomination in the sight of God. Yet—and this is the point we must see—they people claimed that theirs was a "feast unto the Lord" (Exodus 32:5).

Is the Church any different today, when Christmas with Santa Claus and a decorated tree, Easter, with painted eggs and festive baskets, are claimed to be "feasts unto the Lord"? Calling Sunday the "Lord's day" does not make it the Sabbath. "Like father, like son," the Church continues in the "sin of Jeroboam."

Mystery Babylon

Another example of *mixture* to consider: during the forty years in the wilderness, our forefathers carried the tabernacle of God. However, some of them were not content with this, so they *added* something. They made unto themselves a Babylonian tabernacle that was carried also: "But ye have borne the tabernacle of your Moloch and Chiun your images, the star of your god, which ye made to yourselves" (Amos 5:26, Acts 7:42,43). These were but other names for the sun-god Baal and the mother goddess Astarte/Ishtar.

We should take heed. Because of this *mixture of ways*, the songs of worship, sacrifices, and offerings of our forefathers were rejected by Yahveh. And so *we* cannot follow Gentile ways and at the same time have the blessings and power of the Holy One of Israel. Perhaps the reason the Church has not been casting out demons, healing all sickness and disease, and raising the dead is because she has followed *"the **way** of the Gentiles."*

Over the centuries these pagan ways were so cleverly mixed with Christianity that the Babylonish influence became hidden—a mystery—"mystery Babylon." However, Yeshua warned us about "wolves in sheep's clothing" (Matthew 7:15). These wolves of paganism disguised in the outer garments of Christianity have paved a way of a *deadly mixture*—one that has led countless millions down the broad way that leads to destruction (Matthew 7:13). Thus, when Yeshua commanded the Twelve to "keep away from pagan ways," it was to ensure that they, and those who would follow in their footsteps, would not fall under the bondage of Babylon. Of this Babylonian woman of bondage, Yeshua is still saying, "Come out of her, my people, that ye be not partakers of her sins" (Revelation 18:4).

Adam and Eve proved for all eternity that eating from the tree of *"Good and Evil"* (Genesis 2:17) is to eat from a deadly mixture. Eating from this tree will not only give us indigestion, it will eventually kill us! Life eternal requires that we enjoy an unmixed diet from the tree of *Life*!

Yeshua would have us be among the few who find and follow the narrow way leading to that life (Matthew 7:14). However, to find and follow His way of life, we cannot go in "the way of the Gentiles!"

Restoring Israel's Kingdom

11

Ephraim, Once Again A Mighty Man

When will the Kingdom of Israel be restored to the people of Israel? What part might we play in the Father's restoration process?

These questions have perplexed Believers and caused them to plead for an answer since they were first asked of Yeshua some two thousand years ago.

Why?

Because Yeshua's response to their question included a "mystery." He told His disciples that the Father knows the **moment, hour, and day when Yeshua is going to restore the Kingdom to Israel**. He also said, that it was not for them to know this predestined time. Rather, it was their job to be His witnesses, both in Jerusalem, and in all Judea and Samaria, and even to the remotest part of the earth (Acts 1:8).

Fortunately, today it is possible to have greater insight into the

117

answers to these critical questions![50]

However, our first step in unraveling this "time for the Kingdom" mystery, and in understanding our own personal part in the restoration process, requires that we first fully understand who we are in relationship to Yeshua, and to the historical people and nation of Israel.

As Believers, each one of us sees ourselves as having been "born again" into Yahveh's family. But, what is **our** link to the forefathers of Israel? How are **we** connected with those who stood in the very presence of Yahveh at the foot of Mount Sinai? (Exodus 19:16-20). What gives **us** the credibility to be counted by the Holy One of Israel among the people of Israel? Also, what unites us with Messiah's original group of disciples, or as David Stern refers to them in his Jewish New Testament, to His "emissaries?" Just what is our relationship with those chosen few who spent three and a half years in intimate fellowship with the God of Israel, when He walked in the form of a man on this earth?

Answers to the these questions are found in the Words of the Prophet like unto Moses, and in the Words of that Prophet's original emissaries.

In Torah, Moses declared to the chosen people of Israel that, "The Lord your God will raise up for you a prophet like me [Moses] from among you, from your countrymen, you shall listen to him....and I will put My Words in his mouth, and He shall speak to them all that I command him. And it shall come about that whoever will not listen to My words, which He shall speak in My name, I Myself will require it of him'" (Deuteronomy 18:15-22).

Who is this Prophet through whom the Holy One of Israel promised to speak?

It is none other than Yeshua.

Yeshua was fulfilling this prophecy given to Moses when He

---

50 See Chapter 17, *The Messianic Vision*, which outlines our Father's plan to realize His Messianic Vision, that of manifesting His presence—in His earthly Kingdom—in the midst of a **united** people. The outline includes His prerequisites for restoration of His Kingdom to Israel, and His prescription for the reunion of His people.

said to the Father, "The Words which Thou gavest Me I have given to them [His original band of emissaries]; and they received them, and truly understood that I came forth from Thee, and they believed that Thou didst send Me....I do not ask Thee to take them out of the world, but to keep them from the evil one....I do not ask in behalf of these alone, but for those [Believers down through the ages] who also believe in Me through their Word" (John 17:8-20).

Our concern is that we listen to the Words the Father gave Yeshua, which Words He in turn gave to His emissaries. For, those who do not receive these Words, of them the Father Himself will "**require** it." The Hebrew word *darash*[51], which is here translated *require*,[52] can be best understood in the context of this passage to mean that, Yahveh will require an accounting of each one of us as to how we *shama*[53] meaning listen, or harken, to these Words.

From this we conclude that the answer to our "Who are we?" question is: "We are included among those in this generation who are following in the footsteps of the original emissaries, by believing in their Words which were given them by Yeshua.[54]

Having made the point that we are required to listen or harken to the Words that Yeshua gave to His emissaries, which Words they in turn gave to us, the next questions to answer are: To what Words

---

51 Strongs #1875. darash, daw-rash'; a prim. root; prop. to tread or frequent; usually to follow (for pursuit or search); by impl. to seek or ask; spec. to worship:--ask, X at all, care for, X diligently, inquire, make inquisition, [necro-] mancer, question, require, search, seek [for, out], X surely. Used 160 times in 152 verses.

52 Re·quire (r¹-kw°r") *tr.v.* re·quired, re·quir·ing, re·quires. *Abbr.* req. 1. To have as a requisite; need. 2. To call for as obligatory or appropriate; demand. 3. To impose an obligation on; compel. -- re·quir"a·ble *adj.* --re·quir"er *n.*

53 Strongs #8085. shama', shaw-mah'; a prim. root; to hear intelligently (often with impl. of attention, obedience, etc.; caus. to tell, etc.):-- X attentively, call (gather) together, X carefully, X certainly, consent, consider, be content, declare, X diligently, discern, give ear, (cause to, let, make to) hear (-ken, tell), X indeed, listen, make (a) noise, (be) obedient, obey, perceive, (make a) proclaim (-ation), publish, regard, report, shew (forth), (make a) sound, X surely, tell, understand, whosoever [heareth], witness.

54 It is imperative that we recognize that not only Yeshua is the Prophet like unto Moses but that we have, and our forefathers before us had, the Word that the God of Abraham, Isaac and Jacob put in His mouth. Unfortunately, many would have you believe that we do not have the true or valid Word in which we can place our hope. These attacks on our basic foundation come in all sizes, shapes and forms, and from many directions, and they have been addressed in several House of David Heralds. See listing of Heralds in the Appendix.

are we to listen or harken?   And, what is it that the original emissaries believed that we are required to believe?

We begin our answer by using Abraham as an example. And we ask:

What did the Father require that Abraham believe?

He reckoned Abraham's belief in His Word—"That his descendants would be as numerous as the stars of heaven"—as "righteousness" (Genesis 15:6).   And, if we have the faith of Abraham, we too will believe what Abraham believed.[55] Likewise, if we are to believe what the original emissaries believed, we must believe what Yeshua told them: that our ultimate mission is the restoration of the Kingdom to Israel...

Restoring the Kingdom to Israel

The Apostle Luke described a time when Yeshua was praying in a certain place, and when He finished, one of His disciples said to Him, "Lord, teach us to pray just as John taught his disciples." In response Yeshua taught them, "When you pray, say, 'Father, hallowed be Thy Name, Thy kingdom come...on earth as it is in heaven'" (Luke 11:1-4). What is Yeshua telling both His disciples, and us, to pray for? Is He telling them/us to pray that we go to heaven? No, He is instructing them/us to pray that His kingdom come here on the earth!

Some five centuries of silence followed the Biblical declaration, "Behold, I am going to send you Elijah the prophet before the coming of the great and terrible day of the Lord" (Malachi 4:5). Then, the event that heralded the New Covenant occurred: Zacharias, the father of John the Baptist, was filled with the Holy Spirit, and he prophesied, "Blessed be the Lord God of Israel—for He has visited us and accomplished redemption for His people, and has raised up a horn of salvation for us in the house of David His servant" (Luke 1:67).

---

55 See HDH, *Apprehending Abraham's Blessings; Who Is Israel?*, Chapter 1, Believing What Abraham Believed.

In fulfilling Zacharias' prophecy the angel Gabriel visited Mary. And, he told her about Yeshua, the Son she would bear for the Father: "He will be great and will be called the Son of the Most High, and His Father will give Him the throne of His father David, and He will reign over the house of Jacob forever. His kingdom will never end" (Luke 1:32).

Yeshua told us to pray that His Kingdom would come here on the earth. And Gabriel explained that Yeshua's Kingdom is the Kingdom of Jacob/Israel, and that Yeshua would rule over the house of Jacob/Israel forever.

Further, Yeshua said of Himself, "I was sent only to the lost sheep of the house of Israel" (Matthew 15:24). And, He said in John 10:7: "My sheep know My voice and I know them, and they follow Me."

Meditate for a moment on this testimony: "My sheep know My voice and I know them, and they follow Me." This assertion by Yeshua, has not applied to great numbers of people over the past two thousand years, and it does not apply to very many people on the face of this earth today. But it does apply to those who are following in the steps of Yeshua's emissaries—they being **those to whom He gave His kingdom.**

Yeshua said to His emissaries, "I confer on you a Kingdom just as My Father conferred one on Me" (Luke 22:29). He also said, "Do not be afraid, little flock, for your Father has been pleased to give you the Kingdom" (Luke 12:32). And, "Truly I say to you, that you who have followed Me, in the regeneration when the Son of Man will sit on His glorious throne, you also shall sit upon twelve thrones, judging the twelve tribes of Israel" (Matthew 19:28).

Yeshua gave His Kingdom to His emissaries—the very Kingdom which was given to Him by the Father to rule over forever—the House of Jacob/Israel.

Yeshua said when He was 12 years old, "I must be about My Father's business." What was His Father's business? Yeshua explains this later, when He sent out His emissaries, telling them to,

"Preach the Kingdom." And, He instructed them **not** to preach this message in the way of (manner of, or like) the Gentiles. And, He gave them the job of taking this message of the Kingdom to the lost sheep of the house of Israel—a job that remains unfinished to this day[56] (Matthew 10:5-7; 10:23, Luke 9:1-6; John 4:7-42).

What did the emissaries (in whose footsteps we are to follow) understand to be Yahveh's plan and goal concerning them and all Israel?

We begin to see the answer in Luke's description of Yeshua's entrance into Jerusalem, just days before His death: "As He was going, they were spreading their garments in the road. And as He was approaching the descent from the Mount of Olives, the whole multitude of the disciples began to praise God joyfully with a loud voice for all the miracles which they had seen, saying, 'Blessed is the King who comes in the Name of Yahveh'" (Luke 19:36-38).

It was "Kingship" that gave the ruling Pharisees a problem with Yeshua. They feared that the people would crown Yeshua—make Him a King—which would cause war with Rome—which would result in their loss of control of the temple and what little authority they had.

The expectation of virtually all first century Jews was that when the Messiah came, He would deliver Israel from Roman oppression, and become King over an Israel that was united, even as it was under Kings Saul, David and Solomon. This is why the people who recognized Yeshua as the King of Israel were expecting Him to immediately restore the Kingdom to Israel.

Yeshua's Prayer For Us

The Seventeenth Chapter of John contains the prayer of Yeshua before He went to the cross. Yeshua said, at the start of His ministry, "I must be about My Father's business." In John 17:4, He said, "I have glorified Thee on the earth, having accomplished the

---

56 See Chapter 10, *The Way of The Gentiles.*

work which Thou hast given Me to do." And in the next four verses He describes the work He was given to do: "...I manifested Thy name to the men Thou gavest Me out of the world. Thine they were and Thou gavest them to Me and they have kept Thy Word. Now, they have come to know that everything which Thou gavest Me is for them. For the Words which Thou gavest Me I have given to them and they received them [understood them]. And they truly understood that I came from Thee and they believe that Thou didst send Me."

As Yeshua continued His Gethsemane prayer, He said, "I ask on their behalf—I do not ask on behalf of the world, but of those whom Thou gave me, for they are Thine. I have given them Thy Word; and the world has hated them, because they are not of the world, even as I am not of the world. I do not ask Thee to take them out of the world, but to keep them from the evil one....As Thou didst send Me into the world, I also have sent them into the world....I do not ask in behalf of these alone, but for **those also who believe in Me through their Word**" (John 17:14-20).

It is of prime importance that we see that Yeshua prayed, not only for His original emissaries, but also for all those emissaries in future generations who would believe in the Words given the original emissaries—which Words they recorded for our benefit.

How Do We Fit Into The Divine Design?

This is where and how we fit into the Divine design. This is how we automatically come under the mantle of prayer and purpose that Yeshua placed over His original emissaries.

Yeshua, having stated that His emissaries understood the Word of the Father that He had given them, next went to the cross. After His resurrection from the dead, Yeshua came along side two of His emissaries who were on the road to Emmaus. But, they did not recognize Him. As they walked together, and talked about Yeshua and His death, one of the emissaries said, "We thought that He was going to restore the Kingdom to Israel" (Luke 24:21).

Where did they get that idea?

They got it from the fact that all Israel was looking for the end of pagan oppression, and to the establishment of Israel's Kingdom. Besides, Yeshua repeatedly spoke of that Kingdom.

Also, after His resurrection, Yeshua presented Himself alive to His emissaries, appearing to them over a period of forty days. And He again spoke of the things concerning the Kingdom (Acts 1:2). Then came the time for His departure.

"Lord, Is Now the Time That You Are Going To Restore The Kingdom To Israel?"

Yeshua's emissaries were gathered together with Him on the Mount of Olives. They undoubtedly sensed that they were about to witness a momentous event. Standing there with the One whom they had for years followed, they had but one last question for Him: "Lord, is **now** the time that You are going to restore the Kingdom to Israel?" (Acts 6).

While we may speculate on the reason for and the timing of, this question, there is no speculation about Yeshua's answer. He said: "It is not for you to know the times or the seasons that the Father has **already established**" (Acts 1:7).

Almost 2,000 years ago on the Mount of Olives, Yeshua told His emissaries that the Father already knows the **moment, hour, and day when He is going to have Yeshua return and restore the Kingdom to Israel**. However, it was not for them to know this predestined time.

Why? Had they known that it was some 2,000 years in the future, surely it would have dampened their enthusiasm—it would have deadened their resolve. After all, how would **you** feel, if you knew today that the return of Messiah was still some two thousand years in the future?

Yeshua's answer to them also included the command that His emissaries would be witnesses (the actual word is martyrs).

Where? In Jerusalem, all Judea, Samaria, and to the remotest corners of the earth.

It appears that in this day, the Church has forgotten everything but the remotest corners of the earth. As for Jerusalem, Judea, and Samaria, the United Nations, the United States, the Roman Catholic church, and the World Council of Churches are in the process of taking away this area of the promised Kingdom of Israel. In direct opposition to the Father's Word, they seek to give this portion of the Promised Land to the sons of Ishmael (Palestinians). But, the God of Abraham, Isaac and Jacob/Israel did not give this area to Ishmael and his descendants, nor to Esau and his descendants. Rather, by an oath which He swore on His own Name, He gave Jerusalem, Judea, and Samaria to the descendants of Israel for an everlasting possession! (Hebrews 6:13-17).

Requirements For The Return?

After revealing that the time of the restoration of Israel's Kingdom was to be an unknown factor, Yeshua was lifted up into the heavens. And, the angels, who also were present, asked of His emissaries, "Men of Galilee, why do you stand here looking into the sky? This Yeshua, who has been taken up from you into heaven, will come in just the same way as you have watched Him go into heaven" (Acts 1:11).

Other Scriptures reveal that the fulfillment of this angelic prophecy requires a **united** people, a people standing on the Mount of Olives, saying, "Blessed is He who comes in the Name of Yahveh" (Ezekiel 37:1; 15-28; Luke 13:35; Romans 11). Understand that these people say, and then see. They do not see, and then say.

When Will The Kingdom Be Restored To Israel?

How close are we to that glorious day when that united group will witness Yeshua once again standing on the Mount of Olives?

Do we sense that the Messiah could come in our lifetime—in our generation? Earlier in the 20th century, the theme song of the Pentecostals, Charismatics, and Fundamentalists, was that, by the year 2000, Yeshua would have returned. However, having entered into the third millennium since Yeshua's departure, we now know they were wrong.

Though hindsight is a lot more accurate than foresight, it is possible to gain foresight from Scripture, especially with the leading of the Holy Spirit. So, let us now ask the Spirit to guide us, as we seek to better understand the time of Yeshua's return.

It is difficult to interpret the many numbers that are given in the Scriptures. For example, Daniel mentions the 1,235 days, 49 weeks, and 7 weeks. And we have all seen a lot of theology, doctrines, and predictions built around these numbers. Nonetheless, in speculating as to when Yeshua will return, one of the first questions that comes to mind is: Why the 2000 year wait that we have lived through? Especially when 2000 years ago Yeshua said, "Yes, I am coming **quickly**," and, especially considering Peter's proclamation, that we are **in the last days** (Acts 2:17; Revelation 22:20).

At least we can take comfort in the fact that we are 2000 years later than Peter was! Additionally, we can all agree that we have come to a time in history wherein we are now seeing a fulfillment of the command given to Daniel: "But as for you, Daniel, conceal these words and seal up the book until the end of time; many will go back and forth, and knowledge will increase" (Daniel 12:4).

We have planes, cars, and even space vehicles that allow us to go back and forth. We have computers programs that allow us to study Scripture and to see things that were not readily available to the generations before us. (We do not speak of "extra-biblical" revelation. Instead, when Luther saw "Justification by Faith" in the Fifteenth Century, was that something new? No. It was an illumination of principles that had been there in Scripture all the time. But Luther is the one who saw it, and then other people began to see that principle in a way they had not seen it before.)

The Reestablishment of A Jewish State

There are several events that have happened in the latter portion of this century that point to a likelihood that the time is at hand when Yahveh will restore His Kingdom to Israel. Event number one is the reestablishment of a Jewish State. We are seeing the fulfillment of prophecies that Judah would return first in unbelief: "Yahveh, our Lord, will save the tents of Judah first" (Zechariah 12:7). And, "I will give you a new heart and put a new spirit within you; and I will remove the heart of stone from your flesh and give you a heart of flesh. And I will put My Spirit within you and cause you to walk in My statutes, and you will be careful to observe My ordinances....Then you will remember your evil ways and your deeds that were not good, and you will loathe yourselves in your own sight for your iniquities and abominations....On the day that I cleanse you from all your iniquities, I will cause the cities to be inhabited, and the waste places will be rebuilt" (Ezekiel 36:26-34).

The Messianic Jewish Movement

The second event is the Messianic Jewish Movement.

In the first century, Judaism, with its temple, priesthood, and sacrificial system, divided into two major branches: Christianity, with its sacrifice and grace, and Rabbinical Judaism, with its Law, feasts and traditions. And, for the past nineteen centuries, there have been Rabbinic Jews who have recognized Jesus as their Messiah. In the past, conversion to Christianity wrongfully required that they give up the observance of Torah, the Feasts of Israel and Jewish traditions. Then, in the early seventies, several small groups of Jews, independently of each other, came to the conclusion that, while they would accept Yeshua as their Messiah, they would not give up their Jewish identity. Instead, they would incorporate their observance of Torah, the Feasts of Israel, and many of their Jewish traditions with their new found faith in the Messiah of Israel. Thus was the Messianic Jewish Movement born.

127

The Messianic Israel Movement

The third event is the Messianic Israel Movement[57].

During the past nineteen centuries, there have been Christians who recognized the value of observing Torah, the Feasts of Israel (and some Jewish traditions). They have, and presently are, even today, giving up their faith in the Deity of Yeshua (wrongfully required of all who would convert to Rabbinic Judaism), and converting to Rabbinic Judaism to observe Torah and the Feast of Israel.

However, in the late seventies, there were Believers who began to see their identity as Israelites, and to see that they too were an integral part of the people of Israel. Slowly, they began to realize that they were the other house of Israel—Ephraim. They also recognized the value of observing the principles of Torah, the Feasts of Israel, and of incorporating some of the Jewish traditions into their faith in, and walk with, Yeshua.

These two Movements continue to struggle along, despite their bouts of "sibling rivalry." Yet, slowly, ever so slowly, they are maturing and beginning to walk in the knowledge that both are a part of the United Israel that will soon herald the return of Messiah, and ultimately be used of Yahveh to help bring to pass the restoration of the Kingdom to Israel.

One of the most obvious signs of this truth is the fact that, **you** are reading this book. And, that you know, or are beginning to believe, that **you** are an Israelite. Thus, **you** serve as a proof that the prophet Hosea delivered an accurate prophecy concerning the punishment to the people of the Northern Kingdom of Israel—that they would not be Yahveh's people any longer because of their idolatry, but that the day would come in which Yahveh would turn this judgment around, and the children of Ephraim/Israel would become the "sons of the Living God."

Yes! We are among the forerunners who have been granted the

---

57 See *The Hope of Messianic Israel*, page 259.

unmerited grace of seeing that punishment come to an end.

The Punishment Of Ephraim

The Prophets Hosea and Amos explained why and how Israel would be punished for its iniquity: "Israel is swallowed up; They are now among the nations. Like a vessel in which no one delights" (Hosea 8:8). And, "...I will shake the house of Israel among all nations as grain is shaken in a sieve, But not a kernel will fall to the ground" (Amos 9:9).

Bala, the Hebrew word for *swallow,* which word Hosea uses in his description of Ephraim's punishment, has the connotation of someone eating a piece of food, and having it become a part of his body. For example, today, try to find, or identify in your body, the food you ate last week. Even so, Ephraim was destined to be punished, by being swallowed up by the Gentile nations, so to become an indistinguishable part of them. This punishment has been in effect until this generation, and during this time of blindness, **Ephraim has not known who he is!**

From Yahveh's dealings with the Prophet Ezekiel we gain an understanding of the duration of Ephraim's punishment. For Yahveh told Ezekiel to "Lay on your left side and put the sin of the House of Israel upon yourself. You are to bear their sin for the number of days you lie on your side for I have assigned to you a number of days corresponding to the number of years of iniquity [of Israel]...390 days which equates to 390 years. Thus you shall bear the iniquity of the House of Israel"

We know that Yahveh was talking to Ephraim/Israel because He goes on to say, "After you have finished this, lie down again on your right side and bear the sin of the House of Judah. I have assigned you 40 days, a day for each year" (Ezekiel 4:4-6).

Ezekiel lived 135 years **after** the Northern Kingdom of Israel (Ephraim) had become "no more." Yet, it is evident that Yahveh had not forgotten about them, because through Ezekiel, He deals with the length of the punishment for Ephraim's iniquity. The people of the northern ten tribes did not repent of their paganism, and Yahveh was adamant concerning the fact that He is a jealous God, and that they were to have "no other gods" before Him. Yet, He is "a compassionate God; who would not fail them nor destroy them nor forget the covenant which He had sworn to their fathers" (Deuteronomy 4:31; 5:9).

Like father, like son. Ephraim continues to allow pagan, heathen Gentile ways, to creep into his relationship with his God.

The Punishment of Judah

We gain a better understanding of the duration of Ephraim's punishment by taking a look at Judah's punishment:

Ezekiel was instructed to lie on his right side for 40 days, a day for a year. Thus, we see that Judah was to receive 40 years of punishment. But unfortunately, this forty years is only **part** of Judah's punishment. We know this from the account of the two sisters, Aholah (Samaria/Ephraim) and Aholibah (Jerusalem/Judah), which is given in the twenty-third Chapter of Ezekiel. These two sisters engaged in prostitution while they were young and still in Egypt. Additionally, Aholah/Ephraim was engaged in prostitution with the Assyrians. It was this harlotry with their Assyrian neighbors that led to Aholah's downfall.

During the century preceding the final destruction of the City of Samaria, the Northern Kingdom was integrated into the Assyrian Empire. Piece by piece. various portions of the Northern Tribes became vassals of Assyria, until they were entirely absorbed by Assyria. When Ephraim's Capital, the City of Samaria, finally fell in 722 B.C., it was just the last little bastion of the Northern Kingdom.[58] It did not take a war for most of Israel to become Assyrian. This fact is confirmed by Yahveh's statement: "I handed her over to her lovers, the Assyrians, for whom she had lusted" (Ezekiel 23:9). Since the Ephraimites had lusted for these Gentile

---

58 See Chapter 10, *The Way Of The Gentiles.*

ways, Yahveh gave them over to the Assyrians, to ultimately be scattered among the Nations, and thus to become Gentiles.

Recalling the demise of Aholah, Yahveh said to Aholibah, "You saw your sister in her lust and prostitution, yet you have been more depraved than your sister. You have gone the way of your sister, so I will put her cup in your hands. You will drink your sister's cup, a cup large and deep and it will bring scorn and derision for it holds so much."

Her sister's cup contained 390 years of punishment! And, adding 390 years of punishment to the 40 years which Judah initially received, gives a total of 430 years of punishment for Judah.

When did Judah's punishment start?

Nebuchadnezzar, king of Babylon, subdued Judah in 595 B.C.. After this date, they no longer had political or religious control over their own territory, Jerusalem, nor over their temple. Therefore, if we take 596 B.C. as the first year of their punishment, then 430 years later would bring us to 166 B.C.

What happened in 166 B.C.?

The Maccabean's revolted against the Greeks.

In coming to 166 B.C., we come to the time of the Maccabean's victory over the Greeks, and to the miracle cleansing of the temple—the time when they found only enough oil in the temple to last for one day. But, miraculously this one day supply of oil is said to have lasted for eight days, giving them time to make a fresh supply of oil. This miracle is celebrated today by the Jews as the Feast of Chanukkah (Feast of Dedication). Judah's punishment was over. They had regained religious and political control over their temple and a large portion of their territory.[59]

The Length Of Ephraim's Punishment?

Now let us go back to Ephraim, who was assigned 390 years of punishment. Right?

_____
59 See the HDH, *The Price Of Peace*, and, *Celebrating Hanukkah*.

131

No. Unfortunately, Ephraim would receive far more than 390 years. Yahveh's fourfold declaration given in the Twenty Sixth Chapter of Leviticus establishes unrepentant Ephraim's fate:

"If also after these things, you do not obey Me, then I will punish you **seven times** more for your sins....If then, you act with hostility against Me and are unwilling to obey Me, I will increase the plague on you **seven times** according to your sins....Then I will act with hostility against you; and I, even I, will strike you **seven times** for your sins....Then I will act with wrathful hostility against you; and I, even I, will punish you **seven times** for your sins" (Leviticus 26:18, 21, 24, 28).

When Yahveh declares a punishment, you are going to get it. Regardless. If you sow, you are going to reap. According to Yahveh's rules you are going to get the punishment—even if you repent. And, if you **do not repent, you will receive a seven-fold punishment!**

Judah received a punishment of 430 years. And, when those of Judah went to Babylon (that being their punishment), they repented. To this day, the Jewish people (as a whole) do not have idols. And since they repented, their punishment lasted only 430 years.

But, hapless Ephraim has never repented. So, the Northern Kingdom received a seven-fold punishment: 390 years times seven, for a total of 2,730 years of punishment. 2730 years! That's a long time!

Exactly what was Ephraim's punishment?

Yahveh said the Ephraimites would be scattered among the nations and would "lose their identity." They would become "*Lo Ammi*"—"Not A People" (Hosea 1:9-10; 2:2, 23).

But, ill-fated Ephraim, in addition to the 2730 years of punishment, was to receive an additional punishment. For Yahveh said, "I will first **doubly** repay their iniquity and their sin, because they have polluted My land; they have filled My inheritance with the carcasses of their detestable idols and with their abominations" (Jeremiah 16:18).

This double punishment does not refer to Judah, because he wase not guilty in this regard: Who made the golden calves? Who changed the feast days? Who made houses on high places, and made priests from among all the people who were not of the sons of Levi? It was Ephraim (1 Kings 12:28-32). So Yahveh said He would first **doubly** repay Ephraim for his iniquity.

Now, using the same 390 years as a basis, we see that Ephraim is given a second punishment, one that consists of 780 years of punishment.

Yahveh spoke of Ephraim's **double** punishment through Hosea, who was a prophet to the Northern Kingdom: "I will ransom them from the power of Sheol—I will redeem them from death. Death, where are your thorns? Sheol, where is your sting?" (Hosea 13:4).

There was hope for Ephraim. A time would come when Yahveh would **ransom** him.

Misguided Ephraim received a sentence of 2730 years, and, a sentence of 780 years. However, he was given a big break, in that the two punishments ran **concurrently**. Like a child who was grounded for seven weeks, and also barred from watching TV for the first two weeks, so Ephraim was destined to be the recipient of two simultaneous punishments.

As we will later see, one was to be affected on a corporate, or national level, and the other would be realized on an individual basis.

When Did Ephraim's Punishment Start?

In determining the date of Judah's punishment, we did not pick the year 585 B.C., which was when Nebuchadnezzar sacked Jerusalem and destroyed Solomon's temple. Rather, we started from the year, 595 B.C. when Judah no longer had political and religious control over his territories. Therefore, we will apply this same measure to Ephraim. And, while the city of Samaria was finally destroyed in 722 B.C., the majority of the Northern Kingdom had become a vassal state of Assyria by 734 B.C.

Confirmation of these facts is substantiated by *the Cuneiform*

Text of Tiglath-Pileser III, which chronicle his Gaza-Damascus Campaign in 734-33 B.C.

When the armed hordes of Assyrians completed their campaign against Bet-Omri (Israel), Israel was mortally wounded, decimated by deportation, beaten back into a tiny corner of the Northern Kingdom. With the exception of Samaria, all its cities had been annexed, and the country had been divided into provinces over which Assyrian governors and officials exercised strict control.

All that was left of Israel was a dwarf state, a tiny pinpoint on the map: the mountain of Ephraim with the royal city of Samaria.[60]

Thus, if we take the date of 734 B.C., and add 780 years (the double punishment), we come to the year 46 A.D.!

What happened about that time?

End of Ephraim's Double Punishment

That was when the Gospel was beginning to be preached to the "Gentiles." Remember, for the first ten to twenty years, the church was all Jewish—it was even called a sect of Judaism (Acts 24:5; 28:22). Then around 46 A.D., Paul, who was given the primary mission of going to the Gentiles, began his active ministry. Thus began the end of Ephraim's double punishment.

Those of Ephraim, those lost sheep who came to know Yeshua's voice, received a great blessing. Thus began a time wherein those who had once "filled Yahveh's inheritance with idols" could now themselves be filled with His Holy Spirit. Yeshua began to fulfill Yahveh's promise to ransom them. Paul referred to this promise that Yahveh had made through the Prophet Hosea, saying, "But when this perishable must put on the imperishable and this mortal must put on immortality, then will come about the saying that is written, 'Death is swallowed up in victory. Death, where is your sting?'" (11 Corinthians 15: 54-55; Hosea 13:4).

What was Paul doing in Corinth? He was going about his

---

60 See *The Bible As History*, by Werner Keller 1955, pages 245-249, translated from the German, published by William Morrow and Company, New York, in 1956.

ministry to the "Gentiles"—**to the Ephraimites who had been swallowed up by the Nations.**

James, in his address to the Council at Jerusalem, makes two very interesting statements regarding the swallowed up ones: "With this the words of the Prophets agree, just as it is written, 'After these things I will return, and I will rebuild the tabernacle of David which has fallen, and I will rebuild its ruins, and I will restore it. In order that the rest of mankind may seek Me, and all the **Gentiles who are called by My name,** says Yahveh, who makes these things known from of old.' Therefore it is my judgment that we do not trouble those who are **turning to Yahveh from among the Gentiles**" (Acts 15:15-19).

James uses the word "turning," which indicates a process, rather than a done deal, or, an accomplished fact; and, James is referring to **Gentiles** who are in the process of turning to Yahveh. The Greek word *epistrepho,* which is translated *turning,* could just as well be translated as ***returning!*** Strong defines "*epistrepho (ep-ee-stref'-o)* as, "to revert (lit., fig. or mor.):—come (go) again, convert, (re-) turn (about, again)."

Consequently, the Holy Spirit, concerning the "mystery of the Gentiles," has James say, "Therefore it is my judgment that we do not trouble those who are **returning to Yahveh from among the Gentiles.**"

From this understanding, we, from whom the blindness to our identity has been removed, can see one more proof text of Yahveh fulfilling His promise made in Hosea—the promise to redeem those of the Northern Kingdom of Israel.

Yeshua said, "The time is fulfilled, and the Kingdom of Yahveh is at hand; repent and believe in the Gospel" (Mark 1:15). For the past 2000 years, the manifestation of the Kingdom of Yahveh has been on an individual basis. We have not had a corporate, or national Kingdom of Yahveh on earth. After all, if we had a National Kingdom of Israel—comparable to the Kingdom of David and Solomon, with one altar and one capital city—we would not have splintered into some 5,000 denominations and cults.

Why have we not had a National Kingdom?

Because Ephraim's corporate, or national, punishment had not been completed.

When Will Ephraim's Punishment End?

When will Ephraim's corporate punishment be ended?

If we count 2730 years from 734 B.C., we arrive at the year 1996. If we use the year 722 B.C. as a base, we come up with the year 2008.

Please note: This is not to say that Yeshua will return and reestablish His Kingdom in this twelve year time frame! Unlike the now infamous book, *88 Reasons Why Jesus Will Return In 1988,* we are **not** giving reasons why Yeshua will return during this period. Rather, we are saying that, at the end of Ephraim's punishment, Yeshua is free to restore the corporate Kingdom to Israel.

The reason?

Because the punishment of Israel is at an end. And, it is reasonable that Ephraim would **not** have been rewarded with the restoration of the Kingdom while he was being punished!

Surely, when Yeshua returns, His people will be freed. And He must adhere to His own Word, and not return until the punishment He mandated for those of Ephraim is completed. Remember, Yeshua, when He was being asked about the date the Kingdom would be restored, just prior to His accession from the Mount of Olives, knew that the Kingdom would not be restored to Israel until the punishment was completed.

Admittedly, we cannot be absolutely sure as to the exact beginning, nor the exact end, of Yahveh's decreed punishment. And, it is not our purpose to pinpoint **exact** dates, but to establish principles of understanding. As to the actual dates of Ephraim's punishment, we absolutely know that: there is a moment in time when it began, and there will be a moment in time when it ends. We also know that Ephraim's punishment could not have started any later than 722 B.C.. And, that it was only in the last quarter of this century that Messianic non-Jewish Believers began to see that there were two houses of Israel, as described in Scripture (Ephraim and Judah). Further, it is evident that these two houses have not as yet been reunited as one undefiled house. The people of Israel have not yet taken full possession of the land given to their father Abraham. And, the Greater Son of David is not ruling over them. So it is that they began to see, as Ephraimites, that they were full fledged members of the people of Israel to whom the Holy One of Israel would restore His Kingdom! (Isaiah 8:14; Ezekiel 37:22-25).

We know that the punishment of Ephraim began no later than 722 B.C., and we know from history that his punishment has been in **full force** until recent years. What we do not know for sure is when Yahveh will deem that the punishment is fully completed. However, there are quite a few events that point to the time frame of 1996-2008:

First we note that Yeshua said, "The generation that sees the fig tree blossom will see His return" (Matthew 24:32-34). We can look at a generation in Scripture as being 25 years, 40 years, 100 years, or even 120 years.

In highlighting a few "generation examples," we start with the meeting of the First Zionist Congress in Basel, Switzerland in August 1897. There, Herzel said, "At Basel I founded the Jewish state ...In five years, perhaps, and certainly in fifty, everyone will see it." (His fifty year prediction was only eight months short of the actual date of the foundation of the Jewish state in May 1948.)

Another meaningful date is 1917. It is the year of the Balfour Declaration—which declaration set in motion the return that would result in the birth of the Jewish State. Further, 1917 was the year in which General Allenby liberated Palestine and Jerusalem from the Gentile (true pagan) rule of the Turkish Empire, and thus made it physically possible for Jews to return in sufficient numbers to found a state.[61]

The year 1948, when the Jewish state was founded, was also a significant year; as was 1967, when the old city of Jerusalem was liberated, and the borders of the Jewish state were greatly expanded.

The year 1967 is significant for another reason—albeit, perhaps a personal one. It was during this year that a chain of extraordinary events commenced which culminated in the founding of the ministry of the House of David in the Seventies—it being a ministry to those of Messianic Israel. And, the Father has been using House of David to inspire an accumulation of insight, from Scripture, which is resulting in the "teaching of the two houses of Israel.

Can we tie these various dates together? If we use a 100 year generation, then, from Herzel's proclamation we would come to a 1996-1997 time frame. And, if we use a 120 year generation we would be carried well past 2008. However, with 1917 as a base year, we have a hundred year period of time when, not only the punishment will be completed, but the time period which saw the foundation of the Jewish State, the liberation of the old city of Jerusalem, and could very well see significant gatherings of Ephraimites to the land.

Forty years from 1967 brings us to 2007, one year shy of 2008, which marks 2730 years from 722 B.C., which probably marks the latest date that the punishment of Ephraim will be fully completed.

Also, two thousand years from the birth of Yeshua (which most sources agree was in 4 B.C.), brings us to the year 1996. And, in Hosea 6:2, Yahveh says of Ephraim, "He will revive us after two days, he will raise us up on the third day (the millennial Kingdom) that we may live before Him.

Six thousand years from creation (4004 B.C.) brings us again to the year 1996. And, there were some big celebrations in Jerusalem in 1996. They celebrated the 3000-year birthday of the founding of the city of Jerusalem by King David.

Last but not least, 1996 marke the first year of the first Jubilee

---

61 See Chapter 15, *A Mandate For Ephraim.*

generation from Yeshua.

A House of David Perspective

Viewing these dates from a House of David perspective, we see that, forty years from 1948 brings us to 1988, the year when Batya's first book, *In Search of* Israel, the foundational manual on the teaching of the "two houses," was published. Twenty-five years from 1967 brings us to 1992, when Batya's second book, *The Olive Tree of Israel,* was published, and the date from which the *House of David Herald* has since been published on a monthly basis. And fifty years from 1948 marks the first Jubilee of the founding of the Jewish State, and brings us to 1998 when Batya's third book *Who Is Israel? And Why You Need To Know,* was published. 1998 is also the year in which the Messianic Israel Alliance came into being—which will surely prove to be a Jubilee gift for the State of Israel.

The above instructional material is being used by affiliates of the *Messianic Israel Alliance* to fulfill the prophecy: "For after I [Ephraim] turned back, I repented; and after I was instructed, I smote on my thigh; I was ashamed, and also humiliated, because I bore the reproach of my youth" (Jeremiah 31:19).

While it is interesting to contemplate numbers and their meaning, it is far more important that we realize that, we who have rediscovered our identity are forerunners called to the cutting edge of what Yahveh is doing in the earth today. We are the scouts going ahead of an invincible army—an army that will be used to accomplish our Father's Messianic Vision. It is unmerited grace that has brought us to this time and place. It is unmerited favor that has given each of us the unique opportunity to instruct those Ephraimites who entered the Kingdom on an individual basis, to now become part of the corporate Kingdom—the Israel of Yahveh!

If the time period of 1996-2008 is the correct time for the end of Ephraim's punishment, it also is a time for a glorious new beginning! For it marks the commencement of the tremendous task of instructing millions of Ephraimites as to their identity—that we might also make them aware of the job that lies before us.

We have seen the tents of Judah restored first. Can it be long before we hear the Father roar like a lion—calling Ephraim to come trembling from the west (where an east wind had scattered him)? The day cannot be far off when the Father brings him back in such numbers that even the lands of Gilead and Lebanon cannot contain him. Ephraim will yet be like a mighty man. Then together with Judah, they will be victorious over their enemies (Isaiah 11:14; Jeremiah 18:17; Hosea 11:10; Zechariah 10:10,7).

It is imperative that each of us takes full advantage of the opportunities Yahveh gives us to witness concerning His Kingdom. It is essential that we keep our eyes on the truth that Yeshua came to give us the hope of life eternal. And that He has a Kingdom, which currently is not of this world. However, the day is coming when the kingdoms of this world become His Kingdom.

What will it take to accomplish His Messianic Vision? Yeshua said that He is not returning until they say, "Blessed is He who comes in the name of the Yahveh" (Luke 13:35). That means Yeshua will find a welcoming party on the Mount of Olives. That party will not be headed by Arafat, nor by Rabbinical Jews who deny Yeshua. It will be hosted by people who love Him, and know Him. Also, it will not be a mixed multitude: a group of Catholics here, Baptists there, Assembly of God off to themselves, and so on. Instead, it will be a group representative of the twelve tribes of Israel, a people who are united in the knowledge of their identity and purpose (Isaiah 56:3).

In regard to His return, Yahveh commands us three times, in Mark 13:33-37, to:

1. Keep on the alert!
2. Stay on the alert!
3. Be on the alert!

Remember the children's story about the horseshoe nail? "For the want of a nail, a shoe was lost. For the want of a shoe, a horse was lost. For the want of a horse, the rider was lost. For the want of a rider, a troop was lost. For the want of a troop, a company was lost. For the want of a company, a battalion, a regiment, a division, and an army were lost. For the want of an army, the war was lost."

Why did they lose the war?

Because of the lack of one little horseshoe nail.

Each and every one of us is far more important than a horseshoe nail. It is essential that we each do our individual jobs, and man our individual watch post.[62] Just like the horseshoe nail had to keep the shoe on, so we have our job to do. You can have 1000 watchmen, but if one watchman doesn't man his post, there is a hole in the wall. And, we do not want any holes in our wall.

What Are We To Do?

Collectively, the job we have to do is to be the watchmen that preserve Israel. And, we are the forerunners in the foremost of these watchmen! Therefore, let us take full and timely advantage of all the opportunities the Father gives us to be those watchmen. To this end, let each of us include in our daily prayers: "Father, what can I do today to advance Your kingdom here on earth?"

Remember our question of the Father is: "What can I do?" It is not: "What should the besieged people of the Jewish State, most of whom do not know the Messiah, do to deliver themselves and the land promised to all Israel?"

Instead, we must ask: "What should we—who **do** know the Messiah—do to deliver our besieged brother, and to liberate the land that He promised to all Israel?"

We do not know just how, nor for sure when, Yahveh will accomplish all the details required to restore His people to His land. However, we do know that the events that are transpiring in the Middle East do not come as any surprise to Him. We can be

---

62 See the HDH, *Vow Of A Watchman; Who Is Israel?* Chapter 21, *Called to be Watchmen.*

absolutely confident that, even though player tryouts and training operations are still being conducted, all the parts have been determined, and all the lines have been written, for the final act of this six thousand year old human drama being directed by the God of Israel. Now, we have the unmerited opportunity to have decisive roles in the final acts of this drama, which are even now being played out.

As players are selected for parts, and then given the opportunity to play them out, we will see the works of Yahveh's hand begin to emerge, and His purposes fulfilled. There will be those whom Yahveh will entrust with the power and authority to carry out His purposes under His step by step guidance.

Let us pray that we may be found among these trusted ones. May each forerunner successfully complete his tryouts, training, and learn his lines, so that when the time comes, and we are called to play our part, that it will be an "Oscar" winning performance.

Let us never forget that it is far, far, better to be prepared and not called upon, than to be unprepared and called upon.

12

Ephraim Should Know More About Judah

Yahveh's ultimate goal is to manifest His presence—in His earthly Kingdom—in the midst of a united people.

To accomplish this, He chose a people from the seed of Abraham, through Isaac and Jacob, and He called that people "Israel." His chosen people went down into Egypt, being seventy in number, and there they grew into a nation. Then Yahveh brought them out of Egypt and into the Land of Promise.

Under the consecutive reigns of Kings David and Solomon, they reached the pinnacle of their glory as a united kingdom. However, after the death of Solomon, the twelve tribes of Israel divided into two houses: the house of Judah and the house of Ephraim.

These two houses continue to be fundamentally divided to this day. Presently, we find Judah among the Jewish people, and primarily, Ephraim is found among the "nations." For Jacob said Ephraim would become a "melo goyim," a "fulness of Gentiles."[63]

63　The *ArtScroll Tanach Series* says the word used, *m'loh,* means a "fullness" and, "Connotes
(continued...)

143

To save those of scattered Israel (see Ezekiel 34), to restore "both the houses of Israel" (Isaiah 8:14), Yahveh sent His Son, Yeshua to give the hope of eternal and abundant life to those whom Yahveh had called and chosen. This hope, of a gathered and reunited remnant becoming a restored kingdom of Israel, will become a reality when the greater son of David establishes His throne here on earth—when he begins His actual reign over the reunited kingdom of Israel.

How can we, as individuals, help to reunite that kingdom?

By following in the footsteps of the Apostle Paul.

Paul, in Romans Eleven, saw that a combination of Jewish acceptance of Messiah, as well as the ingathering of the full number of former Gentiles from among the nations, would herald this end-time kingdom. This Apostle to the nations was willing to pay the high price of his own salvation to gain the reward of a restored kingdom of Israel. His ministry to the "Gentiles," or "wild olive branches" of Israel, had the added benefit of making the Jews jealous, that some of them might be saved.

Paul addressed those of the "wild" side of Israel's family tree (Jeremiah 11:10,16; 2:18,21; Romans 11)—meaning the non-Jews who were being grafted into the "Rich Root" of Israel's Olive Tree (which "Root is Yeshua: Revelation 22:16)—as well as those Jewish branches that remained in Messiah's tree. Together, Paul wanted them to follow in his footsteps.

Unfortunately, in the nineteen hundred years since Paul's witness, both houses, one believing in a present Messiah and one in a future Messiah (Judaism), have contributed to building walls of misunderstanding. One solid wall that has been built by the non-Jews is that of presenting a Greek/Romanized Christ immersed in a paganized smorgasbord of theologies.

---

63 (...continued)
abundance...meaning: His seed will become the abundance of the nations....They will have to inhabit lands of other nations." See *Genesis*, Volume 6, page 2121. Also see Strong's words # H4393 and 1471. Additionally, note that *melo* is used in Psalm 24:1, being translated, "The earth is the Lord's and the *fullness thereof.*"

This "Greek Jesus" is much more difficult for Jews to accept than would be a Hebrew Yeshua, who more closely portrays their image and concept of the Messiah of Israel. So, it is only wisdom for those of Ephraim to begin by reuniting the remnant in their own house. And, to search for a way to present the truth of the Gospel in a Hebraic manner to Judah. This search will cause the non-Jew to receive back from his Jewish brother and sisters many ancient truths about the heritage of the people of Israel. And we will be better prepared to reach out to them in love and mercy, and then to talk about putting both houses back together.

Coming from the Jewish side of this search for love and mercy is Rabbi Yechiel Eckstein. Yechiel is an Orthodox Jewish Rabbi, and founder and President of the International Fellowship of Christians and Jews. In the introduction to his book, *What Christians Should Know About Jews and Judaism,* Rabbi Eckstein likens the relationship of Jews and Christians to the two Cherubim on the Ark of the Covenant. Very prophetically, Yechiel says:

"It is only when the two cherubim reach out and touch one another that we will see the glory and salvation of our God."

Unfortunately, over the past two thousand years, the wild olive branches (Ephraim) have continued to behave in a very "wild" manner toward their Jewish brethren. They have failed miserably at following Paul's example. For the Jews, the Ark with it's Cherubim remains lost. They are without Temple and sacrifice. Fortunately, Yahveh has a plan in progress to restore His Kingdom to the united House of Israel. That plan is as follows:

✡ From the throne of His father David, Yeshua is currently ruling over the House of Jacob.

✡ The Father has established the time, season or epoch that will signal when the Kingdom will be restored.

✡ Yeshua has a core of disciples that are trained in the Word given Him by the Father. These disciples are raising up successors in each succeeding generation, who believe in Messiah through the words of His original disciples.

✡ Thus, there will be disciples in the generation destined for the restoration of the Kingdom. They will be ready, willing and able to accomplish the desire of their Master. It is from this predestined generation that the partial hardening or blindness will be removed—and these disciples will be gathered from both the Houses of Israel. They will be gathered from all twelve tribes. From Judah will be removed his blindness to the Messiah, and from Ephraim his blindness to his roots (Jeremiah 31:18-19).

✡ These disciples will witness both in Jerusalem, and in all Judea and Samaria, and even to the remotest part of the earth. They will witness to the truth that it will be through the unity of the two Houses of Israel that the world will believe. Then, the end will come, and the Kingdom of Yahveh will be manifested on earth.

If we believe this may well be the generation destined for the restoration of the Kingdom to Israel, then we need to answer two questions: What are we going to about it? And, what price are we willing to pay?

The correct answer to both questions is: LOVE! We must love our brother Judah. The price we must pay, if we are going to be successful, is a price of love.

Sound Advice From An Orthodox Rabbi

Rabbi Yechiel Eckstein tells the story in his book, *What Christians Should Know About Jews and Judaism,* of a young man who visited his rabbi. The young man became so overwhelmed by the emotional experience that he cried out, "Rabbi, I love you dearly." The rabbi, who was both touched and amused by his student's sincerity, asked him, "Tell me, my son, you say that you love me, but where do I hurt? What ails me?" To this the perplexed young man responded, "I do not know where you hurt, Rabbi, but, nevertheless, I love you dearly." The rabbi then replied, "But how can you say you love me when you do not even know where I hurt and what brings me pain?"

Yechiel's story illustrates the truth that we cannot truly love our brother Judah until we know where he hurts. We cannot help until we know what brings him pain.

Let us listen to Yechiel as he speaks at an Israel Symposium, and recounts some of his thoughts, beliefs, and experiences. The following excerpts from his message will give us a better understanding of our brother Judah, of what he believes, of what brings him joy, and of what brings him pain.

"Recently, in my role as a mediator between Christians and Jews, I was called to mediate in regards to a Christian company called the Family Entertainment Network. They are producing bible stories on video for children. And they are using TV infommercials as a marketing tool for their videos. In a half hour program they present selected segments from their video series to motivate the viewing audience to purchase their videos.

"These animated videos were deeply offensive to Jews. They portrayed Yeshua as a blond, blue eyed, soft featured Anglo-Saxon. And they presented all of those who did not accept Him with big hooked noses, unkempt long black curly hair. A totally different image from Yeshua—as if Yeshua was not a Jew.

"Also there were segments of the video that used selections from the King James Version of the Scriptures to paint a very unfavorable picture of the Jews who did not accept Yeshua. One example was how they conspired to kill Yeshua.

"Sadly, the primary targets of this message are children, ages five to twelve.

"What struck me about this affair is that the Christians who produced this material were in my mind not anti-Semitic. However, they were unaware of those pages of Christian history that most Christians never studied, yet they are the pages that Jews are primarily familiar with.

"However, this situation is quite similar to that of the situation surrounding the movie The Last Temptation of Christ. In it, there were insensitivities on the part of many Jews to

Christian sensibilities.

"What this shows me is that two thousand years is a long time to be apart, to be separate. And that all sorts of misunderstandings can arise during that period.

Yahveh Does Not Hear The Prayers of Jews?

"A number of years ago Baily Smith, then the head of the Southern Baptist Convention, made the comment that God Almighty does not hear the prayers of Jews. It became a big issue at the time, so I took him and some Southern Baptist leaders to Israel. And, I spoke at his church in Dell City, Oklahoma. I spoke frankly about the history of the Jewish people and their images of Christians. I told them about the Spanish Inquisition, the Crusades, the Holocaust, and the State of Israel. After I finished, the congregation was clapping, and Baily Smith came over to me and said: 'Isn't Rabbi Eckstein terrific? We have to bring him back for one of our crusades.'

"The whole congregation was agreeing, 'Bring him to the crusades, bring him to the crusades.'

"I heard the word 'crusades,' and I was ready to run.

In that moment, I realized again, that to him the word crusade meant one thing, and to me the word crusade elicited an entirely different emotion. Yet, he was not intending to be offensive or instill that emotion in me.

The Cross: Symbol of Yahveh's Love For Christians An Object Of Fear For Many Jews

"One more example, that is more powerful than any other, involves the symbol of the cross.

Father Ed Flannery, one of the first Catholic's involved in Christian/Jewish dialogue, wrote a book in the early Sixties in which he described why he became involved:

"One day he was walking down the street with a Jewish

woman. Suddenly she stopped talking. He could sense she was uncomfortable. He thought maybe he had said something to offend her, but she assured him that he had not said or done anything offensive.

"Later, Father Flannery pressed the woman as to what had happened. She answered, 'Do you remember when we were walking on Elm Street, and we passed that church with a big cross? I am sorry Father, but every time I see a cross I am afraid. I shudder. I am reminded of what the cross meant to my forefathers, and how they were taken to the cross and brunt and martyred because they refused to accept the cross.'

"Father Flannery asked himself, 'How could this symbol of our God's ultimate love be understood by this Jewish woman as an object of fear?'

That is when he began to study the pages of Christian history that he had never studied before. These pages are the only pages of Christian history of which this Jewish woman was aware.

"I see Christians and Jews as two ships passing in the night. We each want to make this world a better and holier place. But often we fail to do so. The stereotypes and images that we have of one another just go right by the true essence of one another.

The Challenges We Face As Christians and Jews:

"First to reverse our sad and tragic history by really coming to understand the other—not as we perceive the other but as the other perceives himself. We need to stop and let the other community and individuals define themselves.

"Second is to demonstrate true love. It is often easy to love a community as an idea or as an ideal. I have come to know many Christians over the years, who love Jews as an idea. They sometimes love Jews as a biblical ideal. This is a good starting point. But, it is a lot harder to love us with our flaws. We are flawed, we are sinful. Many of us are secular, and it is a lot harder to love us in reality than as an idea.

"We must come to a place where we can love one another unconditionally.

"I have met many Christians who have loved in the hope that _____. Who love in the expectation that _____. Who love on the condition that _____.

I'll let you fill in the blanks. However, the essence of Christian love, as I understand it, is to love unconditionally. And, then to let God move.

"I have been in many churches where the Pastor will ask the congregation, 'How many people did we bring to Christ this week?'

"I feel like saying, 'According to my understanding of Christian theology you didn't bring anybody to Christ. It is God through the Holy Spirit who brings people to Christ.'

"The Christians who feel their goal is to bring the world to Christ are wrong. The Christian great commission is to preach of God's love through Yeshua to the whole world. And God, in His time, in His mysterious way, as Paul describes in Romans Eleven, will do what He wants to do through the Holy Spirit. Through the Holy Spirit He will work on individuals to bring about the changes He desires. It will not be man's doing but God's doing, and God can be trusted.

"In essence, the second goal is to love unconditionally and to leave things to God.

"The third point is to demonstrate unselfish love. A boy scout schleps (escorts) an old lady across the street, who doesn't want to go across the street. He isn't showing love to her. He is harassing her.

I've met many Christians who want to love Jews the way they want to love Jews, not the way Jews want and need to be loved.

Why Are We So Chosen?

"We are witnessing God's presence in history today, in a way that, in my opinion, is no less powerful, and no less demonstrable than when He entered into history and delivered the Israelites from Egyptian slavery. I asked myself, and my congregation, 'What did we do to merit the privilege of being part of this generation. The generation that has seen the rebirth of the State of Israel. Why should we be the ones to witness the reunification of Jerusalem? That we should be the ones to see a community of black Jews, that have not had any contact with the rest of the Jewish community for two thousand years be plucked out in one twenty-four hour period to return to their homeland to join their brothers and sisters. What did we do to merit seeing the Jews of Russia repressed and oppressed for decades being allowed to come to home to Israel.' I do not know. But, one thing is very clear to me, God is calling his children home. We are seeing that He is true to his Word.

Six Million Bones In The Valley of Sheol

"The Jewish people lost six million of their fathers and mothers, brothers and sisters in the Holocaust. One third of the of the world's Jewish population perished. We Jews looked down into the valley of Sheol that was in Europe, and we saw six million dry bones. This was no less compelling than what Ezekiel saw in his valley of dry bones. And, we asked as Ezekiel did, 'Will these bones again live?'

"As Jews we wondered if we could recover from such a life blow. And, behold a miracle occurred. Flesh and sinew appeared on those bones. And, the Jewish people experienced resurrection—they came to the State of Israel!

For Jews, The Road To Jerusalem Is Paved With The Ashes of Auschwitz, Buchenwald and Treblinka

"The link between death and resurrection constitutes the core of your identity as Christians. It is not enough for you as Christians to say that Yeshua died on the cross on Friday. What makes you a Christian is your ability to say, 'He rose from the dead three days later.'

Israel Is Our Easter Sunday

"The rebirth of the State of Israel is our Easter Sunday. It gives us hope for the future, and the will to carry on. Israel is our proof that God still loves His Jewish people—that He has not abandoned them. And, that the promises and covenants He made with our forefathers are still intact.

Seeing Israel: Through The Eyes of a Black Pastor

"My work and ministry were born, without my even knowing it. It began one evening in a hotel room in Jerusalem.

"I grew up in an Orthodox home. My father was an Orthodox Rabbi, the chief Rabbi of Canada. I studied in Yeshivas, and Orthodox Jewish schools all my life. After my ordination in New York I went to Columbia for my doctoral. It was my first time not only being in a school with non-Jews, but in a school with women. I became the Director of Interreligious Affairs for a group called the Anti-Defamation League. And, one of the first things I did was to bring a group of twenty-five Christians to Israel.

"I must tell you that all my life I thought Israel was only related to the Jewish people. I was never aware of the fact that there were Christians who felt anything about Israel.

"This was my first experience at seeing Israel through Christian eyes. My roommate on the twelve day trip was an eighty-six year old black Baptist minister from Virginia. And, I said to myself, 'This is going to be a long twelve days.' I had nothing at all in common with this man. He was poor, and had been saving money for ten years so he could afford to go to

Israel before he died. Finally his children got together and picked up the balance of the ticket so he could go. And, as fate would have it, this man was my roommate.

"On the morning of the first day in Jerusalem I went out on the veranda overlooking the city. I put on my tallit, tefilin, prayer shawl and phylacteries, and said my morning prayers. Tears came to my eyes as I looked over the beautiful city of Jerusalem and realized I had come home.

"I'm sure that my roommate saw me, but he didn't say anything.

"That night I came back to the room a little bit late, and, he didn't see me walk in. I saw him kneeling by the bed with hands lifted upward to heaven. He was crying like a baby. He kept saying, 'Lord, thank you. I am luckier than Moses. I am luckier than Moses. Moses only got to see the Promised Land. I got to walk in it.'

We Both Cried Our Tears Of Joy

"I realized at that moment that this eighty-six year black Baptist minister from Virginia, and this twenty-five year old, newly ordained, hot-shot white Rabbi from New York, had far more in common than I ever could have imagined. We both cried our tears of joy for the privilege, the undeserved privilege of being able to walk in the Holy Land."

We pray these nuggets from Yechiel will give you food for thought. And, that they will encourage you to more effectively reach out to your brother Judah.

Quite naturally, there are profound theological differences between the Believer and the Orthodox Jew. Nevertheless, like Yechiel and the eighty-six year old black Baptist minister from Virginia, we have much in common.

If we, as Ephraimites, are going to successfully lead the way in making the house of Judah and the house of Ephraim the united house of Israel, then we must concentrate on hearing our brother, and on learning how to love him.

A Word To The Wise

However, in seeking to love the people of Judah, let us not add to the problem by mistreating the people of Ephraim. Let us be wise enough to treat both houses with absolute equity. Let us judge both peoples with righteous, absolutely equitable judgment, for only then will they reunite.

Let us show mercy to Judah and understand that he has have—for a season—been "blinded" to the truth about his Messiah (Isaiah 8:14; Romans 11:25). And lets us have an equal mercy for those of Ephraim, who also have been blinded—for a season—to the truth of their Israelite roots (Genesis 48:19; Isaiah 8:14; Romans 11:25; Jeremiah 31:18-19).

13

From Roman Roads To The World Wide Web

T here is an appointed time for everything. And there is a time for every event under heaven" (Ecclesiastes 3:1). Appointed times. Yeshua came at an appointed time, and the Kingdom will be restored to Israel at an appointed time (Mark 13:33; Acts 1:6).

"Yeshua came into Galilee...saying, 'The time is fulfilled, and the Kingdom of God is at hand; repent and trust in the gospel.' And as He was going along by the Sea of Galilee, He saw Simon and Andrew, the brother of Simon, casting a net in the sea; for they were fishermen. And Yeshua said to them, 'Follow Me, and I will make you become fishers of men. And they immediately left the nets and followed Him. And going on a little farther, He saw James the son of Zebedee, and John his brother, who were also in the boat mending the nets. And immediately He called them; and they left their father Zebedee in the boat with the hired servants, and went away to follow Him" (Mark 1:14-21).

Why was Yeshua's time period unique? Why did He say, "The time has come?" (Mark 1:15). Why was that particular time considered "full?" What was different about the time of the first century that distinguished it from any prior century? Moreover, what is the significance of the fact that, immediately following His announcement that the fullness of time was at hand, He began to assemble His disciples?

Why? For one reason, the first century saw the height of "*Pax Romana*," the so-called, *Roman Peace*. It was a time of relative tranquility, in that, Rome enforced their peace on the civilizations that encircled the Mediterranean sea.

Moreover, history has shown that the ancient areas that knew this "peace" also were the primary areas that were targeted to first hear the "Gospel of the Kingdom."[64] Thus, hindsight reveals that the "Good News" could readily be spread at that time because of one salient fact:

Protected Roman roads.

Protected highways and safe sea lanes allowed for a certain new window of opportunity in their day: Because of mighty Rome, no more did robbers and pirates rule over the helpless traveler. No. Rome ruled. The short sword worn by her soldiers guaranteed safe passage for all who walked her ways. And, her guarded highways and harbors made it possible for the fisherman being called by the God of Israel to fulfill Messiah's command, that being to "Go tell."

Even so, the Roman roads of yesteryear helped the Early Believers fulfill their mission, and thus helped make a "way" for all who would believe in Yeshua through the word of the Apostles (John 17:20). In their day, the Early Believers, the Apostles Barnabas and Paul included, traveled newly conquered paths. They dared formerly dangerous roads made accessible by Imperial Rome, all for the glory of the God of Israel.

---

64 See *Who Is Israel?*, In Map Section see map of *Jewish Converts To Christianity 45-300 A.D.* (from *Atlas of Jewish History* by Gilbert). This map reveals that this same area includes the seven churches of Revelation 1-3, plus many synagogues in which Believers in Messiah were predominant during that period.

However, the Roman roads likewise made a way for other teachings to go forth. Quickly, they became a source of mixed blessing, for many types of teachers trod them.

Even so, today, there are many Messianic teachers who speak against the negative "Christian" beliefs that, in reality, have roots that trace back to pagan Roman teachings. But most often, these teachers fail to be balanced in their appraisal of the teachings of both non-Jewish Israel and Jewish Israel.

Many have written about this "Roman problem." Many have condemned "Constantine's Conspiracy."

These people contend that, at the council of Nicea, the Emperor Constantine took control of the "Church," and thus established many anti-Jewish attitudes and laws—all of which ultimately came down those Roman roads.

Sadly, if one seeks to condemn the "Church," one does not have to look long nor hard to find fault with the so-called "Early Church Fathers." But the truth is, in addition to being plagued by errors the Christians carried down Roman causeways, we also are beleaguered by errors that have come to us from Babylonian byways: they being the roads traveled by a dispersed Judah.

For, during their sojourn in Babylon, the people of Judah developed the Babylonian Talmud, a virtual storehouse of laws, legends and ethics, written by Jewish sages and rabbis—which writings often contradict Scripture (Mark 7:9,13; Isaiah 8:20; Jeremiah 8:8; Matthew 15:6; Titus 1:14).

The Road To Zion

Nonetheless, for those of us who seek to restore the "broken brotherhood" of Judah and Ephraim, we must handle the issues that have for so long encouraged division between Jewish Israel and Ephraim Israel with absolute equity. We must be completely fair in the way we treat the Father's "two chosen families" (Jeremiah

33:24).[65] And, if the truth be known—even as Ephraim Israel has gone astray, even as those destined to become a "fulness of Gentiles," have in may ways become like the Gentiles[66]—so it is that those of Jewish Israel also are guilty of having "broken covenant" with the Father.[67] For, speaking of "the house of Israel and the house of Judah," the Father says, His was a covenant which "**they** broke...'" (Jeremiah 31:31-32).

"Both houses of Israel" have "stumbled" (Isaiah 8:14; Romans 11:25); both broke covenant with their Maker. Moreover, their own brotherhood remains broken. As the *New International Version Study Bible* says, Zechariah wrote his Book between the years of 520-480 B.C., and in his Book, he speaks of breaking his "staff called Union, [thus] breaking the brotherhood between Judah and Israel" (verse 11:14). And thus, Zechariah signified "the dissolution of...the unity between the south and the north."[68]

Zechariah symbolically "broke" their brotherhood some two hundred years after Ephraim had been scattered among the Nations —and after Judah returned from Babylon. (Some erroneously claim the two houses were reunited at that time.[69])

Moreover, though Yeshua imputed a certain "oneness" among His people (John 10:16; 17:11,21; Ephesians 2:11-22), still both houses have failed to implement that "oneness." They continue to be a "divided" house, and thus, they fail to stand as a fully restored kingdom (Mark 3:24-25; Ezekiel 37:15-28).

Today, the divided kingdoms of Israel continue down separate roads. Thus our concern with getting those of both houses to begin to ask for the Roadway to Zion.[70]

Our Father speaks of a day wherein His once scattered sheep will be reunited: "'In those days and at that time,' He declares, 'the sons

---

65 See HDH, *The Price of Peace*, and the article, *Just Weights and Measures*.

66 Gen 48:19; Hosea 1-2; 8:8; Amos 9:9; Jer 2:18,21; Rom 11:25.

67 See 1 Kings 11:26-39; 12:21.

68 See NIV *Introduction to Zechariah*, page 1405, and verse 11:14 footnote.

69 See *Who Is Israel?*, Chapter 15, *Is Judah All Israel?*; Jer 3:14-18; 31:20; 50:4-5,20; 2 K 17:23; Zec 8:3,7,13; 9:13; 11:14; 1 Chr 5:26; Dan 9:7; 1 Sam 17:45; Isa 11:13-14; Obad 1:18; Eze 37:22-26.

70 See HDH, *The Crossroads at Laodicea*.

of Israel will come, both they and the sons of Judah as well; they will go along weeping as they go, and it will be Yahveh their God that they will seek. They will ask for the way to Zion, turning their faces in its direction; they will come that they may join themselves to Yahveh in an everlasting covenant that will not be forgotten." Moreover, the Father laments, "My people have become lost sheep; their shepherds have led them astray. They have made them turn aside...and have forgotten their resting place" (Jeremiah 50:4-6; also see Ezekiel 34).

We must help the scattered sheep of Israel find the way that will lead them back to Zion, back to their resting place.

Roman Roads And Two Ways Streets

It is assumed that those who see themselves as non-Jews, and yet as part of Israel, give proper credit to those of Judah for the part they have played in being a "witness" for the God of Israel.[71] Our concern is that those of Ephraim Israel be treated with the same equity. Therefore, in regard to "Christian teaching," to be fair, we will now take a "merciful" look at the results of the teachings that once came down the footpaths in question.

The fact is, for better or worse, in a little over three hundred years, the Good News the Apostles were commanded to take forth essentially became the official religion of the reigning Roman Empire. Though the message was distorted (even as has been the message taken forth by Jewish Israel), still the essence of Ephraim Israel's message was that the One true God had sent His only Begotten Son.

Thus was established the beginnings of a faith that would survive a thousand years of darkness, as barbarians engulfed the empire from the north. Thus was established the root-source of a faith that would survive an aggressive Islam that relentlessly pushed Christianity into western Europe.

---

71 See HDH, *Torah and The Two Witnesses.*

Then came the Reformation, coupled with a European cultural renaissance, which in turn resulted in the English, Spaniards, French, Germans, Italians, Dutchmen and Belgians, etc., taking the Bible and the sword, and virtually "evangelizing" and colonizing the world during the next five hundred years.

Today, as a second millennium draws to a close, those who claim to be "followers of the fishermen" number over two billion strong. And, though we can legitimately criticize most who claim (or have claimed) to follow (or have followed) in their footsteps, still, collectively, theirs is not a shabby record. For, it is no small feat to become the dominant faith of the world.

And yet...

So far, these followers have absolutely failed to restore the kingdom to Israel. For, while they have preached a "Good News" message, they have not fully preached the "Gospel of the kingdom." And Yeshua specifically declared, "This gospel of the kingdom shall be preached in the whole world as a testimony to all the nations, and then, the end will come" (Matthew 24:14; 4:23; 9:35).

Thus the question we need to ask today is the same one the disciples asked Yeshua some two thousand years ago: "Lord, is it at this time that You are restoring the Kingdom to Israel?" (Acts 1:6; also see Acts15:16; Amos 9:11).

If our generation is not the generation appointed for this restoration, then we too, like those who went before us, will undoubtedly have future generations that will criticize our shortcomings; they will examine the paths we have trod. However, if, as many believe, this is the generation that will see the return of Messiah, as well as the restoration of the Kingdom to Israel, then we have a job to do that rivals the job given to our first century brethren!

Selah! Let us pause and meditate!

For us to better understand this job, let us look at an end-time prophecy of Daniel.

The Stone Cut Out

In Daniel chapter two, Daniel describes to Nebuchadnezzar how the image he had seen in his dream represents four kingdoms: The head made of gold represents Nebuchadnezzar's kingdom, he says, and its breast and its arms of silver represents a kingdom that follows Babylon (generally understood to be Medo-Persia); also, its belly and thighs of bronze represents a third kingdom (generally understood to be Greece). Its legs of iron, its feet partly of iron and partly of clay represents a fourth kingdom (generally understood to be Rome, and a restored Rome).

Daniel then tells the King, "You continued looking until a stone was cut out without hands, and it struck the statue on its feet of iron and clay, and crushed them. Then the iron, the clay, the bronze, the silver and the gold were crushed all at the same time, and became like chaff from the summer threshing floors; and the wind carried them away so that not a trace of them was found. But the stone that struck the statue became a great mountain and filled the whole earth" (Daniel 2:32-35).

Ultimately, Daniel gave the King an understanding of his dream. Concerning the "cut out stone," he said:

"In the days of those kings [represented by the image] the God of heaven will set up a kingdom which will never be destroyed, and that kingdom will not be left for another people; it will crush and put an end to all these kingdoms, but it will itself endure forever. Inasmuch as you saw that a stone was cut out of the mountain without hands and that it crushed the iron, the bronze, the clay, the silver, and the gold, the great God has made known to the king what will take place in the future; so the dream is true, and its interpretation is trustworthy" (Daniel 2:45-45).

For now, we will only deal with the identity of the "stone" mentioned in this fascinating prophecy. We will examine how, if correctly interpreted, this mystery might very well impact the mission of Messianic Israel in our day.

Daniel says this stone is cut out without hands from a mountain. In symbolic language, a mountain represents a kingdom (Jeremiah 51:25; Daniel 2:34; Amos 6:12). Cut out of a larger mountain, this stone strikes the image and becomes a great mountain/kingdom that filled the whole earth (Daniel 2:35).

Daniel says this stone is "God's Kingdom" (Daniel 2:44). Therefore, the mountain from which the stone is cut, would necessarily include the old Davidic Kingdom, for God promised a future to David's Kingdom.[72]

World powers have usually come to their power by revolution, conquest, or violence of some kind. However, we are told that this stone (or portion of David's kingdom) was to be cut out without force or power, during a time when all four kingdoms represented by the image were in existence.

This prophecy is being fulfilled in our day.

In 1870 Italy (Rome) emerged as a modern power, Greece became a truly independent nation in 1944, Iran, or Medo-Persia, gained independence in 1942, and Iraq, or Babylon, emerged as a sovereign state in 1932. Thus, all four of these ancient kingdoms are once more independent, free nations, and that, after centuries of their near oblivion.

Of necessity, it must be some time after 1944 that the Father cuts out a piece from the ancient Davidic Kingdom, and begins to reestablish His corporate Kingdom here on earth.

(Note: There are people who have accepted, and are in, the Father's Kingdom, but, as yet, He has not sent His Son back to establish and to rule over His actual Kingdom on this earth. So we find ourselves, as Yeshua did during His first visit, a citizen of the Kingdom of God, but dwelling in the kingdoms of this world.)

Since this stone cut out of a larger mountain strikes the image and becomes a great mountain/kingdom that fills the whole earth, we can reasonably assume that these events occur over a period of time.

---

72 Exo 19:5-6; Deu 4:20; Titus 2:14; 1 Pet 2:9-11; 1 Chr 14:2; 17:14; 28:5; 29:23; 2 Chr 9:8; 13:5,8; Isa 9:6-7; Luke 1:32-33; Eph 5:5; Heb 1:3; 3:6; 8:1; 10:12.

First, the stone is cut out, then it strikes the image, and, in the process of becoming a great kingdom, it crushes the kingdoms of iron and clay, bronze, silver, and gold, and they became like chaff from the summer threshing floors; and the wind carries them away so that not a trace can be found (Daniel 2:34-35).

The Stone Cut Out—Is It The State of Israel?

Many believe, and it is certainly plausible, that the United Nations was used by God to literally "cut out" a small piece of the Davidic Kingdom. For on November 29, 1947, the United Nations divided His land: part was given to Trans-Jordan, part to Egypt, and a part to the Jews. Then on May 16, 1948, the State of Israel came into existence. And, it came into existence without force. It happened at a time in history when the four kingdoms of the image were once again on the stage of world history. Further, on the very first day of its existence, Israel struck the image, as she valiantly fought for her very existence against an Arab league that included the gold and silver kingdoms.

Fifty-two years have passed since that fateful day. And, if Israel is the "Stone," then we have to acknowledge that its process of growing into a great Kingdom and completely smashing the four kingdoms has definitely slowed in the past few years.

Moreover, recent history has shown that Judah cannot accomplish this mammoth task alone.

The Jewish State of Israel needs our help.

Helping Judah

How does the God of Israel say He will help Judah?

Yeshua tells us that, "A kingdom divided cannot stand" (Matthew 12:25; Mark 3:25; Luke 11:17). Therefore, the next item on Yahveh's agenda is that of making the Stone Cut Out a great, reunited kingdom—one that will absolutely rule over its enemies (Genesis 22:17). But, to do so, He first must fully reunite the

163

people of Israel—He must make Ephraim and Judah one nation. And, to accomplish this, Ephraim must once again be made a "mighty man." Moreover, he must be made to hear the Father's "whistle," it being the sign that He is regathering Ephraim from the nations, and bringing him into the land of Israel to Gilead and Lebanon, until no more room can be found for him (Isaiah 11:11; Hosea 11:11, Zechariah 10:7-10).

None of us can know exactly how these prophecies will play out under the Father's direction; nor how they inter-twine with the many other unfulfilled prophecies. However, this we do know: Before millions of Ephraimites can be used to fulfill these prophecies, before they can become an effective force, and thus be utilized by the Father to destroy His enemies and establish his physical Kingdom—they first must know who they are, and what is their mission.

This means, the task of identifying Ephraim is a job that must be accomplished before we can further advance in the end-time game plan.

Why Judah Needs Help

While Judah admittedly needs our help, still, there are some giant obstacles in the way of our providing that much-needed help.

Looking back, we can see that the Yom Kippur War in 1973 was Israel's watershed. That war seemingly was a giant step towards fulfillment of Israel's divine destiny.

However, materially Israel does not today enjoy the advantages she once gained in 1973. She has have retreated from the Sinai, parts of the West Bank, and it is not clear where the land for peace process will end. Will she give up the entire West Bank? The Golan? The beaches of Tel Aviv? Further, the IDF (Israel Defense Force) has lost the esprit de corp it once had. Israel no longer enjoys the same military advantage she once had over its Arab neighbors. However, the State of Israel continues to be a force to be reckoned with!

Unfortunately, there also has been a downward spiral of the moral fiber of the nation. Signs of moral decay grow with each passing year: Newspapers are filled with stories of murder, child abuse, wife abuse, mafia and white collar crime. Politicians and civil servants are constantly exposed for stealing public funds—with Orthodox politicians starring in many of the headlines.

Another evil is the fascination of many of Judah with eastern religions, the occult, and the exotic. Israeli youth stream toward the East: India, Thailand, Napal. The "in" thing is parties that feature occult practices. Even the Orthodox compete with the secular for the services of fortune tellers. Occult practices include TV programs showing Israeli entertainers causing their own hearts to cease beating, while doctors, in utter amazement, observe the medically impossible phenomenon on monitoring equipment. Afterwards, the entertainers explain that they were having an out of body experience, and, having made a spiritual visit around the room, they tell people in the audience what is in their pockets.

Another phenomenon is the sightings of UFO's. In January (1997) the evening news showed hundreds of Israelis, out in the desert, trying to attract flying saucers. Looking to the night sky, they chanted "Kadosh, kadosh, kadosh (Holy, holy, holy)."

Another evil is sexual perversion. Israelis are bombarded with homosexual information in personal newspaper ads, on radio, and TV talk shows wherein homosexuals demand their "rights." Yael Dayan, Knesset member and daughter of the famous general, Moshe Dayan, has taken up their cause, claiming both King David and Jonathan were homosexuals.

Also, massage parlors and independent prostitutes advertize extensively in the papers, and hard porn can be seen from the highway on an outdoor theater screen as one drives on Tel Aviv's main downtown expressway.

Many feel they are miserable, broken and going nowhere, yet the only place they know to turn—if they think the God of Israel might be the answer—is to Orthodox Judaism. And sadly, the mean-spirited, rock-throwing, name-calling, spray-painting, actions of many of the Orthodox have only served to further turn seekers away.[73]

The Stumbling Stone? Yeshua

There is a giant obstacle that those of Messianic Israel face as they try to reach out to help those of Judah who do not believe Yeshua is the Messiah. That stumbling block is the fact that we **do** believe in Messiah Yeshua. For, our faith clashes with the ideal of the Jewish State—which is that its citizens be "Jews." It also clashes with the ultimate Orthodox definement of Jewishness as being: a Jew cannot believe that Yeshua is the Messiah of Israel, therefore, Christians are no more welcome as citizens, or permanent residents of the Jewish State, than are Arabs.

Recently, this division was aggravated by "a well known Evangelist" whose ministry sent out a million copies of his book, "The Peace," to Israeli households. His action stirred many factions in Israel. The Orthodox demonstrated by burning his book in bonfires, by blowing the shofar in front of the Prime Minister's residence, and by making threats of violence against Messianic groups, both Jewish and Christian—which groups have likewise joined the chorus of voices that speak against this evangelistic endeavor. All agree, the Evangelist made the act of maintaining a Christian physical presence in Israel an even more difficult task.

From the above review of the State of Israel (no pun intended), obviously, at this point in time, a natural door is not open for the return of "Ephraim" to the Land. And yet, we need to return to the Land in numbers that will fulfill Biblical prophecy (Zechariah 10:7-10). We need to return in quality numbers that will make a significant difference in the material and moral balance in the

---

73 The primary sources for much of the information about Israel's current condition is, *The Jerusalem Post International Edition*, New York, and the *Maoz* Newsletter, published by the Tel Aviv based Messianic Jewish Ministry of Ari and Shire Sorko Ram.

Middle East (Jeremiah 50:4). For, we will yet be called upon to show that the Holy One of Israel is not the false god called "Allah," but instead, is the God of Abraham, Isaac, and Jacob (Isaiah 11:14).

Is The Door Stuck, Or Are We Not Ready?

Admittedly, there are many obstacles to the fulfillment of Scripture concerning the gathering and reunion of all Israel. Presently, there is much that opposes our return to the Land. For the most part, individually, we cannot do a great deal to solve these problems. However, before the Father opens the door of opportunity for us, there is a question that we need to ask ourselves.

What would we do today if the door were opened?

We need to ask this question so that we might realize that our present problem is not the lack of an open door! No. The problem we face is the fact that we do not have the "instructed, knowing, understanding," and, properly "repentant," numbers of Jeremiah 31:18-19!

The End of The Mystery

The problem at hand is not our lack of opportunity. Instead, the task at hand is to help Ephraim Israel to come to "know" himself, to know his place as the other house of Israel, and to understand the role the Father has asked him to play in working out the salvation of all Israel (Jeremiah 31:18-19; Isaiah 8:14; 11:13; Romans 11).

And, our good news is that we now have an open door of opportunity! For, in Yeshua's day, there were Roman roads and a certain "fulness of time." And in our time, there is coming to pass a certain "fulness" of Romans 11:25-26:

"For I do not want you, brethren," said the Apostle Paul, "to be uninformed of this mystery, that you not be wise in your own estimation, for a partial hardening has happened to Israel, to last until the fullness of the Gentiles has come in; and thus [or, in this manner], will all Israel [that is to be saved] be saved."

Paul spoke of a certain "blindness" that in his day had already come upon Israelites eyes. For Yeshua said of Himself, "Destroy this temple [sanctuary], and in three days I will raise it up. And the Jews said, 'It took forty-six years to build this temple, and will You raise it up in three days?' But Yeshua was speaking of the temple of His body. So, when He was raised from the dead, His disciples recalled what He had said, and they believed the Scripture and the word which Yeshua had spoken" (John 2:19-22).

Yeshua compared Himself to a "Temple/Sanctuary," and the Disciples "believed the Scripture." What particular Scripture did they "believe"?

The Father said to Israel, "It is the Lord of hosts whom you should regard as holy." And then, He shall become a sanctuary; but to both the houses of Israel, a stone to strike and a rock to stumble over..." (Isaiah 8:13-14).

The Lord of Hosts would become a Sanctuary, and both the houses of Israel would stumble over Him. This is the Scripture the Apostles believed. And, it is this "partial hardening" to the truth of the Sanctuary, that is the "blindness" that causes Ephraim and Judah to stumble. And Paul said the veil would not be lifted "until..."

Paul spoke of a certain "fulness" that would come to the "former Gentiles" (Ephesians 2:11-22). He spoke of the end of a period of time. He foretold a certain "perfection," or "maturing," that they would grow into. He spoke of the veil being lifted from the eyes of those of Ephraim Israel; and thus in essence, reaffirmed Jeremiah's prophecy about Ephraim "coming to know himself" (Rotherham's translation), as well as Isaiah's prediction about the time when Ephraim would cease to "stumble" over the "Sanctuary," and would no longer be "jealous" of Judah (Jeremiah 31:18-19; Isaiah 8:14; 11:13; Romans 11:25).

We live in that promised time. For, the "veil" is likewise being lifted from Ephraim's heretofore darkened eyes. And so, it is time for him to see, time for him to understand, and time for him to act. For, when Messianic Israel begins to take full advantage of the opportunities Yahveh gives (and will continue to gives as we can handle them), we will have the fullness of an Israel who understands its heritage. Then, we will see the day when all Israel that is to be saved, will be saved (Romans 11:26). Then, we will see the door open for our return to the Land promised to our fathers!

The Jewish people of the past two thousand years have represented only one of the two families/nations/ kingdoms that comprise the whole house of Israel. Judah's return to the Land is only a partial fulfillment of the reunion of the "two sticks" (Ezekiel 37:15-28).

Only when Ephraim is returned to his own inheritance in the Land, can we expect to see the fulfillment of the portions of Ezekiel's prophecy that deal with eternal peace and the return of the Messiah. For, long ago, the Father said of Ephraim, "In the place where it was said to them, 'You are not My people,' there, it will be said to them, 'You are the sons of the living God'" (Hosea 1:10).

Yes. All Israel must be restored and returned.

The Next Move Is...

Since we know that a divided kingdom cannot stand, we can reason that a united house, or family, cannot be defeated. Therefore, it is only reasonable that the next item on Yahveh's agenda is that of making the present state of Israel (the Stone Cut Out) a great kingdom—one that will possess the gates of its enemies. But, to do so, He must reunite the people of Israel—He must make Ephraim and Judah one nation on the mountains of Israel.

How is He going to accomplish this task?

Each of Us Has An Essential Job To Do

Our God is the God that does not change. His initial plan remains in effect. The instructions remain: "Go tell!" And, if you know, then it is your job to go tell!

Two thousand years ago, our counterparts took to the Roman

roads, that they might gather the scattered sheep of Israel. Today, we have the opportunity to be modern day couriers, using modern communication routes to awaken Ephraim to his identity and mission. This mission, when brought to its fulness, will see Ephraim taking a decisive role in having the present State of Israel fulfill its destiny!

How can we use the cutting edge of communication technology—the World Wide Web—to obtain our goals? By taking full advantage of the opportunities offered by the Internet.

Today there are many Messianic Israel sites on the web. Visit them. The best starting point is the www.mim.net. This is the site of Messianic Israel Ministries/Messianic Israel Alliance/House of David.

A key element of the site is the *Messianic Israel Alliance Directory*, which gives a listing of Messianic Israel congregations fellowships, synagogues, and ministries in the United States and around the world.

In the past, you may have asked why you have been selected as a forerunner, and why you have been given the unmerited opportunity of seeing the Scriptural truth regarding the two houses of Israel. You now have an answer! As part of Messianic Israel, you can actively aid in the development of the World Wide Web project, and you can be included in the directory of those available to share their knowledge, understanding, and enthusiasm with others.

The Time Is At Hand!

Even as Yeshua's time was "full," and He began to choose His disciples, now as the time of the Gentiles is fulfilled and as the "fullness of the Gentiles is come in," so it is time for Yeshua to again make a choice about those who will follow Him at this juncture in history (Matthew 13:49).

The question that each of us must answer is: What does the Holy

One of Israel expect me to do in bringing to fruition the desire of His heart?

Hopefully, your answer basically follows:

"As for me and my house, we will serve the Holy One of Israel. We will expend our strength and resources in raising up the dry bones of the whole house of Israel; thus helping to inject new life into Ephraim and Judah. We will work to help Ephraim become fully aware of his heritage, and to help Judah find eternal life in Messiah. We will walk this road until Ephraim is transformed into a mighty man, until he truly becomes one with Judah; and until together, they overcome their enemies, and thus fully occupy the land promised our forefathers, Abraham, Isaac and Jacob. We will push forward until we see that the glorious promise made through Ezekiel has come to pass, we will work until we hear our Father recite Ezekiel' prophecy as an accomplished fact:

"Behold, I have taken the sons of Israel from among the nations where they had gone, and I have gathered them from every side and brought them into their own land; and they are now one nation in the land, on the mountains of Israel; and one king is king for all of them; and they are no longer two nations, and they are no longer divided into two kingdoms. And they no longer defile themselves with their idols, or with their detestable things, or with any of their transgressions; but I have delivered them from all their dwelling places in which they have sinned, and I have cleansed them. And they are My people, and I Am their God. And My servant David is King over them, and they have One Shepherd; and they are walking in My ordinances, and keeping My statutes, and observing them. And they are living on the land that I gave to Jacob My servant, in which their fathers lived; and they will continue to live on it, they, and their sons, and their sons' sons, forever; and David My servant is their prince forever. And I have made a covenant of peace with them; it is an everlasting covenant with them. And I have placed them and multiply them, and I have set My sanctuary in their midst forever'" (A fulfilled rendering of Ezekiel 37 21-27)."

171

And The Serpent Poured Out...Water Like A River—World Wide Web Waterfalls

Batya Wootten, in a Herald article entitled *End-Time Pit Falls,* writes the following:

While we are happy to have a web site, we also are concerned about the flood of information we see coming forth in teachings, books, newsletters, and from the Internet. And so we write the following collection of thoughts.

In Revelation 12:15, we read, "And the serpent cast out of his mouth water as a flood after the woman, that he might cause her to be carried away of the flood."

In the last days, the serpent pours out his wrath on the woman, who is Israel, and he makes "war" with her children —in particular, he makes war with those "who keep the commandments of Elohim and hold to the testimony of Yeshua."

The people who help the serpent in this endeavor "have a common purpose." Collectively they are called, "Babylon," and thus, Yeshua warns us to "Come out of her" that we might not "participate in her sins nor receive of her plagues" (Revelation 12:14-17 18:2,4).

Babylon. A common purpose. Seems this has happened before... Yes. The story begins in Genesis:

Now the whole earth used the same language and the same words [and]....They said to one another... 'Come, let us build for ourselves a city, and a tower whose top will reach into heaven, and let us make for ourselves a name, otherwise we will be scattered abroad over the face of the whole earth.'

"And Yahveh came down to see the city and the tower which the sons of men had built. And He said, 'Behold, they are one people, and they all have the same language. And this is what they began to do, and now nothing which they purpose to do will be impossible for them. 'Come, let Us go down and there confuse their language, so that they will not understand one another's speech.' So Yahveh scattered them over the face of the whole earth; and they stopped building the city. Therefore its name was called Babel, because there Yahveh confused the language of the whole earth; and from there scattered them abroad over the face of the whole earth" (Genesis 11:1-9)

Hmm.... They used the same language, and therefore, nothing was impossible for them. And, here we are today, the whole world able to communicate on the Internet, using English, the dominant language of the World Wide Web.

A Flood Sent To Carry Away "Commandment Keepers Who Follow Yeshua"

The method the serpent uses in this latter-day war against Israel is to "spew out a river," to send forth a "torrent." Thus does Psalm 18:4 warn of "torrents of ungodliness," the Hebrew word being one that speaks of a "river." Moreover, this serpentine torrent is sent forth for a specific purpose: "To overtake the woman [Israel] and to sweep her away."

This means, in the last days, a flood will come forth from Satan's mouth, and it will come for the specific purpose of "carrying Israel away." This flood of words is sent to carry Israel off course, for it is a flood, and thus, it is a river of words that will take her where Godly rivers ought not to go.

Specifically, the Israel who "keeps the commandments of Elohim and holds to the testimony of Yeshua" are the ones whom Satan seeks to drown with his deceptive doctrines. Thus, for those who believe in Messiah and His claims, and who seek to keep His commandments, it will be for them even as He warned: that In the latter-days, the false one will seek "to mislead, if possible, even the elect" (Matthew 24:24).

A River of Knowledge: Good and Evil

We presently see, in many different forms, a flood of

information coming forth: teachings, books, the Internet. We also see a growing company of non-Jewish Believers who are discovering their so-called "Jewish roots."[74] Mostly, they are a people who are very dissatisfied with the history and actions of the "Church." Also, they are a people who are "starved" to hear the Word of the Holy One; they are "famished" for His truth. For them it has been even as He said of ancient Israel: "'Behold, days are coming,' declares Yahveh Elohim, 'when I will send a famine on the land, not a famine for bread or a thirst for water, but rather for hearing the words of the Lord" (Amos 8:11).

This verse applies to two groups of peoples. It applies to those who have heard the Word, and yet, refused to "hear." These hear but do not act. Repeatedly the Father sends them His Word, and, they refuse to respond. Thus, their hearts become hardened.[75] It also applies to a people hungry for the truth! In fact, they are the very ones whom the evil one wants to sweep away! Moreover, they are not lukewarm Laodiceans that are about to land on the ground like so much spittle. No. They are children of Israel—children who are panting for a drink from the Holy One!

So we feel compelled to warn: Beware, you who are laboring to come out of Laodicea. Beware, you who bemoan the sins of Babylon! For the target of the serpent's flood is none other than you!!!

Do not be swept away! Do not be deceived! Do not trade in the sins of a wayward Church for the sins of wayward Judaism! Beware! For even as it was true for Cain, so it remains true for you that "Sin is crouching at the door; and its desire is for you, but you must master it" (Genesis 4:7).

We must master the flood of deceptive information that is

---

74 In the olive tree of Israel, Yeshua is the "Root" (Rev 22:16). And, this tree has two branches: "Ephraim Israel and Judah" (Jer 11:10,16; 2:18,21; Gen 48:19; Rom 11:25). Thus, "Judah" is but a *branch* in the Olive Tree. To truly look to our "Rootsource," we need to look to Messiah Yeshua, and not to the traditions of men.

75 See Psa 95:8; Pro 28:14; Isa 63:17; Lam 3:65; Matt 19:8; Mark 3:5; 6:52; 8:17; 10:5; 16:14; John 12:40; Eph 4:18; Heb 3:8,15; 4:7.

currently being directed at those of Israel who would "keep the commandments," and at the same time, "hold to the testimony of Yeshua." So it is that the Book of Revelation speaks so often of those who must "overcome."[76]

Running To and Fro Until Dissipated

Speaking of the end-time, Yeshua warns, "If anyone says to you, 'Behold, here is the Messiah,' or 'There He is,' do not believe him. For false messiahs and false prophets will arise and will show great signs and wonders, so as to mislead, if possible, even the elect" (Matthew 24:14,23-24).

Note that the words "false messiahs and false prophets" are in the plural. In other words, people will be saying, "Look, here is the Messiah," and others will be saying, "No, there he is." And all those who are taken in by their calls will be going back and forth: "Here," "No, there," they will say as they go to and fro.

This to and fro confusion is described in Gabriel's instructions to Daniel, "Conceal these words and seal up the book until the end of time; when many will go back and forth, and knowledge will increase" (Daniel 12:4).

Knowledge is the Hebrew "da'ath," which is the word is used in Proverbs 22:12, "The eyes of Yahveh preserve knowledge," and in Genesis 2:9, to speak of "The tree of the knowledge of good and evil." And of this tree, the Father warned, "In the day that you eat from it you will surely die" (Genesis 2:17).[77]

In the last days, there will be an increase of knowledge: both good and bad. And, the knowledge laced with evil, as always, will bring with it a certain death.

The angel Gabriel told Daniel that his words were, "sealed until the latter-days." However, "At that time," Gabriel said, "Those who have insight will shine brightly like the brightness

---

76 See Revelation 2:7,11,17, 26; 3:5,12,21; 5:5; 11:7; 13:7; 17:14; 21:7.
77 Strong's word # H 1847, *da'ath*: knowledge, cunning.

175

of the expanse of heaven" (Daniel 2:3,9; 9:21). Here, Gabriel speaks of circumspect intelligence, or watchful, detailed, discerned understanding.[78]

It is for this insight for food from the "life-giving tree," that we must pray, if we do not want to be swept away with the end-time flood of evil information. And, if we are not going to be totally dissipated by a frantic running to and fro —first to hear this speaker and then to hear that speaker— and therefore never really applying ourselves to any one job —then we must pray for ears to hear the Holy Spirit. "And thine ears shall hear a word behind thee, saying, 'This is the way, walk ye in it...'" (Isaiah 30:21).

In Paul's letters to Timothy, we see that our Father "desires for all men to be saved and to come to the knowledge of the truth." And that He does not want us to "fall into...the snare of the devil" (1 Timothy 2:4; 3:7). Thus He counsels us, "But realize this, that in the last days difficult times will come...[there will be men who] hold to a form of godliness, although they have denied its power; avoid such men as these. Among them are those who...[are] always learning and never able to come to the knowledge of the truth. ...these men also oppose the truth, men of depraved mind, rejected in regard to the faith" (2 Timothy 3:1,5-8).

There is coming, and now is, a flood from men who have much learning, but do not know the One Who is the Truth.[79] They have a form of godliness, but in the eyes of Him Who is Truth, they are depraved ones. Beware of them. Run for your life! They bring with them a torrent of unholy doctrines that will sweep you away from the God of Truth.[80] Their waters will not satisfy, but will leave you parched.

---

78 Strong's word # H 7919.
79 See the Herald's, *The I AM, His Son, and the "Trinity,"* and, *Is The "Greek" New Covenant Inspired? Is Yeshua Divine?*
80 See the Herald, *Forsaking Our First Love.*

A Job Assignment For The West

Again, we feel we presently have an open door of opportunity on the Internet. Just as the Roman roads of yesteryear allowed our forefathers to take forth the message of the Gospel, so we believe the World Wide Web will allow us to take forth the message of the restoration of the Kingdom to a repentant, reunited, restored Israel (Acts 1:6; Ezekiel 37:15-28; Amos 9:10; Zephaniah 3:11-13).

Moreover, we believe this is a job that the Father foreordained would primarily be done here, in the West. For it is written that Ephraim will come trembling from the West!

The instruction that brings about the necessary changes in Ephraim begins in the West! Even as Hosea says of Ephraim: "They will walk after Yahveh, He will roar like a lion; indeed He will roar and His sons will come trembling from the west" (Hosea 11:10).

Here, in the West, Ephraim Israel needs to learn to tremble at the Word of the Holy One! He needs to be so awe-inspired at the scope of the vision for a reunited Israel that he quakes in his boots! For only then will he be ready in his heart to go home!

In Isaiah we read: "So shall they fear the name of Yahveh from the west, and his glory from the rising of the sun. When the enemy shall come in like a flood, the Spirit of Yahveh shall lift up a standard against him" (Isaiah 59:19, KJV).

We believe we have been given the job of awakening a western oriented Ephraim. We also believe we need to warn him about the deceiving words being sent against him like a flood. Thus, we are lifting up the Standard. We lift up Him who is able to stem the tide.

Presently, we are stepping out on newly conquered pathways. And, our faces are set like flint toward a Jerusalem that is the eternal capital of a restored House of Israel.

We hope we will see you on the road located at: www.mim.net, or www.messianicisrael.com, or www.messianicisrael.net, or www.messianicisrael.org.

14

The Jubilee Generation

The seventh angel sounded; and there were great voices in heaven, saying, the kingdoms of this world are become the kingdoms of our Adonai [Lord], and of his Mashiach [Anointed One]; and He shall reign for ever and ever" (Revelation 11:15).

How does the Holy One of Israel, the God of Abraham, Isaac and Jacob, plan to accomplish this age-ending event? How will He realize His Messianic Vision, which is to manifest His presence—in His earthly Kingdom—in the midst of a *united* people.

To reach this goal, obviously one of His larger challenges is "uniting His people, Israel."

The above is taken from Chapter 17, *The Messianic Vision.*[81] While this Chapter gives a good answer to the "how" question, it does not give the fullest answer to the "when" question.

Undoubtedly, our generation is closer to the return of Messiah, and to the establishment of His Kingdom here on earth, than any previous generation! But how close is that? And what is so special about this generation that we should believe that we are "*the* generation"?

The generation that experiences this age-ending event will

---

81 See Chapter 15, *The Messianic Vision.*

realize fulfillment of Yeshua's mission:

"And He came to Nazareth, where He had been brought up; and as was His custom, He entered the synagogue on the Sabbath, and stood up to read. And the book of the prophet Isaiah was handed to Him. And He opened the book, and found the place where it was written, 'the Spirit of the Lord is upon me, because He anointed me to preach the gospel to the poor. He has sent me to proclaim release to the captives, and recovery of sight to the blind, to set free those who are downtrodden, to proclaim the favorable year of the Lord....' And..., 'Today this Scripture has been fulfilled in your hearing'" (Luke 4:18-21).

According to the rabbinical custom of Yeshua's day, reference to this verse in Isaiah would have been thought to include the entire passage.

Continuing, we see that Yeshua was declaring that He had been sent "To proclaim the favorable year of the Lord, and the day of vengeance of our God; to comfort all who mourn...giving them a garland instead of ashes, the oil of gladness instead of mourning, the mantle of praise instead of a spirit of fainting. So they will be called oaks of righteousness, the planting of the Lord, that He may be glorified. Then they will rebuild the ancient ruins, they will raise up the former devastations, and they will repair the ruined cities, the desolations of many generations. And strangers will stand and pasture your flocks, and foreigners will be your farmers and your vinedressers. But you will be called the priests of the Lord; you will be spoken of as ministers of our God. You will eat the wealth of nations, and in their riches you will boast. Instead of your shame you will have a double portion, and instead of humiliation they will shout for joy over their portion. Therefore they will possess a double portion in their land, everlasting joy will be theirs..." (Isaiah 61:2-9).

Standing in a synagogue in Nazareth, Yeshua said, "*Today* this Scripture has been fulfilled in your hearing."

Yet, *today*, some two thousand years later, from our finite viewpoint, Yeshua's declaration has not yet been fully fulfilled.

Truly Yahveh's ways are not our ways, especially when it comes to "time."

So, how did Yeshua fulfill these Scriptures?

He set in motion a plan, which in the fullness of time will see every jot and tittle of these verses accomplished.

Further, every generation since has played an integral part of this fulfillment. However, even though prior generations have gained approval by passing the torch of faith to the next generation, they did not receive what was promised. Because, it yet remains for a generation to carry the torch across the finish line, at which time all things will be perfected (Hebrews 11:39-40).

Could we be that final generation? Could we be the "finish line generation," the generation that will see captives being set free, the blind regaining their sight, the lame being healed, and having their land returned? Will we experience the fulness of the "favorable year of the Lord"?

If so, truly we will experience the ultimate "Jubilee!"

The Concept of Jubilee

At the core of the idea of "jubilee" is the Mosaic doctrine, that all things, all creatures in the world do not belong to men at all, but to Yahveh alone.

The biblical law of redemption makes "jubilee" possible. This jubilee law deals with the fact that the land should not be sold in perpetuity, for it belonged to Yahveh, and those in bondage should, and could be, redeemed. The redemption of land and of those in bondage could be accomplished at anytime by a kinsman redeemer. Otherwise, in the year of Jubilee the land would revert back to the owner, and those in bondage would be freed (Leviticus 25:23-55).

Biblically, the year of Jubilee is celebrated in the fiftieth year. In this year, agricultural lands sold during the past 49 years are returned to their original owners, and any Israelite that is in bondage is set free.

Seventeen Jubilees were celebrated from the time Joshua took the land until the destruction of the First Temple. Then upon Judah's return from Babylon, the count began again, and it stopped with the destruction of the Second Temple.

In 1998 the state of Israel celebrated a jubilee of its founding, still it was not a Biblical jubilee. Perhaps the reason Jewish religious leaders have not yet called for a Biblical jubilee is because, according to the Talmud, the Jubilee Year laws are in force *only when all the tribes are living in "Eretz Israel"* (TB Ar. 32b).

Again, we ask, could we be that jubilee generation?

The answer is, "Yes!"

Why? Because the first jubilee generation saw the first advent of Israel's Messiah. Therefore, would not the second jubilee generation be an appropriate time for His return? Would not a jubilee generation be the time to make the kingdoms of this world the Kingdom of our Messiah? Surely that would be fulfilling the very essence of Yahveh's jubilee principals—by asserting His ownership of all the earth, and its population, and for all creation to acknowledge His Lordship. At that time every knee will bow and every tongue will confess that He and He alone is Lord!

How do we know that Yeshua came in the first jubilee generation? Further, how do we know that we are the second jubilee generation?

Defining A Generation

To begin, a generation is the period from a man's birth to the birth of his son. It also can refer collectively to the people who lived in a like period.

Scripturally, the average length of a generation is most often assumed to be forty years. For, in the wilderness all the men over twenty died within a forty-year time frame. The forty year span of the rule of David and Solomon, and of four of the judges, adds support for a forty year generation.

However, we also find Scriptural support or a hundred year generation: Yahveh told Abraham that his descendants would be in a foreign land four hundred years and then He would bring them out in the "fourth generation."

Matthew's genealogy further complicates the problem of determining the length of a generation. His genealogical list gives forty-two generations from Abraham to the birth of Yeshua (Matthew 1:17). It gets complicated when we try to determine the time span of these forty-two generations. If we use hundred year generations, we have a 4200 year span. If we use forty years, we have a 1680 year span. However, neither of these time spans fits with known history. Further, the general agreement among biblical scholars is that Yeshua was born in 5 or 6 B.C., and that Abraham was born in the period of 2000 B.C. to 2200 B.C.

The answer that solves this dilemma and also fits with history is:

From the flood to the Exodus from Egypt, generations were 100 years long, afterwards, they were forty years long. This reasoning, when applied to Matthew's genealogy, gives us eight, one-hundred year generations: Abraham, Isaac, Jacob, Jacobs twelve sons, and four generations in Egypt—and thirty-four forty-year generations. Using this rationale ($34 \times 40 = 1360 + 800 = 2160$), and back-dating from 6 B.C., we arrive at 2166 B.C. as Abraham's year of birth. This is the exact date given by the NIV Study Bible Old Testament Chronology for Abraham's birth. Further, this perception of generations would place the flood some seven to eight hundred years earlier, and well within the time frame that is acceptable to the majority of scholars.

After Yahveh had virtually destroyed the ancient world with the flood, we find that His plan to have a people for His own possession is to be accomplished through the descendants of Noah's son, Shem. This means Shem's son Arphaxed, represents the first generation of the post-flood world. And, from Arphaxed to Abraham there are seven generations. Add these seven generations to the forty two generations from Abraham to Yeshua, and we have forty-nine generations. *Thus, Yeshua then came in the fiftieth generation, or the first jubilee generation*: 6 B.C. to 34 A.D.

This in turn means the first generation after Yeshua would have begun in 35 A.D., which year is also thought to be the year of Paul's conversion.

Paul conversion is key to the almost 2000 year effort to renew the world *spiritually*, and to regather Yahveh's people. This mission stands in contrast to the mission of Noah's sons, which was to repopulate the world *physically*.

And, the next *fiftieth generation from Yeshua, meaning the second jubilee generation*, began in 1996 A.D.!

So, today, in 2000 A.D., we live in the fourth year of the fiftieth generation from Yeshua, and in the one hundredth generation from the flood!

Part Three

Gathering The Remnant

15

A Mandate For Ephraim

A common concern among those of Messianic Israel is: "I have read all of your books and Heralds. And, I understand the teaching about the two houses of Israel—Ephraim and Judah. So, what do I do now?"

Answering the "what do we do now" and "where do we go from here" questions was a prime focus of the AMI 99 and AMI 2000 Conferences in Orlando, Florida. (For an in-depth study of these questions, we encourage you to order the conference tapes.[82])

Many are asking, "Now that I understand about the two houses what does the Father expect of **me**? What can **I** do about uniting Ephraim and Judah?"

The key to answering these questions is found in understanding how Yahveh will reunite the two houses of Israel. His plan for reunification is outlined in Ezekiel's prophecy about the two sticks. Since Israel's Kingdom was unified only during the short period of the reigns of Saul, David and Solomon's reign, we know that its fulfillment is yet future. So, let us begin our search for answers by taking another look at this prophecy:

---

82 See Messianic Materials Listing.

Ezekiel 37:15 follows: "The word of the Lord came again to me saying,

16 And you son of man take for yourself one stick and write on it, 'For Judah and for the sons of Israel, his companions;' then take another stick and write on it, 'for Joseph, the stick of Ephraim and all the house of Israel his companions.'

17 Then join them for yourself one to another into one stick, that they may become one in your hand.

18 And when the sons of your people speak to you saying, 'Will you not declare to us what you mean by these?

19 say to them, 'Thus says the Lord God, "Behold, I will take the stick of Joseph, which is in the hand of Ephraim, and the tribes of Israel, his companions; and I will put them with the stick of Judah, and make them one stick, and they will be one in my hand."

In these verses, Yahveh first tells Ezekiel to put the two sticks together, then, in verse Nineteen, Yahveh declares that He will put them together and make them one in His hand.

The task that Yahveh outlines for Ezekiel is divided into three steps. Step one is the "Take Step'" Ezekiel is instructed to "take" two sticks and prepare them to be joined. This preparation consists of identifying each stick. Step two is the "Put Step." Ezekiel is to "put" the two sticks together in his hand in such a way as to make them one. The third step is the "Instruction Step." Ezekiel is told to "explain" to the people the meaning of preparing and joining the two sticks.

In verse Nineteen, the time comes for Yahveh to make the two sticks one. How does He say He will do that? In step one, the "Take Step," Yahveh takes the stick of Joseph, which is in the hands of Ephraim, and the tribes of Israel his companions. Note that Yahveh is doing what Ezekiel did. He is identifying in detail the stick of Ephraim, one of the two sticks. However, Yahveh does not "take" or "identify" Judah. Yahveh simply moves to step two, the "Put Step." He "puts'" the stick of Ephraim, which He has just "taken" and "identified," with the stick of Judah.

Was the failure to take, or identify, Judah an oversight on Yahveh's part? Or, will the joining (or putting) take place at a time when Judah has already been "taken" and is readily identifiable? In our day Yahveh has "taken" Judah and identified him as a part of Israel, by reestablishing him in the land. Therefore, the stick that needs to be taken and identified before the "putting" can take place is the stick of Ephraim. And, in our day, the number of Ephraimites who understand their identity is extremely limited.

In Roman's 11:25 Paul explains that a "partial blindness or hardening happened to Israel." For Ephraim, this hardness included blindness to his roots. For Judah it was blindness to the truth that Yeshua is the Messiah. But, just as we are seeing the blinders come off Ephraim, we are also seeing a Jewish acceptance of Messiah unparalleled since the first century. However, in Yahveh's schedule the joining of the two houses into a single nation takes place before the Greater Son of David is recognized by all Israel as their King (Ezekiel 37:20-22).

Where Are We Today?

We are in the very early stage of Yahveh's "taking" and identifying the stick of Ephraim. For, it is time for him to see the truth of his identity as the other house of Israel (Jeremiah 31:18-19). A more complete understanding of Ezekiel 37:19 confirms that is where we are today. The Hebrew word *laqah*,[83] which is translated *take*, could also be translated *select* or *summon*. The Hebrew word *natan*,[84] which is translated *put,* could very well be translated *make* or *constitute*. These alternate translations more accurately portray what Yahveh is saying in verse Nineteen:

"Thus says the Lord God, 'Behold, I will *summon* the stick of Joseph, which is in the hand of Ephraim, and the tribes of Israel, his

---

[83] Strong's number for *laqah* is H3947.
[84] Strong's number for *natan* is H5414.

companions; and with the stick of Judah, I will *constitute* one stick, and they will be one in my hand.'"

This more accurate translation is far more revealing and descriptive. It shows us that Yahveh is *summoning* Ephraim. He is bringing him forth to receive instructions—instructions concerning Yahveh's *constitution* of the united house of Israel.

Since Yahveh is *summoning* and identifying Ephraimites, for the purpose of serving as His instruments in *constituting* a united house of Israel, it surely behooves us to correctly understand what Yahveh is expecting us to do individually and corporately. An important first step in gaining this understanding is discerning where we are in Yahveh's program or timetable for restoring the Kingdom to Israel.

Yahveh, while identifying Ephraim, must inform both sticks that by themselves they are not the entire Israel of God. This is a big task, even for God. The Jewish people have no doubts at all that they, and they alone, are the only inheritors of the promises of Abraham, Isaac, and Jacob. On the other hand, the Church has over 1,586 faiths,[85] many claiming to be the authentic representation of the God of Israel here on earth.

How is Yahveh going to overcome these errant mind sets?

Like other prophecies, it will be far easier to look back at the fulfillment than to look ahead. Since Ezekiel's prophecy about the two sticks remains unfulfilled, we have no choice but to look ahead. However, we can get some insight as to how Yahveh may fulfill this prophecy by looking at how He is fulfilling other like prophecies.

The prophecy that immediately precedes the "two sticks" is Ezekiel's "vision of the valley of dry bones." This prophecy, with Jeremiah's, "I will restore the tents of Jacob"—Mark's, "Fig Tree"—Joel's, "The nations will divide Yahveh's land—and, Isaiah's, "A nation will be born in a day"—are prophecies we have,

---

85 *The* December 1988 edition of the *Encyclopedia of American Religions* lists 1,586 faiths in the United States alone.

or we are seeing be fulfilled in our generation (Jeremiah 30:18; Mark 13:28; Joel 3:2; Isaiah 66:8).

True to His Word, Yahveh is beginning to restore the "tabernacle of David," by first bringing Judah back to the land (Zechariah 12:7, Acts 15:16,17). He is accomplishing this restoration using a combination of the efforts of men, mixed with Divine intervention.

How Has Yahveh Used Men To Fulfill Prophecy?

There are three key efforts, or episodes, in which Yahveh has used men to influence the regathering of Judah and the establishment of the State of Israel. Let us look at them to decide if the Father may be using men and similar events to fulfill the prophecy of the two sticks as it regards Ephraim.

The three key episodes were:

1. The First Zionist Congress.

Theodore Herzel's summation of the accomplishments of the First Zionist Congress in Basel, Switzerland in August 1897:

"At Basel I founded the Jewish state. If I were to say this today, I would be greeted by universal laughter. In five years, perhaps, and certainly in 50, everyone will see it."

2. The Balfour Declaration.

In November 1917, as British forces, having taken Gaza and Beersheba, were advancing towards Jerusalem, British Foreign Minister Arthur Balfour wrote a one-sentence letter to Lord Rothschild as representative of the Zionists. It said:

"His Majesty's Government view with favor the establishment in Palestine of a national home for the Jewish people, and will use their best endeavors to facilitate the achievements of this object, it being clearly understood that nothing shall be done which may prejudice the civil and religious rights of existing non-Jewish communities in Palestine, or the rights and political status enjoyed by Jews in any other country."

This sentence became known as the Balfour Declaration and was endorsed by the League of Nations in 1922.

3. The liberation of Palestine and Jerusalem by the British in December 1917. Together with Herzel and the Balfour Declaration gave the Zionist, and their supporters, the heart to set in motion the return that would result in the birth of the State of Israel in 1948. The capture of Palestine by the British made it physically possible to return.

The Liberation Of Jerusalem, The Fulfillment Of Prophecy

How did Yahveh accomplish the liberation of Jerusalem which was the fulfillment of Isaiah 31:5?

"Like flying birds so the Lord of hosts will protect Jerusalem.

He will protect and deliver it;

He will pass over and rescue it" (Isaiah 31:5).

Isaiah recorded this prophecy some twenty five-hundred years ago, and we have had the unmerited privilege of seeing its fulfillment during this century. It is a fascinating story, and an excellent lesson of how Yahveh mixed man's efforts and divine intervention to accomplish His promise.

It was June 1917, and three years of the Great War had gravely affected the morale of the British Empire. Lloyd-George, the Prime Minister of Britain, clearly saw that his people need a spiritual uplift. The solution? He reasoned that Palestine and Jerusalem held a special place in the morale and psychology of a Christian people bogged down in a costly and dragging war. Lloyd-George wanted Jerusalem as a "Christmas present for the Empire." He concluded that In Palestine, great victories might be won by the right man, and the right man was General Sir Edmund H. H. Allenby, commander of the British 3rd Army in Europe.

Where did Lloyd-George get such an idea? From a practical standpoint wouldn't Berlin have been a far better present than Jerusalem? And why Allenby? Did the Prime Minister understand the significance of Allenby's name? Did he know that as a young man that Allenby had received a personal prophecy that he would be involved in the liberation of Jerusalem? Coincidence or divine intervention?

Allenby assumed command of the 200,000 man Egyptian Expeditionary Forces on June 29, 1917. He had less than five months to deliver Jerusalem as a Christmas present. His biggest obstacle, apart from the German-Turkish forces that occupied Palestine, was water.

Highlighting the importance of water was a curious Arab prophecy to the effect that the Turks would be driven from Jerusalem only "when a prophet of the Lord brought the waters of the Nile to Palestine." And this Allenby did with a pipeline across the Sinai that brought water to the boundaries of Palestine. Additionally, Allenby had thirty thousand camels assigned to hauling water.

Even this remarkable logistical effort could only fully support Allenby's striking force's requirement for water as far as Beersheba. If Jerusalem by Christmas was to become a reality, then Turkish held Beersheba must be taken with its wells intact.

In the ensuing battle for Beersheba a charge in the last hour of daylight by a brigade of Australian Light Horse rode over the Turkish defenders, and entered the town. The fruits of this gallant exploit were that the wells were secured almost intact, although all the wells had been prepared for demolition. The charge had saved the wells. And, without the wells further operations might have suffered fatal delay. Beersheba had fallen on October 31st. It was still possible to reach Jerusalem by Christmas.

The month of November was consumed pursuing the Turks along the Plain of Philistia north to the main Jerusalem-Nablus road. This action was to cut the Turk's principal line of supply, and force the Turks to evacuate Jerusalem. Allenby was determined, to the greatest extent possible, to avoid any fighting in the vicinity of Jerusalem.

The march on Jerusalem was not without its incidents and

miracles. Late on the afternoon of November 28th the retirement of the British 22nd Yeomanry Brigade was aided by a mysterious phenomenon. As the sun had once "stood still" in the Biblical Valley of Ajalon, so it did again that night in the same location. The setting sun caused a reddish glow throughout the Turkish positions while allowing a peaceful Yeomanry retreat through the shadows on the hillsides of the rising moon.

By December 8th Allenby had carried the principal Turkish defenses west of Jerusalem, and had positioned three divisions in a horseshoe around the city. He deliberately left the Turkish defenders a way out (the Dung Gate) hoping that they could be encouraged to leave the city without a fight.

"Now Is The Time For You To Leave Jerusalem"

The encouragement came as leaflets dropped on the Turkish defenders by a Royal Air Force Squadron. The leaflets, printed in Arabic, read; "Now is the time for you to leave Jerusalem" signed Allenby.

Now for some extremely interesting notes: The Royal Air Force Squadron's motto was: "I will spread my wings and keep my promises." And, Allenby translated to Arabic literally is *alla nabi*, "Allah Prophet" or anglicized: "Prophet of Allah." Again, coincidences or divine intervention?

You will probably not be surprised to learn that the leaflets were effective. By the next morning, December 9th, the Turkish soldiers were gone, and the Mayor of Jerusalem set out with a White Flag Party to surrender the city. However, surrendering the city was not as easy as might have been expected. The Mayor spent most of his morning simply trying to find someone to whom he could hand over the keys of the city. His first appeal was to two cooks of the 2/20th London who—having become lost during the night—blundered into Jerusalem in search of water. Flattered, but feeling unequal to the honor, the cooks declined. The Mayor's second offer was to Sergeants Harcomb and Sedgewick of the 1/19th London, and though they had their picture taken with the Mayor and his party, they too declined the honor. Next, two officers of the 60th Division Artillery declined. Then Colonel Bayley of the 30th Brigade received the Mayor's appeal. Bayley contacted Brigadier Watson of the 180th Brigade, who contacted Lieutenant-General Chetwode, commander of the 20th Corp, who sent Major-General Shea of the 60th Division to accept the surrender—on behalf of General Allenby.

Confused, but undaunted, four hundred years of Turkish rule in the Holy City had ended. Jerusalem was once again under the political control of forces who, served the God of Abraham, Isaac and Jacob. The day of deliverance was not Christmas Day, but the first day of the Feast of Chanukkah.

Was this Marx brothers surrender skit and the date another Divine signature? Was the Squadron motto, "I will spread my wings and keep my promises" a coincidence? And, was the fact that the name Allenby translated into Arabic as, "Prophet of Allah," another coincidence?

Also, what about the sun standing still in the Valley of Ajalon? The Arab prophecy that the Turks would be driven from Jerusalem only "when a prophet of the Lord brought the waters of the Nile to Palestine." And, that as a young man Allenby had received a personal prophecy that he would be involved in the liberation of Jerusalem?

Another major coincidence was that the reading in every Anglican Church in the world (Church of England) for December 9th was Isaiah 31, "Surely, the Lord of hosts had come down and waged war on Mount Zion and on its hill. Like flying birds the Lord had protected Jerusalem. He had protected and delivered it, He had passed over and rescued it."

The Holy One of Israel had performed His word with an uncanny exactness. And, while He made it clear that it was His hand giving victory, He had used men in accomplishing His objectives. Just as He did with Moses at the Red Sea, Joshua at the Jordan and Jericho, and Gideon in his battle with Midian, etc., etc.

Scripture and history are clear. Yahveh works with man in fulfilling biblical prophecy!

Could Yahveh Be Working With Ephraim As He Did With Judah?

We started out by asking can we learn from the regathering of Judah. We have looked at prophecies and three key episodes in which Yahveh used men to greatly influence the regathering of Judah and the establishment of the State of Israel. The purpose was to determine whether Yahveh may be using similar events with the Ephraimites in fulfilling the prophecy of the two sticks.

Ephraim's Zionist Congress?

Could the First United Israel Conference held in Jamestown, New York in August of 1990, followed by several United Israel Conference's held at White Stone, Virginia in 1992, 1993 and 1994, and culminating in the Messianic Israel Alliance AMI 99 and AMI 2000 in Orlando, Florida, be Ephraim's counterpart of the Zionist World Congresses?

At these conferences, which began on the evening of Shabbat, two sticks, or candles were lit, one for Ephraim and one for Judah. At the end of Shabbat, an Ephraimite and a Judahite used the two Sabbath lights to light a Havdalah candle (two candles twisted into one). Then the two individual lights were extinguished, leaving a single united light.

These Conferences can and should give Ephraimites the same heart that the early Zionist meetings gave Judah.

These early conferences have grown. [86]

---

[86] In 1999 the Messianic Israel Alliance held its first Ami (People) Conference in Orlando, Florida.
(continued...)

Ephraim's Balfour Declaration?

Now for an Ephraimite's Balfour Declaration. Remember that Balfour, an Ephraimite, wrote a letter to Lord Rothschild, a Judahite. Therefore, let us read an excerpt from a personal letter, written in the late Eighties, from Rabbi Yechiel Eckstein to Batya and Angus Wootten:

"I have such a high regard for you both and appreciate your ministry . . . Batya, in my opinion, you really make a very solid theological argument in your book, *In Search of Israel,* for the idea that the olive tree of Israel has two branches representing the two witnesses of Ephraim and Judah i.e. Christianity and Judaism. **It is one I can essentially affirm** though admittedly you have your hands full trying to convince Christians of that. Please do not hesitate to call if I can help you in any way. You are both on my heart and I pray for your success and well-being."

Yechiel Eckstein, an Orthodox Jewish Rabbi, is the Founder and President of the *International Fellowship Of Christians and Jews*— a Jewish organization that has the specific mission to encourage Christian and Jewish fellowship.

Batya and Angus are Co-founders and Directors of House of David (which was/is the foundation for Messianic Israel Ministries, and the Messianic Israel Alliance). They have the mission to teach about the two houses of Israel, to encourage Believers to rediscover their Israelite roots, and to promote efforts to restore the Kingdom to Israel.

Balfour's statements that "His Majesty's Government view with favor the establishment in Palestine of a national home for the Jewish people, and will use their best endeavors to facilitate the achievements of this object," gave heart to the Zionist of that day.

---

86 (...continued)
And Ami 2000, also held in Orlando, was attended by Messianic Israelites from around the world.

Surely Yechiel's statement, "Your solid theological argument that the two branches of the Olive Tree, and the two witnesses, are Ephraim and Judah i.e. Christianity and Judaism, is one I can essentially affirm—and, please do not hesitate to call if I can help you in any way"—should give heart to the Ephraimites.

Judah A Help To Ephraim?

Just as the British liberation and occupation of Palestine prepared the way for the establishment of the State of Israel, Judah is also preparing the way for Ephraim. This is true, even though Judah may not understand, or realize, his complete purpose any more than the British realized their God-given purpose.

An excellent example, of how Judah is helping Ephraim to rediscover his identity, is the fact that Judah provided the funds necessary to cover the cost printing of *The Olive Tree of Israel* by Batya Ruth Wootten 1992. At that time, this book was one of the best tools available for instructing Ephraim as to his true identity. And, instructing Ephraimites is what it is all about. For Jeremiah says:

"I have surely heard Ephraim grieving,
'Thou hast chastised (punished) me, and I was chastised,
Like and untrained calf;
Bring me back that I may be restored,
For Thou art the Lord my God.
For after I turned back, I repented;
And after I was **instructed**, I smote on my thigh;
I was ashamed, and also humiliated'" (Jeremiah
31:18,19).

Have you every "smote" yourself on the thigh and said, "How could I have **missed it?**" or "Now I **understand,** or now I **see?**"

This is the time for the **instruction** of Ephraim, so he can see how he **missed it,** and so that he can **understand** and be able to **see!**

And who does Yahveh plan to use to instruct Ephraim? We can

find the answer in our mirrors!

What then are we to do? We are to instruct Ephraim!

Remember, Yahveh's ultimate plan is to bring heaven to His people on earth. It is not to bring His people on earth to His Kingdom in Heaven. We are not of this world. Therefore, our treasures and our hope are in the Kingdom to come. So, we should devote a significant portion of our time, effort and resources to the return of the Lord and the establishment of His Kingdom on earth.

The rewards of an overcomer will not go to the lukewarm, those so wrapped up in the affairs of this world that they become part of it. Rather, the overcomers will be those who are on fire to serve the Lord. It is for each of us, great or small, young or old, rich or poor, man or woman, black or white, to be zealous for the Lord. And, to be alert to His return, and open to the opportunities that He gives each of us to serve His purposes.

Restoring Israel's Kingdom

16

Restoring The
Kingdom To Israel

Is *now* the time for the restoration of Israel's kingdom? Will
Yeshua return in *our* generation? To make these questions
more personal, we ask:

Will *you* live to see His return?

All Believers affirm that this age-ending event will take place at
some point in history. However, if we personally believe that the
culmination of history is at hand, surely it will dramatically change
our priorities, how we utilize our time and resources. Since we
were instructed by our Master to remain on the alert for His return,
we do not want to be found unprepared when He arrives. Instead,
we want to be commended for fulfilling our assigned position.

"But of that day or hour no one knows, not even the angels in
heaven, nor the Son, but the Father alone. Take heed, keep on the
alert; for you do not know when the appointed time is. It is like a
man, away on a journey, who upon leaving his house and putting
his slaves in charge, assigning to each one his task, also

commanded the doorkeeper to stay on the alert Therefore, be on the alert—for you do not know when the master of the house is coming, whether in the evening, at midnight, at cockcrowing, or in the morning—lest he come suddenly and find you asleep. And what I say to you I say to all, 'Be on the alert!'" (Mark 13:32-37).

Since it is unlikely that we will accomplish a task that we have not even recognized as being ours to do, let alone prepared ourselves to do it, we each need to establish in our own hearts the basis upon which we will determine our life missions and goals. Will we base them on an assumption that our generation is just running another leg of the race? Or, will we give place to the possibility that we could be the ones to cross the finish line?

Should we give place in our life planning for the possibility that we will live to see Yeshua return? Further, if we do embrace this hope, what should we do about it?

Surely our generation is closer to the Messiah's return and the establishment of His Kingdom here on earth than any previous generation! But, how close is that? Also, what is so special about this generation that we should believe we are *the* generation"—the one that will experience the "favorable year of the Lord"?

Thus far we have addressed this question several times and, the conclusion remains that, in the year 2000 we are in the fourth year of the fiftieth generation from Yeshua, and the one hundredth generation from the flood. And, our generation is not only the Jubilee Generation, it is also, as we have shown, the generation that is experiencing the end of Israel's (Ephraim's) punishment. For, after twenty-seven-hundred and thirty years, Ephraim's veil of blindness to his heritage is at last being removed. He is being freed from the sentence of being a people who were "not a people." [87]

What Time Is It?

Is time running out? Is the end of the final hours of time Yahveh

---

[87] Hos 1:9, Eze 4:3-6; Lev 26:18,21; Isa 8:14; Rom 11:25; Gen 48:19.

allotted to man for his earthly sojourn about to strike? Is His prophetic timepiece about to strike *"Return"*?

If we have a more clear understanding of what time it is on Yahveh's prophetic timepiece, we can better answer these questions. We also can come closer to determining the time of Yeshua's return. For there is a Divine clock that is slowly but surely ticking off the time remaining before the return of the Messiah and the establishment of His Kingdom here on earth.

To determine the hour we note several prophetic events that serve as indicators of Divine time. For example, the events foretold by Zechariah in the latter chapters of his Book are obviously end time events. And, if we are living in a time when these events are unfolding, it is reasonable to assume that we are living in the end times. Even so, we are seeing the fulfillment of Zechariah's warning that Jerusalem would become a cup of trembling and a burdensome stone to all people (12:2-3).

One Scripture that pinpoints prophetic time is the seventh verse of the twelfth chapter of Zechariah:

"The Lord also shall save the tents of Judah first, that the glory of the house of David and the glory of the inhabitants of Jerusalem do not magnify themselves against Judah."

A question that begs to be asked here is:

If Judah is "first," who is *second*? To have a *first* implies that there is a *second*. So, if Yahveh is saving the tents of Judah *first*, then whose tents will be saved next?

It would be helpful if Zechariah had used more readily defined "labels" in chapter twelve. (Perhaps he did not because many end time events were destined to fall in the category of "mysteries.") However, we do know how to apply Zechariah's label, "Judah." With it, he speaks of those who we know as "the Jewish people." But what about the "house of David," and, "the inhabitants of Jerusalem"? To whom was the prophet applying these titles?

Normally, when we think of the "house of David," we think of the tribe of Judah, since David was from the tribe of Judah. But we cannot make that assumption here. For if Zechariah were using Judah and the house of David as equivalent terms, then the verse would read: "The Lord also shall save the tents of Judah or the house of David first, that the glory of the house of David or Judah, and the glory of the inhabitants of Jerusalem do not magnify themselves against Judah or the house of David."

That doesn't make sense. So, Zechariah must have had a different meaning of these three terms (labels) in mind.

But, what did he envision?

The answer could well be that Zechariah based his label on the fact that David was King over "all Israel" (1 Chronicles 12:38; 14:8), and that David's kingdom, or house, consisted of *all twelve tribes of Israel*—even as the kingdom of Israel, or the house of Israel, consisted of all twelve tribes. Thus, during David's kingship, "the house of David," and "the house of Israel," were synonymous—they were words or terms that had similar meanings.

But, after the death of David's son, Solomon, division came to Israel. Yahveh divided Israel into Northern and Southern kingdoms. It happened when the northern ten tribes, or Ephraim, rebelled against the house of David (which was under the imprudent rule of Solomon's son, Rehoboam). However, the Ephraimites retained the title of "Israel." The two southern tribes were known as "Judah," and it is written that, they alone "followed the house of David" (1 Kings 12:19,20; 2 Chronicles 10:19; 11:4).

But note, this means, from that time on, Judah and the house of David *did not represent all twelve tribes!* And, to understand Zechariah's prophecy, it is imperative that we realize that in their *ideal* state, the "house of David" and "all Israel" would include *all twelve tribes!*

Only in this way can these two terms or titles truly represent David's restored kingdom. Again, David was King over *all* Israel: "*All* Israel and Judah loved David" (1 Samuel 18:16).

When Zechariah wrote his prophecy, the titles "
Judah," and "the house of David," were—in the minds of

many—synonymous. Nonetheless, it is evident that Zechariah was not describing the divided people of Israel as they were in his day. Instead, he was looking to the future, he was looking to a point in time that would have to first begin with a certain Messianic era. Zechariah was looking forward to a time that began...

✡ When Zacharias (John the Baptist's father), being inspired by the Holy Spirit, prophesied: "Blessed be Yahveh Elohim of Israel, for He has visited us and accomplished redemption for His people and raised up a horn of salvation for us in the house of David His servant" (Luke 1:67-69).

✡ When the angel Gabriel informed Mary that she would bear a Son whom she would name Yeshua, and that He would be great, and would be called the Son of the Most High; and that the Almighty would give Him the throne of His father David; and that He would reign over the house of Jacob (Israel) forever; and that His kingdom would have no end" (Luke 1:25-33).

✡ When James, at the only recorded meeting of the Jerusalem Council, said, "Simeon has related how Yahveh first concerned Himself about taking from among the nations a people to bear His name. And this is in agreement with the predictions of the Prophets, as it is written: 'After this I will return and set up again the house of David which has fallen down'" (Acts 15:14-16).

Now James would not be describing David's house as having fallen down if Herod's temple and the Jewish hierarchy of the first century fully represented the house of David. Apparently James and Zechariah were looking for something else.

Zechariah was describing a time when the House of David would depict those following after Yeshua, the Greater Son of David, the Messiah of *all* Israel. He foretold a day when once more the labels, "the house of David," and "the house of Israel," would begin to be truly synonymous. He spoke of the day when Messiah would begin to gather together those who are His own.

Zechariah was prophesying about the restoration of "all Israel," and he was applying the term "Judah" to the Jewish people of today. But, that means two problems remain:

To whom do we apply the term "the house of David"? Who are "the inhabitants of Jerusalem"?

There are several possible answers to these intriguing questions.

We know that Yeshua is presently seated on David's throne in the Kingdom in Heaven.[88] From there, He rules over countless numbers of redeemed Israelites from all twelve tribes. And, among these redeemed ones who have gone before us, having completed their sojourn on earth, there is no argument over who sits on David's throne, nor over who inhabits the kingdom, nor over the kingdom's territory.

The Hallmark of The House of David

However, Zechariah reveals that at least a portion of the house of David is represented on earth during the period about which he writes. But, if so, what hallmark would distinguish those on earth who are counted with the house of David from Judah and the inhabitants of Jerusalem?

Perhaps it is that those whom Zechariah counts with an earthly house of David, like their heavenly kingdom counterparts, understand the identity of the King, people, and territory.

Zechariah's division is not based on who the people are, for all are Israelites, and therefore, potentially part of the ideal, or restored house of David. Further, it appears that Zechariah sees the division that exists among these peoples as something that is keeping them from fully restoring the fallen house of David.

So, we offer one possible answer to these divisions—that we might help end Israel's division and establish Yeshua's Kingdom on earth:

---

88 Yeshua has already "sat down" on His throne. His Kingdom is now, and yet, is to come. Sat down: Luke 1:32; Heb 1:3; 10:12; 12:2; Rev 3:21. Kingdom to come: Matt 6:10; Luke 11:2; also see Isa 27:9; 55:3; 59:21; Jer 31:31-34; 32:38-40; Heb 8:8-12; 10:16.

✡ Those of Judah are mentioned as a separate group because they are blinded to Him who sits on the throne of David.

✡ "The *inhabitants* of *Jerusalem*" is inter-changeable with "those who *dwell* in *Zion*." [89] These are citizens of Zion, "a people of peace," for they have recognized that Yeshua, the greater Son of David, is the Prince of Peace, and so they belong to the "Israel of God" (Isaiah 9:6; Galatians 6:16; Ephesians 2:11-22). However, they are a separate group, because as part of the people of Ephraim, they remain blinded to their heritage as part of the people of Israel.[90]

✡ Those of "the house of David" are Israelites from all twelve tribes who are being gathered by the Shepherd God (Ezekiel 34). And they, like their brethren in the heavenly kingdom, understand the identity of their King, His people, and His territory. They see that they are "one family" (Ephesians 3:14-21).[91]

Zechariah's Three Groups
Ezekiel's Two Sticks

But how do Zechariah's three groups of peoples fit with Ezekiel's "two sticks"? For Ezekiel, like Zechariah, does divide the people of Israel, but Ezekiel's division is a twofold division. One part consists of the "stick of Judah and his companions of Israel," and the other part is made up of "the stick of Joseph, which is in the hands of Ephraim, and his companions of Israel,"

Essentially, this division recognizes the blindness or hardness that has happened to all Israel (Romans 11:25). For those identified with Judah are for the most part blinded to the identity of the Messiah of Israel. And, those identified with Ephraim are for the most part blinded to their heritage as Israelites,

Using Ezekiel's definition, we could identify Zechariah's division as follows:

The "tents of Judah" would be the "stick of Judah and his

---

89 See Jer 3:14; Psa 9:11; Isa 10:21,24; Joel 3:17, 3:21; Zech 12:5-8.
90 See Gen 48:19; Hos 1-2; Isa 8:14; Rom 11:25. Also see *The Hope of Messianic Israel*, this issue.
91 See the Herald, *The Redemption of Jerusalem*, Vol. Six, Book Five.

companions of Israel," represented today by the Jewish people. The "house of David" and the "inhabitants of Jerusalem," being part of Israel, and Believers in Messiah, yet according to Zechariah are not of Judah, would necessarily be counted with the "stick of Ephraim." And Ephraim is represented today by those lost sheep of the house of Israel who acknowledge that Yeshua is the Messiah of Israel (Ezekiel 37:15-21; Matthew 14:24; Ephesians 2:11-22).

Both Zechariah and Ezekiel prophesied about the return and reunion of Israel. And, Judah's return to "the land," and Ephraim's return to his heritage, both indicate the dawning of a new day.

Why Are The Tents of Judah First?

The return of millions of Jewish people to "the promised land" in this century is the literal fulfillment of Zechariah's prophecy that the tents of Judah would be saved first! (12:2). The King James Version renders this key verse, "The Lord also shall save the tents of Judah first, that the glory of the house of David and the glory of the inhabitants of Jerusalem do not magnify themselves against Judah." However, the Jerusalem Bible rendering is more appropriately, "Yahveh will save the tents of Judah first to forestall the arrogance of the house of David and the arrogance of the citizens of Jerusalem from rising to the detriment of Judah."

Over the centuries, the Church, seeing herself as the "new Israel," or "spiritual Israel," has, to put it mildly, been arrogant towards the Jewish people.

Then, following the murder of six million Jews in the holocaust, the nations of the world were supportive (for a brief season) of the establishment of a Jewish State in 1948. Throughout their planning for statehood in 1947-48, those who had been known as Jews for twenty-five hundred years primarily referred to their forthcoming state as "Judea." But at the last moment, the decision was made to name the new Jewish State "Israel." [92]

---

92 Many names were proposed: Zion, Judea, Ivriya, etc. "Postage stamps printed in advance...were
(continued...)

Not only was this new Jewish state named Israel, it was quite apparent that the God of Israel was supporting it. For, miracles occurred during the formative years of this tiny State that equaled many of the miracles recorded in biblical history.

However, the reaction of many in the "Church" to these events was to have an identity crisis. If the Jewish people were Israel, then who was "the Church"? There were several major theological responses to this question. One was to continue to ignore any need for physical identity, and to concentrate completely on a spiritual identity, which identity was based strictly on what one "believed."

We can define this attitude by examining an answer most Christians would give to the question: "How would you explain your relationship with your God?" Atypically, that answer is:

"It is based on what I believe."

In other words, it has absolutely nothing to do with who they are, nor who their ancestors were. It is strictly based on individual relationship which is the result of a personal commitment to God, which in turn is based on what they believe.

Compare this attitude with the typical answer of an orthodox Jew to the same question:

"My relationship with my God, the God of Abraham, Isaac and Jacob, is based on the fact that I am a Jew, and my ancestors were Jewish [they mistakenly think it is based on their maternal ancestors]. In other words, I am part of the people of Israel, therefore I have a relationship with the God of Israel."

Belief, in this case, does not play any part in determining "Jewishness"—other than one negative chord: a Jew cannot accept Yeshua as his Messiah and be recognized by the State of Israel and by most Jewish non-believers in Messiah as still being part of the Jewish people.

Thus, there is one major difference between Christian and Jewish

---

92 (...continued)
marked 'Doar Ivri' (Hebrew mail) since no one knew what the name would be." *Israel: A History* by Martin Gilbert, 1998, William Morrow & Company, *The War of Independence May 1948 to the first truce*, p 187.

concepts of God. The Jew sees his God as the Holy One of Israel, and He is primarily seen in the context of His dealings with His people. He is the God of the patriarchs, the God who delivered his forefathers from Egypt, and, the God who has maintained His people to this day.

On the other hand, the Christian sees God in His New Covenant context. To him, He is the God whose sacrifice on the cross is the ultimate atonement for "whosoever will believe."

Another Christian response to his identity crisis was the popularization in the late sixties of an eighteenth century pre-tribulation rapture doctrine—wherein Yahveh supposedly bails the Church out of tribulation, but leaves the Jewish people to face the music.

So it is that the bulk of Christendom lumbers along, oblivious to history, oblivious to their heritage, and oblivious to their mandate to help reestablish the kingdom of Israel here on earth.

Sadly, many Ephraimite Believers remain blind to their call to be "watchmen" for all Israel (Hosea 9:8; Jeremiah 31:6). And, they have not applied Messiah's healing balm to Israel's scar of division. Neither have they responded to the call to work with Judah, to help rebuild the old waste places, to raise up the foundations of the generations —and thus to be called—a repairer of the ancient breach in Israel—a restorer of paths in which to dwell (Isaiah 58:12; Romans 11:11).

Fortunately, He who gives sight to the blind and causes the lame to walk, and the deaf to hear, is now in the process of awakening "all Israel" to their common destiny in this late, and fateful hour.

Repairing The Breech

In this generation, as in all generations, the Holy One of Israel has His "seven thousand in Israel" (1 Kings 19:18; Revelation 7:4; 14:1).[93] But, could His seven thousand in this generation be those

---

93 Undoubtedly these 7,000, like the 144,000 of Revelation, are figurative numbers. But, they do indicate
(continued...)

whom Zechariah labels as being of "the house of David"? Could they be Israelites from all twelve tribes who are being gathered by the Shepherd God (Ezekiel 34)?

Yes they could. And they, like their heavenly kingdom brethren, understand the identity of their King, His people, and His territory. They see that Yahveh's Israel comprises "one family." They also understand that they yet have a part to play in fulfilling our Father's messianic vision.

The job of being a repairer and restorer is one that Ephraim, together with Judah—as the people of Messianic Israel—will in truth finish! For even now there are Ephraimites who seek to respond to Yahveh's call to once again be a "mighty man." As such, they work to restore the paths that will lead chosen Israel back to a redeemed promised land (Jeremiah 23:8; Zechariah 10:7-10). These Messianic forerunners realize the need to work to *implement* the reunion of Israel long ago *imputed* by Messiah's sacrifice in our behalf (1Corthiains 5:7; Ephesians 2:11-22).

The Restored Kingdom of Israel Will Not Be a Divided Kingdom!

Matthew, Mark and Luke stress the fact that any kingdom divided against itself is laid waste; and that any city or house divided against itself will not stand (Matthew 12:25; Mark 3:25; Luke 11:17).

But this means the reverse is also true:

"A unified kingdom will *not* be defeated."

"A united house *will* stand."

Full restoration of all Israel calls for the reunion of the house of Ephraim and the house of Judah. Likewise, the Jewish concept of a "national relationship" with the God of Israel, needs to be married with the Christian concept of an individual relationship with the

---

93 (...continued)
that the elect, chosen, remnant, are small in number when compared to the total population of the world.

God of Israel. For, those who ultimately dwell in Israel's restored Kingdom will have necessarily experienced both individual and national salvation!

The Shepherd God is giving those of Messianic Israel the opportunity to help gather His lost sheep, that He might have His heart's desire—which is to have a people for His own possession. The end-time remnant is now being gathered as foretold by Jeremiah:

"Then I Myself shall gather the remnant of My flock out of all the countries where I have driven them and shall bring them back to their pasture; and they will be fruitful and multiply....nor will any be missing," declares the Lord.

"'Behold, days are coming,' declares Yahveh, 'When I will raise up for David a righteous Branch; and He will reign as king and act wisely and do justice and righteousness in the land. In His days Judah will be saved, and Israel will dwell securely...'"

And at that time, "They will no longer say, 'As Yahveh lives, who brought up the sons of Israel from the land of Egypt,' but, 'as Yahveh lives, who brought up and led back the descendants of the household of Israel from the north land and from all the countries where I had driven them.' Then they will live on their own soil" (Jeremiah 23:1-8).

There is no question that Yahveh will fulfill every jot and tittle of these prophecies to restore the kingdom to the twelve tribes of Israel.

The question is will all those whom He is calling respond to His call? Will they accept the job?

Know this, He who sits on David's throne has "finished" His work (John 17:4). He now waits for His people to finish the task He began long ago.

We are in the process of bringing back the tents of Judah, but that job is not yet done. Millions of Jewish people still need to return to their land. Moreover, true salvation will only come to them when they know the Messiah of Israel. And the plan of salvation is that Ephraim, the "wild" olive branch, must "provoke" Judah to "jealousy" (Genesis 48:19; Romans 11; Jeremiah 11:10,16; 2:18,21).

Beyond helping Judah, Ephraim also needs to awaken other sleeping Ephraimites to the truth of their own Israelite roots (Jeremiah 31:18,19).

In addition, Ephraim needs to be prepared in spirit to return to his own land (Hosea 1:10).

How much time is left to finish these enormous jobs?

We do not know for certain. However, we do know that, when our Master instructed us to remain on the alert for His return, He knew it would be difficult for us to determine the time of His return. And, we do not want to be off in our timing. So what are we to do?

The only safe and sure course of action is to remain on the alert for His return. For, it is far better to be prepared and not called upon, than to be called upon and found unprepared.

So let each of us determine our life mission and goals based on the very real possibility that we could be the generation destined to cross the finish line. Let us establish our goals knowing that these things will not only affect how we live this life, but will affect us for all eternity.

"Therefore, since we are surrounded by such a great cloud of witnesses, let us throw off everything that hinders and the sin that so easily entangles, and let us run with perseverance the race marked out for us. Let us fix our eyes on Yeshua, the author and perfecter of our faith, who for the joy set before him endured the cross, scorning its shame, and sat down at the right hand of the throne of God" (Hebrews 12:1-2).

Yes, run on, O victorious Israel!

Restoring Israel's Kingdom

17

The Messianic Vision

And the seventh angel sounded; and there were great voices in heaven, saying, The kingdoms of this world are become the kingdoms of our Adonai [Lord], and of his Mashiach [Anointed One]; and He shall reign for ever and ever" (Revelation 11:15).

How does the Holy One of Israel, the God of Abraham, Isaac and Jacob, plan to accomplish this age ending event? How will He realize His Messianic Vision of manifesting His presence—in His earthly Kingdom—in the midst of a **united** people? To reach this goal it is obvious that one of His larger challenges is "uniting His people Israel."

Let us examine this challenge as it currently exists. First and foremost we have the almost three-thousand year old division between the two houses of Israel: Judah and Ephraim, originally the Northern and Southern Kingdoms of Israel. This division is manifested in our day by the division between the Jewish people and Christians, or the Church.[94] Additionally, we have the divisions that exist among each of the houses.

On one hand we have the Church divided by laws and opinions

---

94 See *Who Is Israel?* for a complete history of the two houses of Israel.

into a multitude of denominations and cults with a vast smorgasbord of theology and doctrines. These divisions are a result of generation after generation of forefathers who to some extent, have forsaken the covenants of the Holy One Of Israel and following after other gods—the gods often being themselves or other men. For this reason, we have a multitude of divisions among a people who are blinded to their heritage and destiny.

On the other hand, we have the divisions among the Jewish people who are blinded to the identity of the Messiah of Israel. While their divisions are not as numerous as those among Ephraim, they currently tend to be deeper. The deepest rift is currently being manifested in the land of Israel between those who are supportive of the government policy of trading land for peace, and those who are adamantly against this sellout of their inheritance for what they see as a vain hope of a fragile and temporary peace.

One of the most telling examples of the divisions among the people of Israel was the assassination of Yitzhak Rabin, Prime Minister of Israel, at the hands of a fellow countryman, who claimed to be acting on orders from God. Accenting this division were two signs that hung from the eight-story apartment building where Rabin lived. One read: "No moving from the Golan." The other read: "Peace is my security." And on the day of Rabin's funeral, along the highway traveled by the open-backed Army command car carrying his coffin, religious Jews held out a sign with the biblical injunction: "Thou shalt not kill." But spray painted on a nearby lamppost were the words: "Rabin is a traitor."

The sign which read "Peace is my security" emphasizes the cause of division in the Jewish nation, because those who are against the "Peace Now" movement find it difficult to understand how anyone who has even a minimal comprehension of Scripture and the history of the nation of Israel could be supportive of a Government of Israel which supports the creation of a Philistine, or Palestinian State. Therefore, they conclude that those who support the so called "Peace Process," which has split the nation, do not have even a minimal comprehension of Scripture and history. Or, they are willing to disregard it as payment for pleasure and satisfaction NOW!

The "Now's"

That sign, which hung from the eight-story apartment building where Rabin lived, which read: "Peace is my security," typifies the attitude of those who seek satisfaction and gratification **now,** regardless of the future cost. These "Now" people have placed their faith and future security in a man-made peace process, and in the likes of Yaser Arafat and the PLO, rather than placing their faith and hopes in the Holy One of Israel and in His Word. This is true not only for the "Now's" among the Jewish people, but for the "Now's" among the Church, meaning those who place their faith and future in man's ways, organizations and words, both secular and non-secular, rather than placing their faith and hopes for the future in Israel's Holy One, and in His promises.

When we look at the countless divisions, we can see that Yahveh has a big job on His hands in meeting the formidable, if not impossible challenge of healing the divisions that exist among His people. We can be thankful that "nothing will be impossible with Yahveh" (Luke 1:37). For we know that the fulfillment of His Messianic Vision has its appointed time, at the end it shall speak, and not lie: though it tarry, wait for it; because it will surely come, it will not tarry (Habakkuk 2:3)

A Common Denominator

How will Yahveh accomplish this awesome task of healing the divisions among His fractured people?

What we need to make a "whole nation" from the countless "fractions" of the people of Israel is a common denominator.

To add the fractions of 3/4 + 1/3 one must find a common denominator. Otherwise, the two cannot be added together and made one. First we must determine the lowest common denominator. The next step is to convert the denominators of the fractions we are adding to their common denominator. Then, it will also be necessary to change the numerator so the value of the fraction remains unchanged. We do this on the basis of equality—whatever we do to the denominator we do also to the numerator.

To determine the lowest common denominator in this case, we calculate the lowest whole number divisible by both 4 and 3. In this example, the lowest common denominator is 12.

In the case of the fraction 3/4, it is necessary to multiply the denominator 4, by 3, to obtain the common denominator of 12. Then, to preserve the value of the fraction we also multiply the numerator 3 by 3, thus obtaining a new numerator of 9. So, our new fraction is 9/12, which has the same value as the old fraction of 3/4.

We follow this same procedure with the fraction 1/3, multiplying both the numerator and the denominator by 4, and obtain a new fraction of 4/12. However, we can now add 9/12 and 4/12 together, and we obtain a product of 13/12, or expressed as a whole number: 1 and 1/12. In either case they are no longer two fractions, but now are one whole.

Applying this same concept to the fractured people of Israel is a little more difficult, because each fraction tends to see itself as a whole. So, the first step for those among the Jewish and Christian peoples who have been given the unmerited grace to know, or even suspect, that they are part of the **whole** house of Israel, is to realize that **they are a fraction and not a whole**. No longer should they see themselves as Christians and Jews, but rather they must see themselves as Christian/Israelites and Jewish/Israelites, or Ephraim/Israel and Judah/Israel.

No longer should the Jewish people see themselves as Orthodox, Conservative, Reform, and Messianic Jews, but rather they must see themselves as Orthodox Jewish Israelites, Conservative Jewish Israelites, Reform Jewish Israelites, and Messianic Jewish Israelites.

No longer should those Christians who have had the blindness to their heritage removed be satisfied with the label of a denomination. Those who do not feel comfortable with seeing themselves as Messianic Israelites, or Ephraim Israel, should at the very least see themselves as Catholic Israelites, Baptist Israelites, Assembly of God Israelites, or _____ Israelites.

And what will the end results be of adding 9/12 + 4/12? It will equal 13/12. The nine tribes (9/12) of Ephraim will be joined with the four tribes (4/12) of Judah to form the whole (13/12) house of Israel. (For the **sake of this illustration only**, we have considered that, for the most part the tribes of Reuben, Zebulun, Issachar, Dan, Gad, Asher, Naphtali, Ephraim, Manasseh were found among the Ephraimites, and that the tribes of Simeon [lost among Judah], Levi, Judah, and Benjamin were for the most part found among the Judahites.)[95]

It is easy to see that the first task (hopefully, we each see it as our task) is to instruct those whom the Holy One of Israel is calling through His Holy Spirit, to an understanding of their heritage and of the fact that they are a fraction, not a whole entity. And, that they need to insure that their denominator is the common, and equal, denominator of being an Israelite.

Jeremiah shows us where to start:
"I have surely heard Ephraim grieving,
Thou hast chastised (punished) me, and I was chastised,
 Like an untrained calf;
Bring me back that I may be restored,
For Thou art Yahveh, the Lord my God.
For after I turned back, I repented;
And after I was **instructed**, I smote on my thigh;
I was ashamed, and also humiliated" (Jeremiah 31:18,19).

People the world over are beginning to "smote" themselves on the thigh and say, "How could I have missed it?" or "Now I

---

95 We recognize that the poplar division has the tribe of Simeon counted with Ephraim.

understand,"or, "Now I **see**"?

For **now** is the time for the **instruction** of Ephraim, so that he can **see** how he **missed it,** and so that he can **understand** and be able to **see!**

Once we are instructed, we are then ready to follow in the footsteps of the Apostle Paul. Paul, in Romans Eleven, saw that a combination of Jewish acceptance of Messiah, as well as the ingathering of the full number of Gentiles from among the nations, would herald this end-time kingdom. This Apostle to the nations was willing to pay the high price of his own salvation to gain the reward of a restored kingdom of Israel. His ministry to the "Gentiles," or "wild olive branches" of Israel, had the added benefit of making the Jews jealous, that some of them might be saved. (See *The Olive Tree of Israel.*)

Paul wanted those of the "wild" side of the family tree of Israel (Jeremiah 11:10,16; 2:18,21; Romans 11), meaning the non-Jews who were being grafted into the "Rich Root" of the Olive Tree of Israel which "Root is Yeshua (Revelation 22:16)—as well as those Jewish branches that remained on Messiah's tree—*together*, to follow in his footsteps. Unfortunately, in the nineteen hundred years since Paul's witness, both houses, one believing in a present Messiah and one in a future Messiah, have contributed to building walls of misunderstanding. One solid wall that has been built by the non-Jews is that of presenting a Greek/Romanized Christ in a paganized smorgasbord of theologies. This "Greek Jesus" is much more difficult for Jews to accept than is the "Hebrew Yeshua," because this "Hebrew" image conforms more closely to their image of the Messiah.

So the plan is that Ephraim will begin by reuniting the remnant in his house, and then, and only then, can the reunification of both houses take place. As Ephraim searches for the truth of his roots he will receive back from his brother Judah many ancient truths about his heritage. He will then be better prepared to reach out to his brother in love and mercy. For it is only when *both* houses are treated with the dignity and equality that they rightfully deserve, that the true message of Messiah will be demonstrated in the earth.

Loving Your Brother

Chapter 12, *Why Ephraim Should Know More About Judah*, outlined the basic foundation that Yahveh has laid to accomplish His ultimate goal of a united people, and it emphasized that knowing and loving your brother was a prerequisite to reuniting the whole house of Israel.

This chapter leaned heavily on input from Yechiel Eckstein, an Orthodox Jewish Rabbi, Founder and President of the *International Fellowship Of Christians and Jews* (The only Jewish organization [that we know of] that has the specific mission of encouraging Christian and Jewish fellowship). Yechiel gave valuable insight into where Judah is today, and how Judah sees Ephraim. Also, Yechiel evaluates Jewish attitudes toward Ephraimites, and some of the ways that Judah is reaching out to Ephraim. The chapter ends with an appeal: "Quite naturally, there are profound theological differences between the Believer and the Orthodox Jew. Nevertheless, like Yechiel and the eighty-six year old black Baptist minister from Virginia, we have much in common. However, if we, as Ephraimites, are going to successfully lead the way in making the house of Judah and the house of Ephraim the **united** house of Israel, then we must concentrate on hearing our brother, and learning how to love him."

A Word To The Wise

In seeking to love the people of Judah, let us not add to the problem by mistreating the people of Ephraim. Let us be wise enough to treat both houses with absolute equity. Let us judge both peoples with righteous, absolutely equitable, judgement, for only then will they reunite.

How do Ephraimites successfully lead the way in making the

house of Judah and the house of Ephraim the *united* house of Israel? As we pointed out, one of the keys to success is hearing our brother, and learning how to love him by treating him with absolute equity. Treat him in the manner in which you would desire to be treated if roles were reversed.

Above all, remember that the removal of the partial hardening and blindness that has happened to Israel—Judah's inability to recognize and accept his Messiah, and Ephraim's inability to recognize and accept his heritage—which Paul states is a prerequisite for the return of the Deliverer who will remove ungodliness from Jacob, is a work of the Holy Spirit! (Romans 11:25-26).

Hindsight is far clearer than foresight, so it is easy to outline what has happened in the past, and to list principles that must be followed to put the two houses back together. But what is the game plan for today? What is Yahveh going to do now? And, most importantly, how might He use us? The bottom line being what does the Holy One of Israel expect of me! And, when all is said and done and my earthly sojourn is completed—for what will I be held accountable?

These are a lot of questions to answer and, for the "Now's," they are questions that will never be seriously addressed. However, for those who follow after the "Prophet likened unto Moses," and in the footsteps of His disciples, they are questions we must each answer to the best of our ability. And, once we have received a response, we must follow through and do our individual parts to implement the game plan.

A Search For Answers

Where do we start in our search for answers? In Chapter 17, *Mandate for Ephraim*, we quoted from a letter that Batya and Angus Wootten received from Rabbi Yechiel Eckstein. Once again, let us look to Yechiel's insight and take another look at his letter:

"I have such a high regard for you both and appreciate your ministry . . . Batya, in my opinion, you really make a very solid theological argument for the idea that the olive tree of Israel has two branches representing the two witnesses of Ephraim and Judah i.e. Christianity and Judaism. It is one I can essentially affirm though admittedly you have your hands full trying to convince Christians of that. Please do not hesitate to call if I can help you in any way. You are both on my heart and I pray for your success and well-being."

Yechiel's statement—"you will have your hands full trying to convince Christians of the truth that the olive tree of Israel has two branches representing the two witnesses of Ephraim and Judah i.e. Christianity and Judaism"—has proven to be accurate. Yet, realizing that Ephraim has little hope of fulfilling one of his key mandates (that of winning his brother to Messiah, by provoking him to jealousy), until he realizes who he is, leads us to recall another of Yechiel's nuggets of wisdom. By the way, in the natural, it will take quite a bit of doing on Ephraim's part to make a Judahite like Yechiel jealous of how he perceives the Christian's relationship with the God of Abraham, Isaac and Jacob. In fact, some Christians who meet Yechiel quickly become jealous of the relationship that they perceive that he has with the God of Abraham, Isaac and Jacob. So admittedly, Ephraim has quite a way to go before this situation is reversed!

Now for Yechiel's nugget of wisdom: "It is not for me, an Orthodox Jewish Rabbi, to tell you Christians how to convert Jews, but if you have been doing something that has not worked for two-thousand years, then it is about time you tried something else."

We cannot argue with this advice. If something does not work, we should quit doing it, and try something else.

Thomas Edison, in his efforts to develop an electric light bulb had many attempts that failed. Had he kept on repeating a failed experiment, he would never have come up with a successful light bulb. Instead, he kept moving forward, because he considered each of those failed attempts a success of sorts; in that he learned from each failure, the primary lesson being what did not work.

So Ephraim's starting point in his search for answers is to realize that he has not as yet developed a light bulb that works. He does not yet have a way to really provoke Judah to jealousy, meaning being jealous to the extent that Judah wants to be reunited with his brother Ephraim.

Who Told You?

The second step we need to take in our reunion plan is to be sure as we launch another experiment—hopefully Yahveh's solution—that we are not building on a faulty foundation. In Chapter 7, *Who Told You?* we pointed out: "We must be concerned about the consequences of being deceived by errors and misconceptions, for lies bring captivity and death, while truth brings freedom and life (John 8:21,32,44; 2 Timothy 2:26). With such high stakes riding on what we believe, we must perpetually ask ourselves: Is what we believe true? Is the foundation on which we are building our understanding of Yahveh, and His people of Israel one of truthfulness?

We must not invent new kinds of wisdom, then use it to build on a faulty foundation. Instead, we must go back to ground zero and build on ancient and original truths!

A Level Playing Field

So, in answering the all-important questions: "What is the game plan today? What is Yahveh going to do now? And, how might He use us? We need to go back to ground zero and to begin to build on original Scriptural truths! **We must refrain from the temptation to continue building on foundations that do not have the ultimate goal of uniting the people of Israel, both Judah and Ephraim in complete equality**. This includes organizations that, while they **may** have done and **may still be doing good works**, some even advancing the goal of improving the relationship between Judah and Ephraim, yet they do not provide the level playing field where each brother is treated with absolute equity. It is imperative that we have a playing field where there is only one set of weights and measures, where Scripture, and not tradition rules, and the Holy Spirit is given the opportunity to function freely.

A good example of a playing field that cannot be used **as it is presently formed,** are the various organizaions that make up the Messianic Jewish Movement. The Messianic Jewish Alliance of America, or MJAA, is a good example of why they cannot be used. To become a member of the MJAA you must be either Jewish, or the spouse of a believing Jewish Member, or one or both of your parents, or grandparent must have been Jewish. However, Ephraimites who do not meet the above qualifications are not completely ignored. They may become "Associate Members." Interestingly enough, in the area of dues there is equality. For Members and Associate Members pay an equal amount![96]

Obviously, from the viewpoint of Ephraim, the Messianic Jewish Alliance is not providing a level playing field, wherein each player (brother) is treated in the manner in which he would desire to be treated if roles were reversed.

The Messianic Jewish Alliance of America playing field not only gives Ephraimites a problem, for many Jewish Believers in Messiah as well as most of mainline Judaism and the modern state of Israel, refuse to play on the Messianic Jewish playing field. (Likewise, mainline Judaism and the modern state of Israel will not allow the Messianic Jews to play on their playing field.)

Interestingly, the Messianic Jewish Alliance of America recently made a plea to non-Jewish Believers to stand with them in prayer and financial support to turn around the shameful situation of keeping Messianic Jews from their homeland and their inheritance. They are extremely upset that Messianic Jews are being denied full membership (citizenship) by the nation of Israel. And they ask that non-Jewish Believers protest this unfair practice by writing both to

---

96 MJAA Membership Application

the President of the United States and to Israel's Prime Minister.

They must have a tongue in cheek attitude as they, on one hand complain about a Judaism that will not accept them as Jewish (since they determine Jewishness on the unscriptural basis that Jewishness comes from the mother and not the father[97]), and a State of Israel that will not grant them Jewish citizenship because they have accepted Yeshua as the Messiah of Israel. And yet, on the other hand, the MJAA treats Ephraimites in the same manner that they are upset about themselves. They will not accept their brother Ephraimites on an equal basis, as fellow Israelites, because they have not met the unscriptural membership requirements established by the Messianic Jewish Alliance of America. Also, they show little concern that Ephraimite Believers in Yeshua face the same difficulties in becoming citizens of the present state of Israel that the Messianic Jews face.

Maybe we are seeing a divine case of "turn-about is fair play."

The solution would be for the MJAA (and all of us for that matter) to heed the advice of Hillel the Elder, who said to the heathen who asked him to teach him the Torah in one succinct principle:

"Do not do to your fellow what you hate to have done to you—this is the sum of the Torah. The rest is elaboration: go and learn it" (Shabbat 31a).

So, while Messianic Judaism may have in many ways advanced certain aspects of the reunion plan in its present form, it is not the playing field which meets Hillel's requirements, and it is not the playing field on which the final reunion inning or quarter can be played-out.

There are many entities that have played important parts in the past century toward the restoration of Judah. If it were not for the British Empire, the United States, and the United Nations there would not be a modern state of Israel. Yet, in the natural, these same entities could well be responsible for the downfall of the very

---

97 See Chapter 8, *Who Is A Jew, A Look At The Bloodline Of Israel.*

nation that they helped to create.

Additionally, there are a potpourri of organizations whose philosophy and mission is to be a friend of the nation of Israel and the Jewish people, such as the International Christian Embassy, Bridges for Peace. etc. These organizations have shown the nation of Israel and Jewish people that Christians can be friends and supporters, without having the hidden motive of conversion. **They have definitely advanced the process of unity**. However, these organizations do not openly accept the teaching of the two houses of Israel, so naturally, they do not have an organizational **goal of uniting both houses of Israel on a level playing field.**

This is true even though there are individuals in these organizations who recognize the truth that there are two houses of Israel, and that the ultimate goal of the Father is to restore the Kingdom to Israel. However, were they to accept these truths on an organizational basis, they would at this stage of the game jeopardize their relationship with the State of Israel and the Jewish people. So, these organizations, in their **present form**, and with their **present goals**, cannot provide the playing field on which the reunion can be accomplished.

We also are forced to rule out the vast array of "Christian" denominations and churches as being a level playing field, because unity to them is having others accept their manmade membership requirements. And, if Israel plays any part in their theology, it is for the most part only on a "spiritual basis."

Prescription For Reunion

The Holy One of Israel's plan to make His Messianic Vision a reality is outlined in Chapter 15, *Mandate for Ephraim*. This Chapter shows why Ezekiel's prophecy about uniting the two sticks is the basis of the Reunion Game Plan. (Ezekiel 37:15-19)

In this prophecy Yahveh first tells Ezekiel to put the two sticks (Ephraim and Judah) together. Then Yahveh declares that **He** will put them together and make them one in His hand.

We know that in Yahveh's schedule, the joining of the two houses into a single nation takes place before the Greater Son of David is recognized by all Israel as their King. The question that we need to answer is, "Where are we today in this "joining process"?

We are in the very early stage of Yahveh's "taking" and identifying the stick of Ephraim, and putting it together with the stick of Judah. It is time for Ephraim to see the truth of his identity as the other house of Israel (Jeremiah 31:18-19). Only then will Judah see that Yeshua is his Messiah.

True to His Word, Yahveh is beginning to restore the "tabernacle of David" by fulfilling these prophecies, using a combination of the efforts of men, mixed with Divine intervention. Chapter 15, *A Mandate for Ephraim*, gives the fascinating accounts of how some of these prophecies were fulfilled.

It depicts just how Yahveh mixed man's efforts and divine intervention to accomplish His promise. It shows how the Holy One of Israel performed His word with an uncanny exactness. And, while He made it clear that it was His hand giving victory, He had used men in accomplishing His objectives. Just as He did with Moses at the Red Sea, Joshua at the Jordan and Jericho, and Gideon in his battle with Midian, etc., etc.

Scripture and history are clear. Yahveh works with man in fulfilling biblical prophecy!

Seeing how Yahveh has worked through men in the past to fulfill prophecy certainly is indicative of how He may well use men to fulfil those remaining prophecies that will result in the reunion of both the houses of Israel, the restoration of the Kingdom to Israel, and thus the fulfillment of His Messianic Vision.

What Can We Do?

What can each of us do to help? Like a good military tactician, let us review Yeshua's strategy. Starting with the small group of disciples given to Him by the Father, Yeshua set in motion a four part plan that would gather the lost sheep of Israel from among the nations, and thus unify the divided and scattered house of Israel.

Phase I: **Recruitment**. Starting in Jerusalem, then in all Judea, Samaria and even to the remotest part of the earth, Yeshua's followers were to accomplish the ingathering of the lost sheep of the house of Israel (Acts 1:8). Activities that fall in this phase include: witnessing, world missions, revivals, evangelistic materials and media, and all forms of evangelization to bring lost sheep to the Messiah.

Phase II: **Training**. Yeshua's instructions were to make disciples of those that were gathered to Him (Matthew 28:19). Activities that fall in this phase include: prayer, fellowship, Biblical schools, Bible studies, conferences and seminars, educational materials and media, and all forms of discipleship instructions.

Phase III: **Maintenance**. Yeshua said, "Tend My lambs and feed my sheep," and, "occupy until I come" (John 21:15-17; Luke 19:13). Activities in this phase include: prayer, fellowship, and all activities listed in Phase II that involve maintaining discipleship proficiency. Also, included in this phase is material maintenance: Maintaining the *ekklesia*,[98] and para-*ekklesia* facilities and personnel, feeding and caring for those in need, healing, and all forms of preservation and substance activities.

Phase IV: **Mission Accomplishment**. Yeshua asked of His Father that His sheep would be one, even as He and the Father were one. He also said that oneness would herald the revelation of the sons of God, and the restoration of the Kingdom to Israel (John 17:21; Romans 8:19-23; Ezekiel 37:15-28; Isaiah 11:11-14). Activities that fall in this phase: fulfillment of yet unfulfilled prophecy—especially regarding reuniting the divided house of Israel. Key Tasks: identify Ephraim, encouraging him to repent of the deeds of his youth (paganism), stimulating dramatic changes in Ephraim, aspiring him to personal holiness, and encouraging

---

98 See HDH Listing for *The Call Of The Ekklesia*.

reunion with Judah (Jeremiah 31:19; Isaiah 11:13-14; 27:9).

The accomplishment of all four Phases is necessary to realize a united Israel. An army cannot fight and win a battle unless soldiers are recruited, trained, and maintained. However, if we never get beyond recruiting, training and maintenance, we will never see the mighty army of Ephraim and Judah swooping down on their enemies and ushering in the Messianic Kingdom (Isaiah 11:14).

The organized Church has been a fantastic recruiter, a fair trainer, a poor maintainer, and has virtually ignored mission accomplishment! The truth of this statement is well illustrated by the following excerpts from the June 12, 1995 issue of the *National & International Religion Report*:

"House Speaker Newt Gingrich's plan to use churches and other charities to compensate for budget cuts to social services will put too large a stain on their resources, ministry representatives say. To make up for the $60 billion in cuts proposed in the House-approved Personal Responsibility Act alone, each of America's 350,000 churches would have to raise an additional $190,000 over the next five years....Gingrich has suggested that every church and synagogue in the country can adopt a homeless person for six months....Dismantling America's welfare system and relying solely on charities and volunteers would cause 'a disaster of a large magnitude'....Christian groups helping the poor have more long-term success than the government because the gospel 'changes lives,'...The nations 250 rescue missions served 75,000 meals a day, provided 24,800 beds per night, and gave 13,700,000 articles of clothing last year."

What would happen if the members of those 350,000 churches tithed and depended on the Father to support the tasks He has given them to do? An additional thought: with 350,000 churches and 250 rescue missions, a ratio of 1,400 churches to one rescue mission—maybe the problem is too many churches and not enough rescue missions.

So, what are "the shepherds" going to do with their

responsibility to "Tend My lambs and feed my sheep"? (John 21:15-17). It is a responsibility that not only has Yeshua given them, but one that the government also would like for them to assume.

What is the Church's answer? According to the same report, nearly 4,000 of the world's evangelical leaders have pledged to aggressively take on new challenges and opportunities to evangelize mankind. In their recent meeting in May in Seoul, South Korea at the Global Consultation On World Evangelism '95, they affirmed the ambitious goal of establishing a church-planting movement among every people group in the world (10,500 people groups remain to be reached) by the turn of the century.

"The massive scope of the task energized and unified delegates. 'We came together around a vision created in us by the command of Christ to make disciples of all nations,' said Robert Coleman of Trinity Evangelical Divinity School, reading from the conference declaration. 'This is the time for which we were born.' Coleman began to tremble with emotion, and the entire gathering 'went wild' in a spontaneous response..."

Earlier it was said that the organized Church has been a fantastic recruiter, but after seeing that 10,500 people groups have yet to be reached, that rating must be down graded to fair or poor. Further, the century turned and these 10,500 groups remain to be reached.

Several years ago there was a Deacon in a small church, which like all churches, saw its prime mission as "saving" the local populace. And, the Pastor was emphatic that every member should be out knocking on doors and passing out tracts on the streets. The Deacon's council was, "Pastor, what we need to do is change the lives of those members we already have. We need to enable our current members to establish the relationship with Jesus, and each other, that Jesus had with the Father. If we did that, we would be fulfilling Jesus' prayer: 'I in them, and Thou in Me, that they may be perfected in unity, that the world may know that Thou didst send Me, and didst love them, even as Thou didst love Me' (John 17:23)."

He went on to point out to the Pastor that, "If we began to accomplish this type of change, in even **some** of our members, we would not be able to keep people out. However, if we did not change lives, we would not be able to keep even our present members in." The change that must happen in peoples lives to answer Jesus' prayer, does not automatically happen when one raises his hand signaling repentance for his sins, and acceptance of Jesus as his Messiah (procedure in many churches) and starts on the long trek of working out his salvation in fear and trembling (Philippians 2:12). A trek that is going to require adequate training and maintenance along the way, if it is going to be successful.

Adding to the Deacon's council, we need to recognize that the complete salvation experience encompasses job accomplishment. Let us, when our hour has come, be able to say as Yeshua did, "Father, I glorified Thee on the earth, having **accomplished the work** which Thou hast given Me to do. And now, glorify Thou Me together with Thyself, Father, with the glory which I had with Thee before the world was" (John 17:4-5).

Those whom the Father will use to accomplish His Messianic Vision will be a people who will not only make "Mission Accomplishment" a priority. But they will include those who are fantastic recruiters, fantastic trainers, and fantastic maintainers, and thus will accomplish their mission. In the past, ignoring mission accomplishment may have been partially due to Yahveh's timing. However, in our day we need to change our focus because ours may be the generation that will end the two-thousand year long relay race by carrying the baton across the finish line!

If Not Us, Then Who? If Not Now, Then When?

Are we that people? If the Lord expects us to include "mission accomplishment" in our efforts to "be about our Father's business," what are we doing about it?

Rich or poor, young or old we all have the same number of hours in our week. And, judgment is not based on whether we have a rich man's gold, or a widow's mite, but it is based on what we do with our resources! Let not our judgment be that spoken over the Church of Laodicea (Revelation 3:15,16): "I know your deeds, that you are neither cold nor hot; I would that you were cold or hot. So because you are lukewarm, and neither hot or cold, I will spit you out of My mouth." Rather, let our judgment be that of Matthew 25:34: "Come, you who are blessed of My Father, inherit the kingdom prepared for you from the foundation of the world."

We must keep our focus on the fact that Yahveh's ultimate plan is to bring Heaven to His people on earth. It is not to bring His people on earth to His Kingdom in Heaven. Further, we are not to be a people who are "of this world." Instead, our treasures and our hope are in the Kingdom to come. And therefore, we should devote a significant portion of our time, effort and resources to the return of the Lord and the establishment of His Kingdom on earth.

The rewards of an overcomer will not go to the lukewarm, nor to those so wrapped up in the affairs of this world that they become part of it. Rather, the overcomers will be those who are on fire to serve the Holy One Of Israel. It is for each of us, great or small, young or old, rich or poor, man or woman, to be zealous for Him, to be alert to His return, and open to the opportunities that He gives each of us to serve His purposes.

Restoring Israel's Kingdom

18

When Will Yeshua Return?

Will Yeshua return and establish His Kingdom on earth in *your* lifetime?

How you answer will have great impact on the choices you make during your brief earthly sojourn.

If you accept the possibility of Yeshua returning during your watch, you will step out on a life changing walk. One of the first changes you should make will be in how you see yourself. For if you understand that Yeshua is establishing *His* Israelite Kingdom here on earth (Luke 1:30-34), you also will know that you are part of the people of Israel (Ephesians 2:11-12; Galatians 3:28-29). And so, you will no longer see yourself as a "Gentile," but as an Israelite; as a forerunner who our Father will use to accomplish the coming reunion of Ephraim and Judah.

As you begin to fulfill our Father's desire to have a Kingdom, He will give you a "knowing" that you are numbered among the fishermen He is presently calling forth to gather His people.

On the other hand, if you conclude that our Faher will not return during your watch, then you will undoubtedly continue to spend your time and resources on the commission given our forefathers throughout the "Church age." That being a mission of recruiting and maintaining, and of looking to the fulfillment of our "hope of glory" in some future generation.

Correctly answering our opening question is a challenge we all face. How we answer could very well affect our eternal destiny, because our worldly testing produces our heavenly rewards (Deuteronomy 13:1-4). If our watch turns out to be the one in which Yeshua returns, we surely do not want to be like the foolish virgins who ran out of oil. Nor do we want to be like the servant whose master came on a day and at an hour which he had not expected.

We would not like their rewards. The foolish virgins had the door closed to them and were told by their master that he did not know them. The unprepared servant was cut in pieces and assigned a place with the hypocrites, where there will be weeping and gnashing of teeth (Matthew 24:49-51; 25:1-12).

Instead, we want to be counted among those who heed the warning, "Be on the alert then, for you do not know the day nor the hour" (Matthew 25:13). So, let us be prepared for Yeshua's return, even if it turns out that He does not return during our lifetime. After all, what will we have lost? But, if we are unprepared when Yeshua returns, we may well be found wanting!

The Date Of Yeshua's Return?

While we may not know the exact day and hour of Yeshua's return, we can make some reasonable assumptions regarding the time and season. For example, today, we are some two thousand years closer to this age-ending event than were the small group of disciples who gathered on the Mount of Olives at the time of Yeshua's departure.

At that time, they all had a very natural question, one which disciples have continued to ask throughout the centuries, *"When are you coming back?"*

Their actual question was, "Lord, is it at this time You are restoring the Kingdom to Israel?" And Yeshua answered them, "It is not for you to know times or epochs which the Father has fixed by His own authority" (Acts 1:6-7).

The Williams New Testament[99] rendering of this verse is, "It is not your business to learn times and dates." The Berkeley New Testament[100] interpretation is, "It is not your affair to know times or seasons." Unfortunately, these translations reflect the attitude of the church, not only in the past, but also today. It may not have been the business of the original band of disciples to know the time of Yeshua's Return—a time which He told them the Father had already established —and yet, it was a time which they were not to know.

It is understandable that Yeshua would not let them know the time, because it would have been some two thousand years in the future!

And, what would our attitude be if we knew that Yeshua's Return was scheduled for the year 4,000 A.D.? To prepare for this event, we would do just what the church is doing, and has done for centuries—recruit and maintain.

Admittedly, this is an essential task. However, there will be a day when the church has basically accomplished this task, and we will have enough recruits to establish the Kingdom. And we may be in that day. For, there are now 6 billion people alive on planet Earth—half of the people who have ever lived on this planet since the dawn of civilization.

Thus, we must consider: "could the actual date of Yeshua's return hinge on predetermined preparations and achievements made by disciples in the generation that will experience this event?

---

99 The New Testament: A Translation in the Language of the Peoples (Charles B. Williams).
100 The Berkeley Version of the New Testament (Gerrit Verkuyl).

Why Did The Father Pick It?

We know **our Father has set the date!** But whatever that date is, *why did He pick it?*

Is it a date picked randomly, without regard to the course of human events? Or is it a date that is predicated on human events—a date determined by the actions and reactions of people? Did our Father pick a particular date because of circumstances He foresaw?

Paul tells us that we have the mind of the Lord, and he encourages us not to be conformed to this world, but to be transformed by the renewing of our mind, so that we may prove what is the will of God (Romans 12:2; 1 Corinthians 2:16). Also we know that "whatever was written in earlier times was written for our instruction...upon whom the ends of the ages have come." (Romans 15:4; 1 Corinthians 10:11). Further, Yahveh says, "Come now, and let us reason together" (Isaiah 1:18).

So our first step in obtaining a reasonable answer about how Yahveh sets dates is to examine the past. Therefore, we now travel back to another historical date setting.

"Yahveh said to Abram, 'Know for certain that your descendants will be strangers in a land that is not theirs, where they will be enslaved and oppressed four hundred years'" (Genesis 15:13)

Where did this "four hundred year" time frame come from? What considerations went into the its establishment?

It would appear that one consideration was that, the iniquity of the Amorites (one of the nine nations in the land promised to Abraham), was not yet "full" (Genesis 15:19-21).

Why Did The Father Deliver Israel From Egypt When He Did?

However, when we go forward 400 years, to the actual fulfillment of this prophecy, we find that the reason given by Yahveh to Moses for delivering Abraham's descendants from Egypt was, "I have surely seen the affliction of My people who are in

Egypt, and have given heed to their cry because of their taskmasters, for I am aware of their sufferings. So **I have come down to deliver them from the power of the Egyptians**, and to bring them up from that land to a good and spacious land, to a land flowing with milk and honey, to the place of the Canaanite and the Hittite and the Amorite and the Perizzite and the Hivite and the Jebusite" (Exodus 3:7-8).

Yahveh came because of their cry for deliverance.

He said, "I have come down to deliver them from the power of the Egyptians." But, how did He accomplish His self-assigned job?

He gave it to Moses!

Moses did the Father's work!

But, what if Moses had said, "I do not want the job; I'm happy here in Midian and I'm not welcome in Egypt. So, thanks for the offer, but please pick someone else."

Moses, could have answered this way, because, all men—even you and I—have the right to decline a mission from Yahveh.

Free Will Or Predestination?

Free will is a hallmark of Judeo-Christian theology. Man's eternal destiny is in his own hands. Man has the right and the power to embrace or disregard the call of Yahveh on his life, and to accept, or reject His guidance to accomplish His call in his life.

Adam and Eve serve as prime examples of two people who chose not to follow the Father's instructions. However, even though they could have chosen *not* to eat from the tree of the knowledge of good and evil, Yahveh foreknew what their decision would be, just as He knows the decisions we will make (Genesis 2:17).

So how did Yahveh fulfill His prophecy that Abraham's descendants would be delivered from Egypt in four hundred years? Did He predestine that they would cry out for deliverance at that time? Did He create "puppets," so Moses, Aaron, the elders of Israel, all the people of Israel, and a Pharaoh and the Egyptians would play their parts so as to affect deliverance? Or, did Yahveh

239

look into the future and see that it would take four hundred years for the Israelites to have their fill of Egypt, and thus of their own free will, would cry out for deliverance. And that, a Moses, an Aaron, the elders and all of the people Israel, would be willing, at that time, to follow His guidance to the extent necessary to deliver them from Egypt?

Granted that Yahveh can affect compelling circumstances to accomplish His purposes—such as the ten plagues with which He afflicted the Egyptians. However, Pharaoh could have let the Israelites go at any time. He did not have to pursue them, and thus lose his army in the Red Sea. Also, Adam and Eve could have rejected the tempter, and not have eaten fruit from the tree of the knowledge of good and evil. And, Judas could have rejected the offer of twenty pieces of silver.

If you believe that man has free will, then it is reasonable for you to believe that Yahveh set the four-hundred year date based on looking into the future, and seeing that circumstances, which He undoubtedly created, would generate the **free will response** from people sufficient to accomplish His purposes at that time.

The Fullness of Time

"When the fullness of the time came, Yahveh sent forth His Son, born of a woman, born under the Law, so that He might redeem those who were under the Law, that we might receive the adoption as sons" (Galatians 4:4-5).

How did Yahveh determine when there was a "fullness of time" for this world-changing event?

Did He predestine a Mary, a Joseph, twelve disciples, a Jewish hierarchy, and a Roman Military Governor who would each accomplish the part assigned to them?

More puppets? Or, once again, did Yahveh look into the future and see that the circumstances which He created would generate the **free will response** from people sufficient to accomplish His purposes?

Did Mary have the choice to say, "I do not want to be impregnated other than by my husband?" Could Joseph have said, "I won't marry a woman pregnant by another?" Did not each disciple have the choice to reject Yeshua's call to follow Him?

Yes they did. Even so, many disciples did reject Him (John 6:66). Could not the Jewish hierarchy have accepted Yeshua as the son of God? Could not Pilate have refused to put Him to death?

If you agree that it is reasonable to assume that Yahveh set past dates by looking into the future, and selecting a time when circumstances which He created would generate the **free will response** from people sufficient to accomplish His purposes—then—it is only reasonable that dates, still future in our day, have been, and presently are, set by Yahveh in the same manner.

What Will Precipitate Yeshua's Return?

Thus we conclude that the date has already been set for the return of the Messiah, and for the restoration of the Kingdom to Israel. It was set when Yahveh long ago looked into the future. He selected a time when circumstances and **free will response** from people will be sufficient to accomplish His Kingdom restoration.

Therefore, the question we need to answer is, *"What circumstances, or events, coupled with the appropriate response are sufficient to precipitate Yeshua's return?*

Peter said Yeshua has ascended into heaven, and that He is going to stay there until all that Yahveh prophesied through the ancient prophets regarding events that must be accomplished prior to the Return, are fulfilled (Acts 3:19-21).

Undoubtedly, the major prophecies that must be fulfilled before Yeshua's return deal with the gathering of the remnant of Israel.

"Behold, days are coming," declares Yahveh, "when it will no longer be said, 'As the Lord lives, who brought up the sons of Israel out of the land of Egypt, but, 'As the Lord lives, who brought up the sons of Israel from the land of the north and from all the countries where He had banished them.' For I will restore them to their own land which I gave to their fathers" (Jeremiah 16:14-15).

How does Yahveh plan to gather the remnant?

"Behold, I am going to send for many fishermen," declares Yahveh, "and they will fish for them; and afterwards I will send for many hunters, and they will hunt them from every mountain and every hill and from the clefts of the rocks" (Jeremiah 16:16).

Yahveh uses every generation to advance His plans, and He considers many factors in establishing times and seasons for specific events.

And for Yeshua's return, a key consideration is to have people who will accept the mission of "fishermen." To have people who will work together to create the climate and circumstances required to accomplish this event.

The ancient prophets tell us that the day will come when Ephraim will receive instructions and will repent for the deeds of his youth (Jeremiah 31:19). Then Yahveh will whistle for him, and he will come trembling from the west (where an east wind blew him) (Jeremiah18:17). Ephraim will once again be like a mighty man (Zechariah 10:7). And he will be as numerous as he was before. He will fill the land promised to the Patriarchs, until there is no more room in Israel, Lebanon, and Gilead (Isaiah 49:20; Zechariah 10:10).

What Precipitated Judah's Regathering?

We have been given the unmerited opportunity to live in a day that has seen many ancient prophecies concerning the regathering of Israel fulfilled. In 1945 we saw the nations of the world, in the form of the United Nations, gather together and divide the land Yahveh promised to Abraham (Joel 3:2). We have seen a land born in a day—the secular nation of Israel in 1948 (Isaiah 66:8). And, over the last century, we have seen our Jewish brothers trekking back to Israel, fulfilling the prophecy that the tents of Judah would come up first (Zechariah 12:7).

However, you cannot have a first without a second, and the

ancient prophecies that deal with the regathering of Ephraim, the other house of Israel, must of necessity be fulfilled in the same general time frame.

But, what circumstances will Yahveh create to generate the **free will response** from people sufficient to accomplish Ephraim's regathering?

Theodore Herzel faced a similar problem regarding the regathering of Judah. Summing up the accomplishments of the First Zionist Congress, that had addressed this challenge in Basel, Switzerland in August 1987, Herzel said, "At Basel I founded the Jewish state. If I were to say this today, I would be greeted by universal laughter. In five years, perhaps, and certainly in 50, everyone will see it."

Amazingly, Herzel's fifty-year prediction was only nine months short of the May 15, 1948 date which saw the formal foundation of the modern state of Israel.

In 1897 Herzel did not see how Yahveh was going to somehow carve out a state for the Jewish people. But he and his fellow Zionists cried out to be delivered from Egypt (the world). They asked for, and labored for, a land of their own. Surely Herzel did not imagine the circumstances that Yahveh would forge to provide and build up a land for them. He did not see that the murder of six million Jews would impel a guilty world to give the Jews their own state. Nor did he see that billions of dollars would be given by Jews and Christians around the world to support and build up this new state, nor that even more billions would be given by the United States.

The results? Over five million Jews (one-third of the world Jewish population) now reside in the state of Israel.

What Will Precipitate Ephraim's Regathering?

While we cannot foresee all the circumstances Yahveh will forge to fulfill the prophecies concerning Ephraim, we can see certain circumstances beginning to unfold. Primarily these circumstances deal with our heritage and identity.

For this reason, in many ways, we who would awaken Ephraim have a greater task before us than did Herzel and the early Zionists. For they were dealing with a people who knew their heritage and were looking for a land.

But with the Ephraimites, we have a people unaware of their heritage; a people who do not have a welcoming land. Still, over the past half century, we have seen an increased interest in Christians in the land of Israel and the Jewish people.

Twenty-five years ago, the name Ephraim, or the House of Ephraim, or stick of Ephraim, would have drawn a complete blank from virtually all Christians. But today, especially among evangelical, fundamental, and unaffiliated Christians, you find many with various levels of understanding of these terms.

Who Are Unaffiliated Christians?

"Unaffiliated Christians?"

According to the *98 Britannica Book of the Year*, there are in the United States 31,678,000 professing Christians who are not affiliated with any church. Worldwide the total is 104,939,000.[101] Imagine, with 5,000 denominations and cults available (that is only the tip of the iceberg), 104,939,000 Christians cannot find one that satisfies their needs. Granted that many of these may be nominal Christians, or maybe extremely picky ones. But what are they looking for? Could their dissatisfaction with the organized Church be one of those circumstances that Yahveh is forging to gather Ephraim? Could it be that from the ranks of these dissidents Yahveh will draw many of the Ephraimites to accomplish the ingathering of all Israel? Surely, the 31,678,000 unaffiliated in the United States would go a long way toward filling up the lands of Israel, Lebanon and Gilead.

Also, we have seen the birth and beginning growth of Messianic

---

[101] *98 Britannica Book of the Year*, 1998, Encyclopaedia Britannica, Chicago, *Religion: World Religious Statistics*, p 314.

Israel, which demonstration is the result of the free will activities of individuals and small groups around the world. These hold to the "Hope of Messianic Israel."[102] Could these forerunners be a key component of the circumstances Yahveh is arranging to accomplish the restoration of the Kingdom to Israel?

Assuming that the answer to this question is "yes," then our next questions is, What response does Yahveh desire from His *forerunners? What free will response can we render to successfully meet His desire to restore the Kingdom to Israel?*

Without God And Without Hope

As discussed earlier the Apostle Paul gives three reasons why the Ephesians (Gentiles, or non-jews) previously had been without hope, and without God in the world. And, those who would enjoy the fulness of relationship with the God of Israel face these problems today:

1) They were separated from Yeshua. They were not saved. However, while we all can agree that not having obtained individual salvation is any individual's greatest problem, it was, according to Paul, not their only problem.

2) Paul also said they were excluded, or alienated, from the **commonwealth of Israel**. In other words, in addition to not having individual salvation, they did not have *national salvation*. For they were not part of a people set apart for the Holy One of Israel.

3) They were **strangers to the covenants of promise**. Paul speaks of the covenants that will one day culminate in the fulfillment of the Messianic Promise—which is the hope of glory; the hope that the fulness of our eternal inheritance will be consummated at Yeshua's coming (Ephesians 2:12).

In the past, Yahveh has worked through His people to accomplish His purposes on earth. Therefore, it is only reasonable to expect that **He will work through His people to accomplish the**

---

102 See the *Hope of Messianic Israel.*

coming reunion of all Israel. And, prudence demands that we believe we are that people, and that this could very well be the generation that sees Messiah's return.

Therefore, in the same manner and with the same zeal that the Church has taken forth the solution to Israel's first and foremost problem —that Israelites were **separated from Yeshua**—we must now herald the solution to the problem of being excluded, or alienated, from the common-wealth of Israel! And, once we have solved both of these problems, we will have solved the third problem. *We will no longer be **strangers to the covenants of promise**!*

A Divine Mandate

Seeing that we are no longer foreigners and strangers, but that we have been given the unmerited grace to be joined with Yeshua, and made aware of our membership in the commonwealth of Israel, and that we are partakers of the covenants of promise, then we have an obligation—a Divine mandate!

Each one of us can, and should proclaim the truth of our heritage: We must proclaim the truth that we not only are joined with the Messiah of Israel, but we are part of His people, Israel! (We pray you will work with and assist Messianic Israel in taking out this age ending message of heritage).

Yahveh has plans for our welfare, to give each one of us a future and a hope (Jeremiah 29:11). The accomplishment of His plans, in a manner pleasing to Him, depends on how we respond as He guides us through the circumstances He has arranged for our lives.

A Cry For Deliverance

Like our forefathers in ancient Egypt, will we cry out for deliverance from our Egypt? In our day, will we take advantage of the opportunity to be numbered among the fishermen whom Yahveh is calling to regather His people Israel?

When Yahveh asks us, "I have surely seen the affliction of My people who are scattered in ever nation, tribe, and tongue. I have given heed to their cry, I am aware of their sufferings. So I have come down to deliver them from the power of Satan, and from the governments of men, and to bring them back to that good and spacious land, just as I promised their fathers— Abraham, Isaac and Jacob. Now who will I send to accomplish this task?"

Will we answer as did Isaiah, "Here am I. Send me?" (Isaiah 6:8).

We are part of that multitude of fishermen that our forefather Jacob foresaw some thirty-seven-hundred years ago. And, Jacob made the Hebrews Chapter Eleven *"Hall of Fame,"* because he blessed Ephraim and Manasseh, the sons of Joseph, saying, *"May they grow into teeming multitudes upon the earth."* However, a more accurate translation of this verse would be, *"May they multiply; may they grow like a multitude of fish; may they be teeming multitudes* (Genesis 48:15-21).[103]

We know that Jacob, along with all who gained approval through their faith, did not receive what was promised. Because as the Father says, He has provided something better for us so that "apart from *us* they should not be made perfect" (Hebrews 11:39-40).

Could we be that *"us?"*

Could we even now be fulfilling Jacob's prophecy as we begin to gather a multitude of fish?

Truly, the fields are ready for harvest (John 4:35)! And working together, we need to insure that all whom Yahveh is calling have the opportunity to receive instruction through study materials and personal contact. For we know that these materials will help change their lives, just as they have changed our lives, and the lives of

---

103 The *ArtScroll Tanach Series* (*commentary from Talmudic, Midrashic* and *Rabbinic* sources; translates the verse, "May they proliferate abundantly like fish" (*Genesis*, Vol. 6, Mesorah, 1982, pp 2115-2117). It also can be translated, "May they multiply; may they grow into a multitude of fish" (translated from *The New Concordance of the Tanach* by Rimona Frank, Hebrew editor). Perhaps this translation fits best, for "fishers of men" would one day be sent forth to gather scattered Israel (Mat 4:19).

others. Therefore, it is incumbent upon us who know to be a witness, preaching the good news of the Gospel of the Kingdom—which in its fulness culminates in the restoration of the Kingdom to Israel.

Being About Our Father's Business

Yeshua is forever about His Father's business— changing lives! Therefore, we forerunners are automatically in the life changing business too. So we need to be about the business of changing lives. And nothing will change someone quicker than personal salvation, coupled with an understanding of his heritage and purpose. Further, as we change the lives of others, we will change! We will change into the "one new man" the Father would have us become. *Let us say, Here am I, Send me.*

19

Preparing For
The Final Battle

A*mong the sons of Israel were the sons of Issachar, men who understood the times, with knowledge of what Israel should do"* (1 Chronicles 12:32).

In our day, do we have sons of Israel who can discern where we are in the unfolding Biblical saga of the people of Israel? Do we have those with an understanding of what Israel should do? Do we understand the mission given to our generation?

Or, are most of the sons of Israel numbered with the "they." *"They have quickly turned aside from the way which I commanded them. They have made for themselves a molten calf, and have worshiped it and have sacrificed to it and said, 'This is your god, O Israel, who brought you up from the land of Egypt!'"* (Exodus 32:8)

Unfortunately, there is nothing new under the sun, it is still the "bull" versus the God of Israel.

We are in a "worship war"—a war over what or Whom will we choose to serve. On an individual level it is a battle for the eternal salvation of our souls. On a national, or corporate level, it is a battle that is waged against our "unity" as "the people of Israel." It is a battle against our being able to attain to a "oneness" like that of the Father and Yeshua, or to settle for the division promoted by our Adversary, the Great Divider.

Individually, our primary challenge is to maintain our personal relationship with Yeshua, and thus to be empowered to run our race in a way that will allow us to successfully work out our salvation (Galatians 2:2; Philippians 2:16; Hebrews 12:1).

While we must have a personal relationship with Messiah to be able to run this race, in addition, at this time in history, we also need to grab hold of our "national identity." For, those of "scattered Ephraim," together with those of Judah who are presently reunited in Messiah, need to be very active members of the family of "Israel."

For it is only those Israelites who have both an individual and national relationship with the Holy One of Israel that have any hope of achieving the "oneness" required to fulfill His desire to have a people for His own possession.

And, this oneness is not some far-fetched "ideal." In fact, we are commanded to come to this place of Divinely ordained unity. And, at some point in history there will be a remnant of Israel that is so unified. It is this remnant who has perfected its unity that will cause the world to believe that Yeshua is the Son sent by our Father (John 17:22-23).

How do we attain this level of unity?

Yeshua says the glory (praise, honor, approval and majesty), which the Father has given to Him, He has likewise given to us, so "that we may be one, just as He and the Father are one." So, we must appropriate that Divinely given position of honor, approval and majesty, and purpose to embrace unity and reject division. Then we too will be able to walk in perfected unity (John 17:21-23).

We must seek this unity, for it is the power found in this "oneness" that will enable the return of "all" Israel to their own soil

—to the Land promised to Abraham, Isaac, and Jacob. And, it is this gathering of the remnant that will bring about the ultimate victory—that of making the kingdoms of this world become the Kingdom of our Messiah! (Revelation 11:15).

Unite is an action word. For its English definition describes, "the process of putting, or bring together to make one, combine or join into a whole." In Greek the word used in Yeshua's high priestly prayer, which is translated unity, is *"heis."* And heis is defined as one—the numeral one.

Therefore, if we are going to bring together a people and unite them, we need to promote the "ones" and reject the "twos" and "threes." We cannot be supportive of organizations, denominations, ministries, etc., that promote and practice heretical doctrine that causes division by separating the people of Israel.

We do this by joining together with those who are striving for our Messiah's ideal of unity. And we reject those who are pursuing the division of our Adversary. We must reject the heretical doctrine that proclaims that the Church and Israel are separate entities with separate covenants. We must reject the heretical doctrine that proclaims that the Jewish people are physical Israel and the Church is "spiritual Israel." We must reject the heretical doctrine that divides Israel into first and second class citizens.

We can only imagine the results that will be obtained by the power of a fully unified Israel (meaning, an Israel united in accordance with our Father's desires and instructions). However, we do see the strength and support that results from "union" with others: family, school, military, workplace, nation, etc..

The good news is that the Father is in the process of unifying us in such a manner!

The pace of implementation is quickening as we prepare to enter the seventh and final millennium of the history of the people of Israel. Even so, our Father has implemented His battle plan which will fulfill the purposes of His creation and accomplish the full reunion of His people, Israel.

However, the key to our successfully taking part in fulfillment of this battle plan is:

First, we must understand our Father's purposes—and—that goal must become our primary focus.

To understand this goal, we need to realize that, while the God of Abraham, Isaac, and Jacob is omniscient, omnipotent, and omnipresent—still, there is one thing He cannot do, and remain consistent with His character. He cannot create a people who will **choose** Him as their God. To **choose** Him, one must have **free will**. And clearly, our Father's heart's desire is to have a people for His own possession—a people who have **freely chosen** Him.

So our job is to do that which our Father cannot do, and that is to **freely chose to be His people.**

The gathering of a called and chosen people—people called by the Holy Spirit and chosen because of their free will response to that call (Matthew 22:13; Revelation 17:14)—and the establishment of a Kingdom wherein Yahveh can dwell with His people—that—is the ultimate goal of His creation plan.

Since reaching this goal is dependent on the free will response of His people, then of necessity, we, **His people, must play a key role in the execution of the battle plan** to restore the Kingdom to Israel.

Again, we are at war. And that means, we have an enemy. And, our enemy has a battle plan. In all probability, there is even a banner on the wall of Satan's War Council Room in Hell that reads:

"It's Division Stupid!"

Why? Because, a divided house, or kingdom, cannot stand (Matthew 12:25; Mark 3:25; Luke 11:17).

To insure that Yahveh's people continue to be divided, Satan has in his arsenal, a pack of lies that he continually uses. His primary strategy is to promote disbelief in the Biblical-Judeo-Christian faith. He does this by promoting false religions and beliefs systems. And, the one that has long proven both extremely popular, and effective, with *all* Israel, is, "worship of the bull."

Make no mistake, the "bull" is alive and well on planet earth. In America, he has set up headquarters on Wall Street and in Washington—with branch offices throughout the world.

He has, through control of the economy, taken control of not only America, but the world. And, he is applying his moral standards, which promote division, to a large segment of society.

Presently, many of the people of the world are riding the bull's golden wave of abundance. While many in ancient Israel worshiped a "golden calf," today we have a modern "Israel" that worships a "bull that makes gold."

They turn over their future financial hope: short range investments for children's education, homes, long range retirement investments, to the "bull." And in return, he promises to "take care of them." Quite naturally, since their hope is now "in the bull," his well being is of utmost importance to them. Thus, it doesn't matter whether our leaders are moral or not. What matters is, "Are they taking good care of the bull?"

It is not important that the majority of the people exalted as role models in the entertainment media (movies, TV, music, sports, etc.) have morals that surely are a stench in the nostrils of the God of Israel. What matters is, "Are they contributing to the welfare of the bull?"

If the economy had been in a shambles, would President Clinton have maintained an approval rating above sixty percent during his "trial"? Would he have survived the impeachment process? Would Jesse Ventura, Governor of Minnesota, have maintained an approval rating above fifty percent after saying, "Organized religion is for weak-minded people"?

The fact that most people are willing to accept the current condition of our society and culture is an indictment against the "believing church." It also proves that the Father's selection plan, of "many are called and few are chosen," is working. Also, this "great falling away" which we are now experiencing, is a certain sign of the end of the age—a sign that soon, Messiah Yeshua will spew an apostate church out of His mouth (Revelation 3:14-22).

The bull's booming economy has created an opulent society that has chosen man over God. Its wealth and opulence have caused a falling away that surely fits the message given to the church in Laodicea. "I know your deeds, that you are neither cold nor hot; I wish that you were cold or hot. Because you are lukewarm, and neither hot nor cold, I will spit you out of My mouth. Because you say, 'I am rich, and have become wealthy, and have need of nothing,' and you do not know that you are wretched and miserable and poor and blind and naked, I advise you to buy from Me gold refined by fire so that you may become rich, and white garments so that you may clothe yourself, and that the shame of your nakedness will not be revealed; and eye salve to anoint your eyes so that you may see. Those whom I love, I reprove and discipline; so be zealous and repent. Behold, I stand at the door and knock; if anyone hears My voice and opens to Me, I will come in to him and dine with him, and he with Me. He who over-comes, I will grant to him to sit down with Me on My throne, as I also overcame and sat down with My Father on His throne" (Revelation 3:14-21)

How do we become "rich" and "put on white garments" and "have our eyes anointed that we may see"? How can we "overcome" and share in the throne of our Lord"?[104]

The answer is to "buy gold." Not the gold of this world from the bull, rather gold refined by fire from Messiah Yeshua. For if you serve the bull, you will be paid in the gold of this world—gold which only has "value" in this world.

However, if you elect to worship and serve the God of Abraham, Isaac and Jacob, you will be paid in gold refined by Messiah Yeshua's fire—gold that has "value" in this world and in the world to come.

So, let us lay aside all "bull worship." Let us instead choose to store up Heavenly treasures that cannot be destroyed (Matthew 6:19-21). Like Joshua, let us "choose this day whom we will

---

104 For more answers, see the HDH, *The Crossroads At Laodicea*.

serve!" Let us choose to serve, with all our hearts, the God of Abraham, Isaac, and Jacob (Joshua 24:15). Let us take hold of His hope for a restored Israel with whom He can forever dwell. Collectively, let us now dedicate ourselves to making that dream become a reality.

Since we, the people of Israel, are destined to play a key role in the execution of the battle plan to restore the Kingdom to Israel, we need to be about our Father's business.

Our ancestors, in their preparations to return to the Land, first gathered "all the host of the Lord" (Exodus 12:41). Likewise, we need to gather all the Lord's Host. And our first task is to identify sufficient Israelites to fulfill the prophecies concerning the gathering of the end-time remnant.

Having gathered the host of Israel, our ancestors marched out of Egypt. They departed with little idea of where they were going or how they were to get there. And, having reached the Red Sea, it was doubtful that they even thought about crossing it.

Then the Father revealed His plan to deliver His people, and defeat the pursuing Egyptians, by parting and closing the Red Sea. But, remember, the Red sea did not part until the Israelites had reach its shores, and according to tradition the first Israelite had walked into the water until it reached his nose.

Likewise, once we have accomplish the task of identifying and gathering our host, and are prepared to leave "Egypt," our Father will reveal the way in which He will accomplish the next phase of gathering the remnant of His people.

To accomplish this identifying and gathering of the remnant, those Messianic Israelites, whom the Father has given an understanding of their heritage and purpose, need to come together and to work together. And the primary expression of this unity and purpose available today is found among those of the Messianic Israel Alliance.

Messianic Israel has as its mission the restoration of the Kingdom to Israel. It can give those who see themselves as part of

Israel the opportunity to participate in the gathering of the remnant. And, give them assurance that they are wisely using the time, talents and resources that our Father has given them, to accomplish His desires.

Given the opportunity from the vantage point of hind-sight, all of us would make adjustments in our past use of our time, talents and resources. Unfortunately, we cannot change the past. But we can change the future! So, let each of us resolve that our future use of time, talents and resources will be made through the foresight provided by the leading of the Ruach ha Kodesh (Holy Spirit).

Messianic Israel, or Messianic Israel Ministries/House of David/Messianic Israel Alliance,[105] provides **you** several ways in which you can take an active part in the regathering of the people of Israel.

Through the House of David you can work with the "school" that provides education, literature, materials, and instructions that will make you, and others like you, effective ambassadors capable of carrying out our Father's plan. On the other hand, the Messianic Israel Alliance (MIA), which is composed of almost two hundred (and growing daily) allied congregations, fellowships, synagogue, and ministries, provides an arena in which you can better reach the "students" and actually participate in the execution of our Father's plan.

Messianic Israel provides a web site, and a web ring that connects the websites of many of the allied congregations, fellowships, synagogues, and ministries. And, it provides support for outreaches in the Land.

For more information about Messianic Israel visit the website at mim.net, or messianicisrael.com, or messianicisrael.net, or messianicisrael.

Messianic Israel Ministries gives you the opportunity to be involved in the logistical support, which includes outreaches in the

---

[105] The House of David was founded in the 1970's. From those who embraced the House of David teachings of the "two houses," there emerged in the late 90's an alliance formed to advance the process of gathering the remnant and restoring the kingdom to Israel.

Land. Through the House of David you can participate in the educational effort. And your involvement with the Messianic Israel Alliance makes you part of the action effort—for, in the MIA, we are actually gathering the remnant and becoming "One Stick" in our Father's hand—a people united by a common hope, and dedicated to fulfilling that hope—*The Hope of Messianic Israel.*

Hopefully, having read this book you now see yourself as a Messianic Israelite, on the cutting edge of what our Father is doing in this generation. Our Father is putting new wine in new wineskins, and He will give you ample opportunities to best prepare for the eternal future He has planned for you.

"For I know the plans that I have for you," declares the Lord, "plans for welfare and not for calamity to give you a future and a hope" (Jeremiah 29:11).

The Father created the world for you! And, it is His fervent desire that you fulfill the plans and hope that He has given you, and that the future you choose is to spend eternity with Him.

This book opened with a question. We end with one more question and an answer:

Are you, like Joshua and Caleb, an Ephraimite and a Judahite, **prepared to be a part** of the people who cross our "Jordan," take the land, and thus **restore Israel's Kingdom?**

My prayer is that your answer might be:

Yes! I am well able!

Restoring Israel's Kingdom

 # The Hope of Messianic Israel

Messianic Israel believes *Yeshua Ha'Natsree* (Jesus of Nazareth) was and is the true Messiah, the Lion of Judah, the Branch Who will fully reunite all Israel; that He died and rose from the dead and lives at the right hand of the Almighty; and according to the ancient Holy Scriptures, Yeshua is Yahveh Elohim appearing in the flesh, as Yeshua demonstrated in Himself (Deu 18:18-19; John 8:58; 10:33; Mat 12:6-8; 9:35; 15:31; Isa 11; 53; Micah 5:2-4; Luke 24:46; Isa 8:14; John 2:22; Acts 3:15-17; Heb 13:20; 1 John 4:2; 2 John 1:7; Rev 5:5; John 1:1).

Messianic Israel believes we are made righteous in Messiah Yeshua (He is the heart of Abraham's unconditional covenant). The sign of the New Covenant is circumcision of the heart, which leads to confession, salvation, faith, grace, and to good works in Messiah. The conditional Mosaic covenant presents the eternal truths of Torah (God's teaching and instructions) to His people, the hearing of which brings about blessing or curse (respond and be blessed, disobey and lack). In the New Covenant, Yeshua's Law is to be written on our hearts by the Spirit (Rom 4:13-16; 5:2; 10:10; 1 Pet 1:19; 2 Cor 5:21; Gal 3:16,29; Titus 3:5; Heb 10:38; 1 John 1:9; Eph 2:8; James 2:14; Deu 28; Ezek 36:26; Jer 31:31-33; Heb 10:16; Gal 2:16; John 5:46; 10;30; 14:2; 15:10).

Messianic Israel is a people whose heart's desire is to fully reunite the olive tree of Israel—both branches— Ephraim and Judah—into one, redeemed, nation of Israel—through Messiah Yeshua. They seek to arouse Ephraim from obscurity, and by example, to awaken Judah to the Messiah—and thus to hasten both

Yeshua's return to Earth and the restoration of the Kingdom to Israel (Mat 6:10; 12:25; 21:43; 24:43; Luke 22:29-30; Mark 13:34; Luke 22:29-30; 2 Chr 11:4; Eze 37:15-28; Jer 11:10,16; 2:18,21; Rom 11:17,24; Eph 2:11-22; Acts 1:6).

Messianic Israel deems the Jewish people to be the identifiable representatives and offspring of Judah and "the children of Israel, his companions," and that non-Jewish followers of the Messiah from all nations have been, up to now, the unidentifiable representatives and offspring of Ephraim and "all the house of Israel, his companions" (Gen 48:19; Hosea 1-2; 5:3; Eze 37:16; Jer 31:6-9; Gen 15:2-5; 26:3; 28:4; Heb 11:9; Isa 56:3,6-8; Eph 2:11-22).

Messianic Israel affirms that the Jewish people have been kept identifiable as seed of the patriarch Jacob, Yahveh's covenant people, to preserve His Holy Torah (Law), Feasts, and Shabbat (Sabbath); that the salvation of the Jewish people through their acceptance of Messiah Yeshua, will be the crowning act of mankind's redemption, and is necessary for the restoration of the Kingdom to Israel. Further, the Father plans that Ephraim, they being the "wild olive branch," stimulate Judah to want what they have; they are called to walk in a way that will make Judah jealous of their relationship with the God of Israel (Gen 48:19; Isa 11:13; 37:31,32; Zec 2:12; Eze 37:15-28; Hosea 1:7; Rom 10:19; 11:11,14; Mat 23:39).

Messianic Israel believes the non-Jewish followers of Yeshua are predominately returning Ephraim, those who were once among the Gentiles as "LoAmmi," "Not a people," but have now been restored to the commonwealth of Israel through their covenant with Israel's Messiah; that, they are no more Gentiles, but fulfill the promised restoration of uprooted Ephraim, and Jacob's prophecy that Ephraim would become "melo hagoyim," the "fulness of the Gentiles." As Ephraim, they have been kept in mystery until recently, being used to preserve the testimony of Yeshua, the Messiah of all Israel.

Their awakening, recognition, and performance as Ephraim, and their union with Judah, is a necessity for salvation of "all" Israel, and the restoration of the Kingdom to Israel (Gen 48:19; Hosea 1:9-10; 5:3; 8:8; Amos 9:9; Jer 31:18-19; Zec 10:7; Rom 9:24-26; 11:26; Eph 2:11-22).

Messianic Israel declares that Believers in Yeshua were not meant to replace Judah as Israel, but as "Ephraim," they are part of the called out ones (*ekklesia*), and in these latter-days, the Father is leading them to, whenever Scripturally possible, join with Judah; that Judah (faithful Jewish ones who will receive Messiah) and Ephraim (faithful non-Jewish Messiah followers) ultimately will fulfill the destiny of the two houses of Israel: that together they might fulfill the prophesies about the one, unified, victorious people of Israel (Jer 31:9; Rom 8:29; Col 1:15,18; 2:12; Heb 12:22-24; Lev 23:2-36; Exo 19:5; 1 Pet 1:1; 2:9; Jer 3:18; 23:6; Zec 8:13; 12:1-5; Mat 25:31-46; Exo 12:48-49; Num 15:15-16; Isa 56:3,6-8).

Messianic Israel maintains that up to this general time "blindness in part" has happened to all (both houses) of Israel, and as the blinders are lifted, non-Jewish followers in Yeshua will gain insight into their role as Ephraim, they will become defenders of Scriptural Torah and of Judah, and due to this character change, many Jewish people will accept Yeshua as Messiah This process has already begun as indicated through the Messianic Jewish movement (Judah), the Christian Zionism movement (Ephraim), and the Messianic Israel movement (union of Judah and Ephraim) (Isa 8:14; 11:13; Rom 11:25,26; Jer 33:14-16; 31:18-19; Ezek 37:15-28).

The reunion and full restoration of the two houses, and, thus the restoration of Israel's Kingdom: This is the hope that burns in the hearts of those of Messianic Israel...

Restoring Israel's Kingdom

Abbreviations and Bibliography

Abbreviations:

ArtScroll: ArtScroll Tanach Series
HDH: House of David Herald
NIV: New International Version Bible
NIV Study Bible: New International Version Study Bible
Strong's: Strong's Exhaustive Concordance
TAB: The Amplified Bible
TWOT: Theological Wordbook of the Old Testament

Bibliography

The following is a listing of writings used in making this book.

Adler, Mortimer J. *Ten Philosophical Mistakes.* New York: Macmillian, 1997.

Ben-Gurion, David *Jewish Identity,* Jerusalem, Israel, Feldheim, 1970

Bertman, Stephen *Cultural Amnesia: America's Future and the Crisis of Memory* Praeger, 2000

Bromiley, G.W, ed. *The International Standard Bible Encyclopedia, 4 Vols.* Grand Rapids: Eerdman's, 1979.

Brown, Frances. *The New Brown-Driver-Briggs-Gesenius Hebrew-Aramaic Lexicon.* Peabody, MA:

Bullock, David L., *Allenby's War, The Palestine-Arabian Campaigns, 1916-1918* , Blandford Press.

DeHaan, M. R.. *The Chemistry of the Blood.* Grand Rapids: Zondervan, 1971, 1989.

Eckstein, Rabbi Yechiel, *What Christians Should Know About Jews and Judaism*

Edersheim, Alfred. *The Life and Times of Jesus the Messiah.* Grand Rapids: Eerdman's, 1979.

Gilbert, Martin. *Atlas of Jewish History.* New York: William Morrow, 1993.

_____*Israel: A History.* New York: William Morrow, 1998.

Green, Jay P. *The Interlinear Bible,* Hebrew, Greek, English. Grand Rapids: Baker, 1979.

Guinness, Paul G. *Hear O Israel* , Vantage Press.

Harris, R. Laird, Gleason L. Archer Jr., and Bruce K. Waltke, eds. *Theological Wordbook of the Old Testament, 2 Vols.* Chicago: Moody, 1981.

House of David Herald. Saint Cloud, FL: 1982-2000.

Interpreter's Dictionary of the Bible, 5 Vols. Nashville: Abingdon, 1962.

Jahn, Herb. *The Aramic New Covenant.* Orange, CA: Exegeses, 1996.

Lamsa, George M. *The Holy Bible From Ancient Eastern Manuscripts.* Nashville: Holman, 1968, 1984.

Leil, C.F.; F. Delitzsch. *Commentary on the Old Testament In Ten Volumes.* Grand Rapids: Eerdman's, 1981.

Lindsey, Robert. *Jesus, Rabbi, and Lord.* Oak Creek, WI: Cornerstone, 1990.

The New Encyclopaedia Britannica, 29 Vols. Chicago: Encyclopedia Britannica, 1985.

The New English Bible With the Apocrypha. Oxford, England: Oxford University Press, 1970.

New International Version Study Bible. Grand Rapids: Zondervan, 1985.

Scherman, Nosson, and Meir Zlotowitz, eds. *Genesis. ArtScroll Tanach Series.* Brooklyn: Mesorah, 1987.

Strong, James. *The New Strong's Exhaustive Concordance.* Nashville: Thomas Nelson, 1984.

Stern, David H. *Jewish New Testament Commentary.* Clarksville, MD: Jewish New Testament, 1995.

Tenny, Merrill, ed. *Zondervan Pictorial Encyclopedia of the Bible, 5 Vols.* Grand Rapids: Zondervan, 1976.

Vaughn, Curtis, ed. *26 Translations of the Holy Bible.* Atlanta: Mathis, 1985.

Vincent, Marvin R. *Vincent's Word Studies of the New Testament.* McLean, VA: MacDonald.

Vine, W.E. *The Expanded Vine's Expository Dictionary of New Testament Words.* Minneapolis: Bethany, 1984.

Webster's Third New International Dictionary, 3 Vols. Chicago: Encyclopedia Britannica, 1981.

Whiston, William, trs. *The Works of Flavius Josephus, 4 Vols.* Grand Rapids: Baker, 1974.

Wilson, William. *Wilson's Old Testament Word Studies, Unabridged Edition.* McLean, VA: MacDonald.

Wavell, General Sir Archibald, *Allenby, A Study In Greatness,* Oxford University Press.

Wootten, Batya Ruth. *In Search of Israel.* Lakewood, NY: Destiny Image/House of David, 1988.

_____*The Olive Tree of Israel.* White Stone, VA: House of David, 1992.

_____*Who Is Israel? And Why You Need To Know.* Saint Cloud, FL: Key of David, 1998

_____*Who Is Israel?,* Expanded Edition. Saint Cloud, FL: Key of David, 2000.

Wuest, Kenneth S. *Weust's Word Studies From the Greek New Testament.* Grand Rapids: Eerdman's, 1981.

Young, G. Douglas. *Young's Bible Dictionary.* Nashville: Masada, 1984.

Young, Robert. *Young's Analytical Concordance to The Bible.* Nashville: Thomas Nelson, 1982.

Restoring Israel's Kingdom

Index

House of David Herald
The Voice Of Messianic Israel

    *Available only on web in electronic format.

For A Free Catalogue And Sample Newsletter Write To The:

PO Box 700217, Saint Cloud, FL 34770
Phone: 800 829-8777 (Orders Only)
Fax: 407 348-3770
Web: www.mim.net
Since 1977
Ministering to "both the houses of Israel" (Isaiah 8:14)

Visit our
Messianic Israel Ministries website:
www.mim.net

All *Heralds* are available for viewing and can be searched on site by keywords. Heralds may be downloaded free of charge by those who are affiliated with the Messianic Israel Alliance —those who publically affirm their agreement with the *Hope of Messianic Israel*.

Biography

In 1967 Angus Wootten retired from the United States Army. In the course of that eventful year he met Sid Roth. Sid was a Jew who was not practicing Judaism, Angus was not practicing Catholicism. These two ultimately ended up being in business together. From the secular side it was an investment business, from the non-secular, it became a business that was mightily used to help fund the foundational efforts of Messianic Judaism.

In the early Seventies, Angus, and his wife Batya, were involved with Sid and a small group of Messianic Jews in the founding of *Beth Messiah*, in the Washington D.C., area—it being one of the first Messianic Jewish Congregations. They also worked with Sid in his founding of the *Messianic Vision*, a ministry to all who were interested in the phenomenon of Jews accepting Jesus as their Messiah, yet retaining their Jewish traditions.

In 1977, to further the purposes of the *Messianic Vision*, Batya established the *House of David* as a bookstore/catalogue company. The "business" was primarily funded by her husband, Angus. The store needed someone to fund it because it specialized in materials and books about Israel, the Jewish people, Christians, and how they all relate. At the time, interest in the subject matter was marginal at best. Some even reacted to it with hostility.

Because Batya felt a responsibility to know what the materials they were offering said, she read countless books about the subject of Israel. Much to her dismay, she discovered a wide variance of opinion about Israel's true role in the world, its future, and most important, about Israel's identity. She felt, to say the least, stymied.

Batya and Angus had endless discussions about "Israel." Then, being in spiritual anguish over the matter, Batya began to cry out in earnest to her Heavenly Father, asking Him for His answer to her ever-present question, *Who Is Israel?"*

Even as He promises to answer us, so the God of Israel answered her. He began to open up the Scriptures to her and satisfied her heart-cry, which led to her writing: *In Search of Israel, The Olive Tree of Israel,* and *Who Is Israel?*

Batya's main passion has been to understand who is Israel, and to help correct the "bad attitudes" "both the houses of Israel" have long had towards one another. On the other hand Angus, with his "take the hill" mind-set, has focused on the "mission" of the people of Israel. His fervor to further the cause of the restoration of the kingdom to Israel led to his writing, *Restoring Israel's Kingdom.*

Restoring Israel's Kingdom is for those who feel a longing in their hearts for "something more." It is to help those who feel a hunger deep within because they are beginning to understand that the "set time" to restore Israel's Kingdom is upon us.

Together, Angus and Batya have ten children and thirteen grandchildren. Working hand in glove, they pioneered the House of David Catalogue (a first of its kind). The House of David, which had always been non-profit, became an official non-profit (5013(c) ministry in 1982. This change, not only in status, but in focus, led to their publishing the enlightening monthly Newsletter, the House of David Herald. They also developed the Messianic Israel web site (www.mim.net)—which led to the founding of the Messianic Israel Alliance—which is an alliance of congregations, fellowships, synagogues, ministries and home fellowships that agree with The Hope of Messianic Israel.

All of their efforts have served—and continue to help serve—to develop greater understanding of, and fresh insight into, the GOD of Israel and His chosen people.

Read their writings and be blessed.

—Who Is— Israel?
Enlarged Edition
by Batya Wootten

This phenomenal book is causing a stir among Bible Believers! Could it be that it is serving as a harbinger of the greatest change in Messiah's Body since the Reformation? Read this Enlarged Edition and find out why so many are getting so excited!!

Who is Israel? Why do *you* need to know?

Because knowing who you are and where you are going is vital to your relationship with the GOD of Israel.

You need to read this book because it will: Inspire and encourage you, even change your life — Help you discover your own Hebraic Heritage — Put your feet on the road to Zion.

Read this Scriptural account of Israel and understand: Israel, the Church, the Bible — The mystery of the "fulness of the Gentiles" — The "blindness of 'Israel'" — The Father's master plan for Israel — This guidebook will explain why you: Feel something is "missing" in your life — Have an unexplainable love for Israel and Jewish people — Feel an urge to celebrate the feasts of Israel.

This handbook will help you to: Move from religion to relationship — Unmuddle the muddled doctrines of Christianity — Properly intercede for "all Israel" — Remove the stones from Israel's road home — Live the *Shema*, the heart of New Covenant faith — Fulfill the latter-day desires of the Father's heart.

The Biblical truths unveiled in this volume will help: Put an end to "Christian" anti-Semitism — Heal divisions in the Body of Messiah — Cure the plague of "Believer's Boredom" — Relieve "rootlessness" in non-Jews who love "Israel."

This book: Leads us back to our First Love — Lifts up Messiah Yeshua — Gives Him His proper place — Shows how He is the epitome of all that is "Israel."

The revelation that unfolds on these pages will enrich your relationship with the Holy One of Israel; it will lead Jewish and non-Jewish Believers (Judah and Ephraim) to become the promised "one new man."

Read them and be blessed.

Contents

ISBN 1-886987-03-3 $14.95 plus ship.   House of David, PO Box 700217, Saint Cloud, FL 34770   1 800 829-8777

Notes

Notes